Bangkok

Recipes and Stories from the Heart of Thailand

Bangkok

LEELA PUNYARATABANDHU

Photography by David Loftus

TEN SPEED PRESS
California | New York

For Isaac

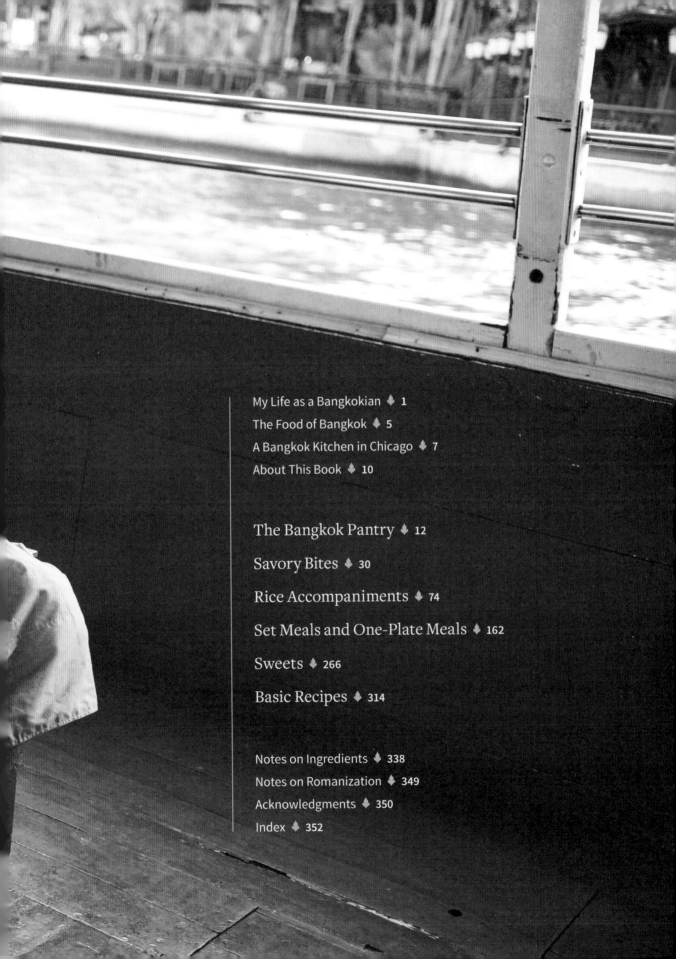

My Life as a
Bangkokian

It was 1945 when my maternal great-grandparents returned with their family to Bangkok following about two years in a nearby province. Their exodus had been prompted by the frequent aerial bombings near their home on the Chao Phraya River, one of the areas of the city most relentlessly attacked during World War II. Although its many bruises were still visible, Bangkok was on its way to healing, and my great-grandparents knew that. And so my great-grandfather decided it was time for him and his household to start anew.

Still haunted by the sounds of air-raid sirens, *khun thuat* (great-grandfather) made sure this latest house wasn't as close to the river as the previous one. A big new house—half cement, half wood—was erected on a half-acre lot of his family's land on the northwest side of Bangkok, farther away from the Chao Phraya. Still emotionally attached to life near the water, he had a manmade canal dug that connected to a natural one, so that half of the house rested on solid ground and the other half on wood and cement stilts over the water. And still troubled by having watched family members scatter to different nearby provinces during the war, *khun thuat* made sure this house was big enough for the entire clan should anyone need a place to stay in times of need.

If you asked me where my life as a Bangkokian began, I would say it began in that house by the canal. Although my parents and my uncles and aunts had their own homes, we all lived either just a few doors down or no more than fifteen minutes away, and we all gathered there all the time. That big house was the sun of our universe. My parents met and got married there. The day I was born at a hospital six miles away, they took me to that house and stayed there until my mother was back on her feet. Most of my cousins grew up there. After my father passed away, Mom and I lived there on and off throughout my grade-school years. My maternal great-grandparents died there, and, years later, my mother also died there.

In retrospect, that half-acre piece of Bangkok shaped my life, made me who I am—including my career in food—more than any other spot in the world. Watching the house steadily dilapidate following my great-grandparents' passing made my heart ache. Then, a few years ago, the house was no more. The only tangible proofs that it once existed are family photo albums, the side street that still bears my great-grandfather's surname, and a copy of the contract we signed when the family sold the land to a developer who promptly demolished the house and built a residential high-rise in its place.

But the picture I have in my mind of that wooden house, with its lush garden alongside a canal, and my love for it will never fade.

❧   ❧   ❧

Every day at that house was like a trip back to the past, and sometimes I felt like I was on the set of a period movie. My great-grandparents, who were born in the 1890s, were very much set in their early 1900s Bangkok way of life. Their house and how they ran their household reflected that.

Nearly everything they planted around the house was edible, for example. In the old days, Bangkokians could never imagine a house without an edible garden, as the garden was their supermarket. What was cooked depended on what a quick walk through the herb garden and an examination of the vegetables and fruits revealed. A day when the mango trees produced new leaves was seen as a small window of opportunity to serve those acidic, refreshing, astringent shoots alongside a chile relish. When the basil bushes got too big and unwieldy, it was time to whip out a wok and make spicy basil stir-fry. Nearly every part of the banana trees could be turned into something. The noni tree in the front of the house contributed not only its bitter leaves for cooking but also soft, smelly, antioxidant-rich fruits that no one in the house liked except *khun thuat* and the rhino fish in the pond (both of whom lived to old age). The rose apple tree was also fertile, and when it flowered, we'd sometimes make a salad with the bright fuchsia stamens of its blossoms. Other times, we'd wait until the flowers turned into fruits and dip those in a fish sauce–shrimp paste–palm sugar caramel. And as long as the coconut trees in the backyard were still bearing fruits—which they never failed to do—we knew a pot of curry from scratch could be made at any moment.

Although I loved spending time in the garden, the parts of the house that had the biggest and the most lasting impact on me were the library and the kitchen.

My great-grandfather, grandfather, and father were bibliophiles who together had amassed a collection of books that turned into a home library so extensive that it couldn't possibly have been read in its entirety in a single lifetime. And I grew up reading many of those historical documents, letters, memoirs, journals, and, yes, cookbooks. My lifelong love affair with old books and ancient manuscripts started in that library when I was a small child. Many of the time-honored recipes unique to Bangkok that you'll find in this book came out of my time in that library.

But as impressive as the library was, nothing could beat the kitchen, which, according to one of my aunts, was a replica of the one in my great-grandmother's childhood home that dated back to the 1820s. It was a traditional Thai kitchen that was part of the main house but had no walls and opened to the garden. It was outfitted with a waist-high two-burner clay stove that was reserved for heavy-duty tasks, such as cooking a big pot of rice or curry or putting a large multitiered steamer to work. There was also a small clay stove on the floor that was used for quicker tasks, such as roasting fresh chiles, garlic, shallots, a thumb-size piece of shrimp paste inside a banana leaf packet, or a small dried fish for a relish or curry paste. Both stoves were powered by wood charcoal, which explains why the traditional Thai kitchen has always been in an open area. Nothing in that kitchen required gas or electricity except for a minibar-size refrigerator.

Instead of a table and chairs, we had a *tang*, a rectangular wooden stool that was more like an oversize coffee table that three or four people could sit on at the same time. That was where we would slice, chop, or grate our ingredients. A seated coconut grater with a protruding toothed blade—dubbed the "bunny" for its rabbit-like appearance—was a constant fixture on that stool.

Outside the kitchen stood a row of large clay jars for collecting rainwater. When they were full, *khun thuat*'s cook would reach into each one with a piece of alum in her hand and swing her arm in a circular motion—a practice called *kwaeng san som*—to get all of the impurities that came with the rain to settle to the bottom of the jar. The rainwater wasn't so much our main source of drinking water as it was the ingredient for flower-scented water, which was essential in the traditional cooking and dessert making of Bangkok.

We even had an old coal oven in which my great-grandmother would make baked desserts using the *fai lang fai bon* method: hot coals underneath to cook the baked goods from the bottom and then a metal sheet on top covered with more coals to brown the surface. It was so difficult to use that no one bothered with it after she passed away, but it remained in its place like an exhibit at a folk museum. Stupid, ungrateful kid that I was, I was ashamed when my classmates came over and saw those "ancient" things. When I went to my best friend's house and glimpsed the new imported oven his mom had just installed in their kitchen—the one I'd seen in the J. C. Penney's catalogs my mom bought from her American friend's garage sale—I was jealous.

But that kitchen was everything to me. And looking back, I realize that if I owe my life and my career in food to any inanimate entity, it would be that house with its traditional cooking corner and its splendid library.

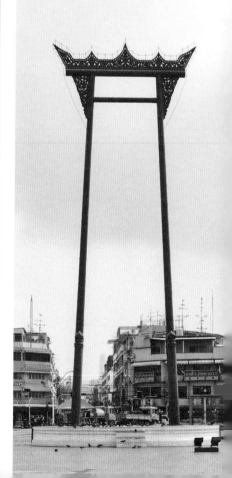

The Food of
Bangkok

As the capital, Bangkok is naturally the first city that comes to mind when people think of Thailand, and as the center of government, Bangkok does represent the entire country. But culturally and culinarily, the city cannot be considered representative of any other place but itself—not even the Central region of which it is part. In other words, Bangkok is unique, and so is its food.

Two key factors have shaped the food of Bangkok, the first of which is geography. Because the Chao Phraya River runs through the city's heart en route to emptying into the Gulf of Thailand, freshwater fish and river prawns feature prominently in the city's culinary tradition. Take fish and prawns out of the traditional cuisine of Bangkok and a great chasm would open. Their popularity is due in part to their abundance. But the archaic religious belief that frowns on the killing of larger animals, such as water buffaloes or cows, because they are useful in rice farming and therefore deserve our gratitude and protection, has also contributed to the dominance of aquatic animals. In adherence with that principle, the ancient inhabitants of the alluvial plain of the Chao Phraya subsisted on a simple regimen of rice, fish, fruits, and vegetables. Although by the time Bangkok was founded, pigs, chickens, and ducks had already been incorporated into the diet, and nowadays even though Bangkokians have no qualms about downing a bowl of beef noodles, the remnants of that river-dependent way of life and cooking can still be seen.

History has been an equally important factor in defining the city's food. Bangkok has always been influenced by foreign cultures through both visitors and settlers, and they have shaped its cuisine at every level, from the royal courts to the grassroots.

The origin of Bangkok traces back to a settlement on the west side of the river that was under the control of the ruling Ayutthaya Kingdom (1357–1767) whose center was located some fifty miles north of

contemporary Bangkok. Although small, the village, due to its strategic location on the river, steadily grew in significance as an important customs outpost. That meant that even then Bangkok was exposed to European, Persian, Chinese, and Japanese influences, as well as to groups that had already established their presence in Ayutthaya, such as the Mon, an ethnic group originally from the Mon State in Burma (Myanmar). Ayutthaya was destroyed in 1767, and the Thonburi Kingdom was established the following year. With the change in rulers, the center of government and trade moved to Thonburi, an area on the west bank of the Chao Phraya that is now part of present-day Bangkok. The kingdom ended after a fairly short run, however, and in 1782, Rama I, the first king of the new ruling dynasty, the House of Chakri, established the Rattanakosin Kingdom on the east bank of the river, and with it, the center of power known as Krungthep Maha Nakhon by the Thais and as Bangkok outside of Thailand. The capital—and the economy—grew steadily through burgeoning international trade and thoughtful modernization into a stunning, vibrant, diverse city on both sides of the river.

Today, Bangkok cuisine can be described as an indigenous Central cuisine with heavy influences from a heady blend of foreign cultures—Chinese, Mon, Persian, Portuguese, modern European, North American, and more—resulting in a beautiful, quirky mix that locals and visitors alike can't get enough of.

A Bangkok Kitchen in
Chicago

I n his 2005 commencement address at Kenyon College, the late novelist David Foster Wallace related the following parable: "There are these two young fish swimming along and they happen to meet an older fish swimming the opposite way, who nods at them and says, 'Morning, boys. How's the water?' And the two young fish swim on for a little bit, and then eventually one of them looks over at the other and goes, 'What the hell is water?'"

Although the main point of that speech is about something quite different, it reminds me of how for a long time I never realized who I was or that I was the product of the environment in which I grew up. I've always been a Bangkokian. I was born there. I grew up there. I went to school there. Both sides of my family have lived there.

It took coming to the United States for me to recognize, for the first time, how the culture of Bangkok had shaped my life and my food—to see the water now that I was pulled out of it. When I first arrived in Chicago for school, I had a hunch that it would be a long stay. I was right. I think my mother sensed that, which might have been why she gave me her collection of cookbooks as a way of solidifying my roots, of helping me understand and preserve my cultural identity. I turned my kitchen in Chicago into a Thai kitchen for that very reason. And that experience has become this book, which is not only a collection of recipes representing the food of Bangkok but also a product of years of re-creating the Bangkok food I know and love in my kitchen in America during the months I'm away from my hometown.

If my Chicago years have taught me anything, it's that with knowledge and resourcefulness, the cuisine of Bangkok—even old dishes from the early days of the city—can be faithfully replicated in the United States.

About This
Book

Decades ago, anyone in Bangkok with a television couldn't have escaped the earworm of a commercial jingle that went, "We've lifted up the ocean and put it right here—Seafood Market! Seafood Market!" The message was unmistakable: Seafood at Seafood Market is so abundant and fresh that even though the restaurant is smack dab in the middle of the bustling concrete jungle of Upper Sukhumvit, known for its posh malls, hotels, and office buildings, you'll feel as if you're feasting at a seafood shack by the beach with your toes in the sand.

This book follows the same ethos. My goal is to bring the vibrant food scene of Bangkok into your world and help you re-create in your kitchen some of what I believe to be the city's best and iconic dishes. It's my hope that by making them, you'll be sitting in your home, yet—no matter where in the world you are—you'll feel like you're enjoying piping hot *tom yam* noodles on a street in Bangkok to the sound of tuk-tuks whizzing by, dining on exquisite fare once made in the royal courts at a beautiful restaurant near the Chao Phraya River, or sitting at my family table sampling the delicious down-home dishes I grew up eating.

Bangkok is one of the best food cities in the world, and paring down a long list of all the magnificent dishes it has to offer is a difficult task. But I've tried my best to make sure the book contains an eclectic yet thoughtfully curated array that presents the cuisine of Bangkok as it truly is—that of a proud city with long-held traditions, a diverse city where foods from many cultures have melded into a cohesive mosaic, a lively city where street dining goes on around the clock, and a modern cosmopolis whose cuisine is ever evolving and ever open to new influences. The dishes in this book are a mix of traditional recipes that are still eaten today, my family's recipes, street-food classics, family-restaurant classics, adaptations of famous dishes from destination restaurants and street stalls, and my own recipes that I've made in my kitchen in the United States for more than a decade. Some of them will be familiar to most Thai food aficionados worldwide; some will be lesser known; some will even be challenging to those unfamiliar with the true taste of traditional Thai food. But to represent the food of Bangkok faithfully, I need to include these dishes.

I have organized the recipes into chapters that reflect the way Bangkokians eat. The first chapter contains some of the pantry items that most Bangkokian cooks always have on hand. Next come the savory bites that cover anything typically enjoyed as a between-meal stand-alone snack, be it intricately crafted bite-size hors d'œuvres from the royal kitchens of old or treats served on bamboo skewers prepared on street corners. Then you have the accompaniments, dishes that are placed alongside the main star of the meal, rice, in a *samrap* (family meal ensemble). Traditionally, a *samrap* includes a few accompaniments, but I have adjusted the serving size of each recipe in the chapter so it can be the lone accompaniment with rice.

A chapter of set meals and one-plate meals follows. Made up of multiple components, a set meal is similar to a *samrap* but is traditionally composed and, therefore, less flexible about what the elements can be. A one-plate meal is a complete meal based on rice or noodles, served on a plate or in a bowl—a kind of fast food, Bangkok style. Next, I have included a selection of sweets that can follow a meal or be enjoyed as a between-meal snack—or whenever you feel like something sweet. The final chapter provides directions for making nearly two dozen ingredients, condiments, noodles, and other recipe components that you'll turn to again and again. Last, I have included notes on how to recognize and where to find the commonly used noodles, vegetables, seasonings, and other ingredients in the Bangkok kitchen.

The Bangkok
Pantry

Rice

You can't talk about the food of Bangkok without talking about rice. Rice is the main dish and everything else that is served with it is there to accompany it, not the other way around.

Understanding this is key to understanding nearly everything else about Thai food. For starters, it helps you recognize that the reason Thai cooks don't hold back when they season rice accompaniments is precisely because they need to account for its blandness. Rice is normally served unseasoned—as a blank canvas ready to take on colors. I'm convinced another factor is at play in the Thai preference for plain rice, however—the love for its natural scent.

When people talk about Thai food, the clichéd "balance of all flavors: sour, salty, sweet, bitter, and spicy" never fails to make its way into the conversation, even though nobody seems to be able to explain what "balance" in this case means. Anyone who is truly familiar with traditional Thai food will know that the scent of food, including the scent of plain rice, is as central to the experience as flavor.

When I first came to the United States as a student, I stayed with a host family for nearly a month until the apartment I had reserved was ready. It was nice to have a roof over my head and kind people who cared for me. However, my biggest challenge during those early days was not having a kitchen of my own and not regularly having rice with my meals. The few times I did have rice, it was converted rice (courtesy of Uncle Ben's), which was a big adjustment for me (I've since made peace with it). So as soon as I moved into my apartment, I bought a bag of Thai jasmine rice from an Asian store and a tiny rice cooker from Target. The moment the rice cooker went ding and I opened the lid, the scent hit me. It was a scent I'd taken for granted my whole life.

Aroi jon raluek chat dai, literally "so delicious it makes you recall your past lives," is an expression used—jokingly—by some Thais to describe food that's so good it instantly returns you to a past life. Well, I don't know if any food can be *that* good; I don't even know if reincarnation is real or not. But I believe in the physiology of olfaction and its ability to trigger long-buried memories—in your current lifetime, that is.

After weeks of being rice deprived, the scent of that freshly cooked pot of jasmine rice took me back to a place I'd long forgotten. It was the night my maternal grandfather and I hung out underneath his front-yard pergola, which was lushly covered with green vines dotted with white, star-shaped *chommanat* blossoms. Perhaps inspired by the full moon, Grandpa suddenly broke into a traditional song whose lyrics were too archaic for me to understand. Still singing, he picked some of the tiny white flowers and gently put them in my hair. There was something about that song, his voice, and the tenderness of it all that made a tomboyish kindergartner, in whose hair you'd more likely to see chewing gum than flowers, feel like a little lady.

I've since learned that the song is called "Ratri Pradap Dao" (Night Adorned with Stars), and it was penned by King Prajadhipok, the seventh monarch under the House of Chakri. It's a serenade to a beloved woman, likening her to the flowers in the garden under the night sky. One of those flowers is *chommanat*, which is praised for its understated beauty. Its fragrance, the song says, is more delicate, sweet, and subtle than intense and titillating, yet inexorably binds you to it once experienced—like the heart of a kind woman.

There's a lot to be said about the scent of *chommanat* blossoms and why the Thai people are so fond of it. Romantic notions aside, there's a scientific explanation. The aroma compound responsible for the warm and subtly sweet fragrance of *chommanat* (*Vallaris glabra Ktze*, also commonly known as "bread flower") is 2-acetyl-1-pyrroline, the very same compound found in the leaves of the pandan plant, one of the most frequently used perfuming agents in Thai cooking, and in aromatic rice such as jasmine, a prized Thai rice cultivar. No wonder a pot of jasmine rice could take me back to that night.

It's not an exaggeration to say that 2-acetyl-1-pyrroline may be the favorite food-related aroma of the Thai people, which is why, unless something already comes with the scent naturally, Thai cooks have figured out a way to introduce it.

Making Rice: Old Way versus New Way

Electric rice cookers have long been ubiquitous in Thailand, even in rural areas. Everybody uses one. But because I come from a family whose patriarch, my great-grandfather, insisted that certain things be done the old way, I witnessed the traditional method of cooking long-grain rice as a child.

My great-grandfather owned a large rice field in Ang Thong Province, a couple of hours north of Bangkok, which he had allowed a family he knew to farm for free so they could have money to live. Around the beginning of the last quarter of each year—the time for the annual rice harvest—these farmers would gift my great-grandfather with large burlap sacks full of just-harvested aromatic rice, enough to last us a year.

My great-grandfather's cook, Auntie Sali, would prepare the rice by boiling it in a large pot in copious amounts of water, pasta style. When the boiling was finished, she would insert a bamboo rod into one of the pot's loop handles, then through the loop handle of the pot lid, and finally out through the other loop handle. Having tightly secured the lid, she would tilt the pot to drain out every bit of the white cloudy cooking liquid. She would then put the pot back on the charcoal stove and swirl it around for a while to steam the rice further in the residual moisture. During the final few minutes, she would let the pot sit undisturbed on the stove so the rice would form a thin crust at the bottom of the pot—a bonus, as she would say.

We would eat the boiled-then-steamed rice with our meal, of course. The milky liquid would be served warm to Great-Grandpa as a premeal aperitif. The crust that formed at the bottom of the pot would be scraped out, dried for a day or so in Bangkok's hot sun, and then deep-fried to create rice crackers for eating alone as a snack or for using in a dish like Rice Crackers with Pork-Shrimp-Coconut Dip (page 48). My great-grandmother would sometimes enjoy hot tea made with sun-dried rice crackers that she grilled over hot coals until puffy and lightly blistered and then steeped in boiling water.

Romantic nostalgia aside, the question remains: Is this a better way of cooking rice? Well, the boiling method has its pros and cons. But I think the reason that Thais have collectively moved on to using the electric rice cooker is precisely because those cons outweigh the pros. Interestingly, the boiling method may actually be more practical in the Western kitchen, since rice cookers are not as common in the United States as they are in Asia. Anyone who makes rice on the stove top may also find the boiling method to be more practical and to yield better results consistently. That's because the risk of using the wrong amount of water and ending up with rice that's too hard or too wet or gummy is nonexistent. It doesn't matter whether the rice is new crop with a higher moisture content, old crop with a lower moisture content, or something in between. The method remains the same.

Boiled rice

1½ cups raw long-grain white rice, preferably Thai jasmine

10 cups water

4 pandan leaves, tied together into a knot (optional but recommended if using old crop or nonaromatic long-grain rice)

If there's anything tricky about this old method of cooking rice, it is knowing when to stop boiling the rice and drain off the water. Boil it until it's perfectly cooked and you'll end up with overcooked rice after the steaming; stop too soon and you'll end up with undercooked rice. My recommendation is to pull the rice when it's about 80 percent done (90 percent if cooking whole-grain rice). That's when the grains have expanded and softened but are still a bit crunchy in the middle, which will show up as a tiny opaque spot in the center when you hold a grain up to the light. (Home cooks in the old days described rice at this stage as looking like the eyes of a frog, *ta kop*.) The moisture remaining in the pot will continue to steam the rice to about 95 percent done on the stove, and the residual heat will take care of the remaining 5 percent when the rice stands off the heat. **Makes a generous 4 cups**

Combine the rice and water in a heavy saucepan at least 8 inches in diameter and tall enough to accommodate the rice and water comfortably. Stir to separate the grains and bring to a rolling boil, uncovered, over high heat. Lower the heat to medium-high and continue to cook, stirring occasionally, until the grains have softened but still have a bit of a bite to them, 7 to 8 minutes.

Put a fine-mesh sieve over a large heatproof bowl and pour the contents of the saucepan into the sieve. (The liquid captured in the bowl can be consumed as a beverage.) Shake off any excess water from the rice, return the rice to the pan, and bury the pandan leaves in it. Put the pan back on the stove, top it with a tight lid, and turn the heat to medium-low. Steam the rice using the residual moisture, rotating the pan and shaking it back and forth (not up and down) a few times as if you are making popcorn, for 3 minutes. Turn off the heat and leave the pan undisturbed, still covered, for 15 minutes. Remove and discard the pandan leaves and fluff the rice with a fork before serving.

Steamed glutinous rice

ข้าวเหนียวนึ่ง KHAO NIAO NUENG

**4 cups raw Thai white
glutinous rice**

Most people think of jasmine rice as the quintessential Thai rice, yet archaeological evidence from four to six millennia ago points to glutinous rice—aka sticky rice—as the main staple in all regions of Thailand. Most scholars believe that it wasn't until the Ayutthaya period that long-grain rice (*khao jao*, literally "rice [for the] royals") became the rice of choice among the elite of the kingdom, while glutinous rice remained the staple of the hoi polloi.

These days, no such distinctions exist, and the kind of rice you choose is all about your preference and what rice accompaniment(s) you are eating. Sticky rice, for example, is the default for grilled or roasted meats of non-Chinese origin, such as Black Pepper Roasted Chicken (page 155) or Grilled Pork on Skewers (page 42).

In my first book, *Simple Thai Food*, I offer three methods for cooking sticky rice: one employs a tiered steamer and the other two completely nontraditional methods involve a splatter guard and a mesh colander, respectively. Here, I walk you through the method of steaming sticky rice in a *huat*, a conical bamboo basket, the traditional mode in Thailand. Although some traditions have disappeared, I don't see the practice of steaming sticky rice in a bamboo basket going away any time soon. Pandan leaves aren't usually used to scent plain sticky rice, but the bamboo cooking vessel—as strange as it may sound—acts as a scenting agent, imparting a tea-like aroma. The traditional use of a *kratip* (bamboo container) or banana leaves to keep cooked sticky rice soft and warm also reinforces the scenting.

You can buy a set made up of a traditional conical bamboo basket and a tall, narrow steamer pot at a Southeast Asian grocery store or online. (While you're at it, pick up a *kratip* from the store, too.) Once you have removed the cooked rice from the basket, don't put the basket in the dishwasher; instead, soak it in water overnight to loosen up any rice that has stuck to its crevices, scrub it, and then, to prevent mold, leave it to dry thoroughly in the sun or in a dry place in the kitchen before putting it away. ♦ **Makes about 8 cups**

To remove excess starch, put the rice in a fine-mesh sieve or colander and rinse under cold running water until the water runs clear. Transfer the rice to a bowl, add water to cover, and let soak for at least 5 hours or up to overnight.

Fill the pot with water as full as you can without the bottom of the basket touching the water and set the pot over high heat. Drain the rice, being careful not to break the grains. When the water boils, place the rice in the bamboo basket and rest the basket in the top of the pot. Steam the rice over rapidly boiling water for 15 minutes. Then, flip the rice by holding the "wings" of the basket firmly and shaking the basket up and down until the rice that was on the top is now on the bottom of the basket. Continue to cook over rapidly boiling water until the rice grains are soft and sticky, yet glossy, 15 to 20 minutes longer. The grains should be separate and still hold their shape.

Serve the rice immediately, or transfer it to a *kratip* and close the lid tightly or to a covered thermos. It should keep soft and warm for 2 to 3 hours until serving.

Fried rice crackers

ข้าวตังทอด **KHAO TANG THOT**

1½ cups cooked long-grain white rice, preferably Thai jasmine

Vegetable oil, for deep-frying

The old-fashioned way of cooking rice (see page 16) often yields a tasty bonus of thin rice crusts on the bottom of the pot. These crusts are broken up into smaller pieces, dried in the sun, and then deep-fried into crispy crackers that can be used in various recipes, such as Rice Crackers with Pork-Shrimp-Coconut Dip (page 48), or for a savory snack with chile jam (page 22) or another spread.

This recipe assumes that you have cooked rice the modern way, either steamed on the stove top or in a rice cooker. Be sure to cook the rice a little drier than usual for these crackers. Wet, soggy rice will yield dense crackers that don't puff up well in the oil. ♦ **Makes 24 crackers**

Line two sheet pans with parchment paper. To be sure the crackers are uniform, use a 1-tablespoon measuring spoon to scoop up the rice and place it on the prepared sheet pans (1½ cups rice equals 24 tablespoons). With damp fingers, form the grains of each spoonful into a single layer, creating a round just shy of 3 inches in diameter and being careful not to press too hard. You want the grains tightly connected and the edges of each round somewhat neat.

Dry the rounds in the sun (covered with a domed mesh food cover, if necessary) or dehydrate them in a 110°F oven, flipping them and rotating the pans every now and then, until they are thoroughly dried all the way to the center. When in doubt, err on the side of overdrying; you won't be sorry. If sun drying, the time it takes will depend on the weather. If oven drying, it should take about 12 hours.

Pour the oil to a depth of 2 inches into a wok or Dutch oven and heat to 350°F. Line a sheet pan with paper towels and place it near the stove.

Working in batches to avoid crowding, fry the rice rounds, flipping them around as they cook, until they are crisp and golden brown, about 1 minute. Using a slotted spoon or spatula, transfer the crackers to the towel-lined pan to drain.

Let cool completely before serving or storing in an airtight container at room temperature for up to 1 week.

Plain rice porridge

ข้าวต้ม   ❖   KHAO TOM

¾ cup raw long-grain white rice, preferably Thai jasmine

¼ cup raw Thai white glutinous rice

8 cups water

½ teaspoon salt

4 pandan leaves, tied together into a knot (optional but recommended if using old-crop or nonaromatic long-grain rice)

Ask ten cooks to describe the best Chinese-style plain rice porridge and you'll probably get ten different answers. If you ask me, this is what I would say: I like to detect the scent of jasmine rice when I open a pot of just-cooked porridge (in other words, I need my 2-acetyl-1-pyrroline). The rice grains should hold their shape and there should be some thick, creamy liquid left—just enough to make the porridge somewhat soupy rather than thick and goopy.

Starting with high-quality raw new-crop jasmine rice and not overcooking it help ensure the porridge meets the first two criteria, and reinforcing the amount of amylopectin (the starch molecule that makes rice gelatinous and sticky) by adding glutinous rice and using lots of water helps it meet the last criterion. Finding new-crop jasmine rice shouldn't be a problem for most people, as the jasmine rice imported from Thailand is almost always new crop. If you use a different type of long-grain rice, you may want to add the pandan leaves as suggested.

It may seem the recipe produces a large amount of porridge, but keep in mind that a cup of rice porridge is much lighter than a cup of steamed rice, as much of it is liquid. It's not uncommon for two or three people with healthy appetites to finish 2 quarts of rice porridge in one sitting. ❖ **Makes about 8 cups**

Combine both types of rice and 6 cups of the water in a 4-quart saucepan, stir, cover, and bring to a boil over high heat. Lower the heat to medium so the liquid boils gently and continue to cook, covered, for 15 minutes. At this point the rice grains will have softened and about two-thirds of the liquid will have been absorbed. Add the remaining 2 cups water, the salt, and the pandan leaves to the pan. Give the rice a stir, bring it back to a boil over high heat, lower the heat to a gentle boil, and cook, covered, for another 5 minutes.

The porridge is now ready to serve. It will become thicker as it stands off the heat. To return it to its original consistency, add water as needed and heat through. Leftovers can be stored in an airtight container in the refrigerator for up to 3 days; reheat and thin as needed before serving.

Chile jam

น้ำพริกเผา NAM PHRIK PHAO

5 dried Thai long or guajillo chiles, cut into 1-inch pieces, soaked until softened and squeezed dry

2 teaspoons white peppercorns

½-inch piece fresh sand ginger or 1 tablespoon finely chopped galangal

1 head garlic, separated into cloves and peeled

1 large shallot (about 1 ounce), cut into small cubes

2 tablespoons dried shrimp, soaked in hot water until softened and squeezed dry

2 teaspoons packed Thai shrimp paste

½ cup packed grated palm sugar

3 tablespoons tamarind paste, homemade (page 316) or store-bought

3 tablespoons fish sauce

3 tablespoons pork cracklings (page 28), finely chopped

1 cup homemade lard (see page 28) or vegetable oil

No Thai relish is more versatile or more widely used than chile jam (*nam phrik phao*). A longtime traditional food of the central plain, chile jam was originally served along with fresh vegetables to accompany rice as part of a *samrap* (see page 11), but Bangkokians have taken to employing this flavorful condiment in countless other ways. They use it as a spread on sandwiches, slather it on crispy rice crackers (page 20) for a snack, add it as a seasoning or accent ingredient to various salads and stir-fries, and dip fried pork rinds or fried fish skins in it, much like one dips tortilla chips in salsa. It even has a long-standing royal connection: the tradition among courtiers of making soft buns with a filling of *nam phrik pao* has been documented as far back as the early 1900s.

But the dish that has given *nam phrik phao* international fame is the iconic *tom yam kung*, an herbaceous Central Thai prawn soup perfumed with lemongrass, galangal, *makrut* lime leaves, and, in its most well-known rendition, a warm, smoky background note of chile jam.

To bring Bangkok into your kitchen, you'll need this chile jam, which is easily purchased at any well-stocked Southeast Asian store. Don't feel bad about buying it; most Bangkokians do the same these days. But if you feel like making this relish from scratch, this recipe is a new favorite of mine based on a recently discovered old family recipe. Unlike the chile jam recipe in my first book, this version is accented with fragrant herbs and derives more heat from peppercorns. But it's the oomph and richness from homemade lard and pork cracklings that makes it a winner.

Sand ginger (*Kaempferia galanga*) can be found at well-stocked stores specializing in East Asian and South Asian ingredients. ◆ **Makes about 2 cups**

In a mortar or a small chopper, grind together the chiles, peppercorns, sand ginger, garlic, shallot, dried shrimp, and shrimp paste to a smooth paste. Transfer the paste to a wok; add the sugar, tamarind paste, fish sauce, cracklings, and lard; and set over medium heat. Fry, stirring occasionally, until the paste has turned dark reddish brown and is the consistency of a loose jam, 15 to 20 minutes.

Remove from the heat and let cool. Transfer to a glass jar, lard and all, and cap tightly. The jam will keep in the refrigerator for up to 1 month or in the freezer for up to 6 months.

Flower-scented water

น้ำลอยดอกไม้ NAM LOI DOK MAI

12 cups filtered, nonchlorinated water or boiled tap water, at room temperature

1½ cups pesticide-free edible flowers with a sweet fragrance (such as Arabian jasmine, nasturtium, rose [use only the fragrant types and only the petals], and/or ylang-ylang [petals only])

My great-grandparents always greeted guests with a silver bowl of cold water—not from the fridge but from a terra-cotta jar that was used to store filtered rainwater. Just one sip of that water would leave guests wondering how my great-grandparents had fit their whole garden of tropical blossoms into a single bowl.

Flower-scented water is not only a symbol of tradition or of the old Bangkokian life but also of elegance and refinement. It lends itself to more practical culinary purposes, as well. Dessert making, for example— especially in the royal courts and aristocratic households—depends on flower-scented water. The classic rice in ice-cold water (see page 166) can never be made properly without this fragrant ingredient, either.

Two imported products available in the United States, artificial jasmine essence and amyl acetate, which artificially mimics the fragrance of the *nom maeo* flower (*Rauwenhoffia siamensis* Scheff.), work adequately in desserts and baked goods. But if you have access to fragrant edible flowers, this recipe explains how to use them to prepare scented water.

The bloom time of the flowers will determine the timing of the scenting process. Study the flowers you will be using to find out when they bloom naturally and use them to scent the water at that time. If you mix different types of flowers, it is best to select varieties that bloom at the same time to ensure maximum scent. In every case, make sure the flowers are in perfect condition, with absolutely no bruises that can give the water an unpleasant smell. **Makes 12 cups**

Select a shallow container to increase the surface area and pour the water into it. Gently place the flowers on the surface of the water, making sure they float rather than sink. Cover the container and leave undisturbed for 12 hours. Using a skimmer, gently remove the flowers. The scented water is best used the same day.

The Kitchen Cupboard

These days, with most modern homes and condos in Bangkok equipped with built-in cabinetry similar to what you find in the United States, you're more likely to see the old-school wooden kitchen cupboard, or *tu kap khao* (literally, "a cupboard [containing] rice accompaniments"), at a folk museum or a restaurant with a retro-themed decor. Things were different several decades ago, however, when a food cabinet was an essential part of nearly every kitchen, including the ultratraditional kitchen of my childhood.

This type of freestanding, shelved cabinet features a main storage chamber with two meshed doors for ventilation. That's where you keep the dishes you make in the morning to eat throughout the day. There are usually some compartments on top of or underneath the main chamber for storing dry ingredients and pantry items. The cabinet has four small feet and each one—and this may be strange to anyone who has never lived in a tropical climate—sits in a little ceramic water moat bowl. This prevents the ants from eating what's supposed to be for people. When I was a kid, these little water moats were objects of great fascination to me. My mother once caught me lying on my belly on the kitchen floor, staring at the feet of our kitchen cabinet for a long time. She later admitted that for a moment she thought I might be unwell in the head. What Mom didn't understand was that I was observing the behavior of ants faced with a life decision of whether to swim across the moat for food or to retreat. What I discovered was that, like humans, some ants made the right choice and some—fatally—were under the illusion they did.

I used to ask myself if, say, one day we forgot to put water in the moats and the ants got to the stuff in our kitchen cabinet, what items I would feel saddest about losing to them. My first thought was always the bowl of lard and pork cracklings, which were ingredients we used daily.

Lard was once the cooking fat of choice among Bangkokians. If you look through Thai cookbooks from the late nineteenth to early twentieth centuries, you'd see that lard is called for in nearly every recipe that involves fat. In the old days, Chinese cooks in Bangkok also used lard as the main cooking fat. The use of vegetable oil is a somewhat recent phenomenon that was initially fueled by the belief that it was a healthier choice. A more practical factor also played a role in the abandonment of lard in favor of vegetable oil: the transition to air-conditioning. Chinese restaurants using lard found that specks of fat in food that once stayed liquid hardened up midmeal due to the cool swirling air.

It's interesting how Bangkokians have come full circle after just a few decades. Cooks in the city are putting lard back in the larder, recognizing now that some vegetable oils aren't as healthful (or friendly to the environment) as previously thought. Crispy omelet fried in lard and topped with pork cracklings has come back to restaurant menus. This new popularity is not surprising, of course, as lard adds flavor to everything it touches.

Making lard also gives us another delicious ingredient to keep in the food cabinet, pork cracklings, which have many uses in traditional and Chinese-influenced Thai cooking. Back in the 1970s, M. R. Thanadsri Svasti, Thailand's one-person Michelin guide, appeared in a television commercial for a well-known brand of table seasoning sauce in which he extolled the virtues of a bowl of warm rice mixed with crunchy pork cracklings and a few dashes of the sauce. He "wouldn't trade it for a plate of steak," suggesting that a common Thai pantry staple was far superior to a Western dish that, at the time, was accessible only to Bangkokians with a lot of money to spare. That phrase became an instant hit in the city, and my aunts and uncles still use it to describe a lowly, everyday homemade dish that they think is more delicious than anything a fancy restaurant can offer.

Pork cracklings and lard

กากหมู-น้ำมันหมู **KAK MU-NAM MAN MU**

2 pounds pork belly fat with no skin or lean meat attached, cut into ½-inch cubes

3 cups water

A number of the recipes in this book call for lard, which takes you back to the time when many of the traditional dishes you now see in Bangkok first came on the dining scene. Although leaf fat, which is the fine, soft fat from around the kidneys of a pig, is widely considered to be the best fat to use, lard made from belly fat or fatback is more suitable for Thai cooking. If you prefer not to use lard in your cooking, you can use vegetable oil in the same amount. ⬥ **Makes 2 cups pork cracklings and 2 cups lard**

Combine the fat and water in a carbon-steel wok or 12-inch deep sauté pan, stir, and set over high heat. About 3 minutes after the water comes to a boil, lower the heat to medium and continue to cook, uncovered and stirring often, until the pork fat turns light brown, about 45 minutes. At this point, increase the heat to medium-high to crisp the pork fat. Once the pork cracklings take on the color of light honey, after about 2 minutes, turn off the heat. Using a mesh skimmer, transfer the cracklings to a heatproof plate to cool; leave the lard to cool in the pan.

Once the lard and the cracklings have cooled, store them separately in airtight containers. The pork cracklings will stay fresh for 2 to 3 days in the refrigerator, though they should be used in a recipe as soon as possible for the best flavor. The lard can be refrigerated for up to 1 month or frozen for up to 4 months.

Faux river prawn tomalley

มันกุ้งเทียม MAN KUNG THIAM

1 pound head-on, shell-on medium shrimp with visible orange tomalley

3 cups water

4 egg yolks

½ cup homemade lard (page 28) or vegetable oil

With so many Asian grocery stores selling Thai ingredients, re-creating the food of Bangkok is easy nowadays. But even the most well-stocked store does not carry river prawn tomalley, an ingredient in several classic dishes. In Bangkok, you can find fresh tomalley neatly packed in a plastic bag ready to use. In the United States, unless I find whole shrimp with lots of tomalley and squeeze it out of them one by one until I have enough for a recipe, jarred shrimp paste in oil with red dye, salt, and artificial ingredients is my only option. This has prompted me to devise this sauce, the best substitute for river prawn tomalley I've found to date on this side of the Chao Phraya. ◆ **Makes about 2 cups**

Peel the shrimp, reserving the shells and tails, and set the meat aside for another use. Squeeze the orange, gooey tomalley from the head area into a 2-quart saucepan and add the now-empty heads, the reserved shells and tails, and the water to the pan. Place the pan over high heat and bring to a boil, then turn the heat to medium and simmer, using a sturdy wooden spoon to press and squeeze the shrimp shells against the side of the pan for maximum flavor and color. After about 10 minutes, you should end up with a soft orange–colored liquid. Remove from the heat and let cool slightly.

Transfer the contents of the pan to a blender and puree. Pour the puree through a fine-mesh sieve set over the same saucepan, then, using a rubber spatula, press against the puree to force as much liquid as possible into the pan. Discard the solids.

Place the shrimp liquid over high heat, bring to a boil, and boil until reduced to 1½ cups. Put the egg yolks in a heatproof bowl that can hold about 2 cups liquid and set it near the stove. Once the shrimp liquid is reduced to 1½ cups, turn the heat to medium, add the lard, and whisk until homogenous. Temper the yolks by slowly pouring about 1 cup of the hot liquid into the yolk bowl while whisking constantly. Then scrape the tempered yolks into the pan and continue to cook, whisking often, until the yolks form tiny curds and the fat separates, 8 to 10 minutes.

Remove the pan from the heat and divide between two half-pint Mason jars or pour into a heatproof shallow glass or ceramic storage container with a lid. Let cool completely, cover, and store in the refrigerator for up to 1 week or in the freezer for up to 4 months. The fat will rise to the top, so when removing sauce from the jar to use in a recipe, make sure you push the spoon all the way to the bottom so that you get both the fatty and the eggy parts. (This is done more easily when the jar isn't too deep, which is why I have suggested two small jars or a shallow container.)

Savory
Bites

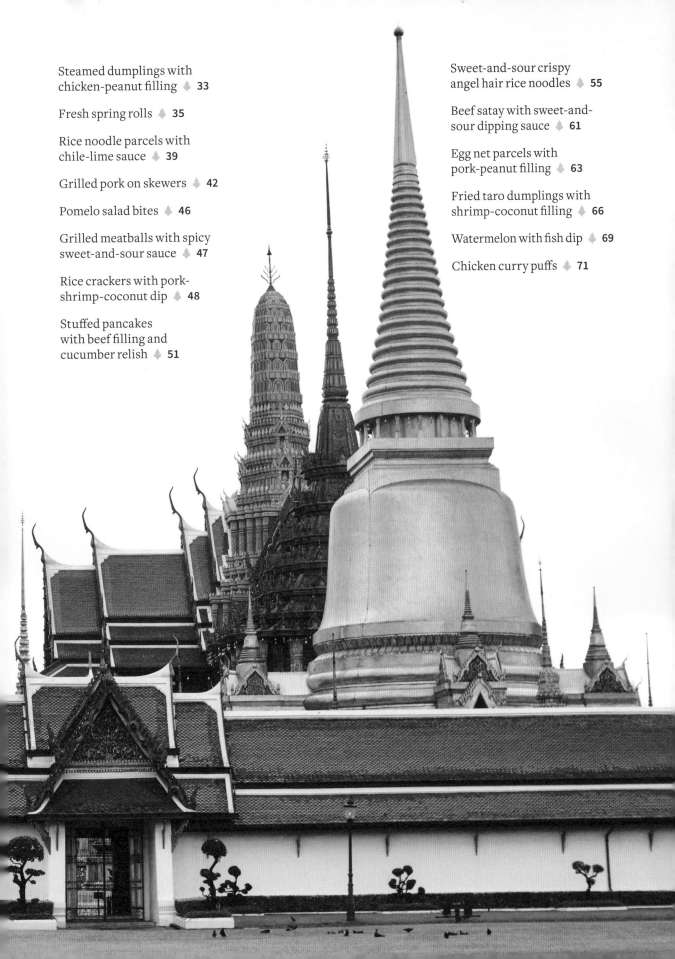

Steamed dumplings with chicken-peanut filling

ปั้นสิบนึ่งไส้ไก่ PAN SIP NUENG SAI KAI

FILLING

3 large cloves garlic

3 tablespoons finely chopped cilantro roots or stems

½ teaspoon white peppercorns

1 tablespoon homemade lard (page 28) or vegetable oil

⅓ cup finely diced shallots

12 ounces skinless, boneless chicken thighs, chopped with a cleaver to a coarse grind or coarsely ground in a food processor

1½ teaspoons salt

2½ tablespoons packed grated palm sugar or 2 tablespoons packed light brown sugar

3 tablespoons unsalted roasted peanuts, finely chopped

DOUGH

1½ cups water

1¼ cups Thai tapioca starch

¾ cup Thai rice flour, plus more for working with the dough

½ cup Thai glutinous rice flour

½ teaspoon salt

2 tablespoons vegetable oil

Banana leaf, wiped clean with a damp cloth, for lining steamer tier (optional)

SIDES

¼ cup fried garlic oil (page 322)

¼ cup fried garlic (page 322)

About 24 green lettuce leaves

Plump fresh bird's eye chiles, as many as you like

½-inch bunch cilantro

This recipe has been in our family for three generations. The dumplings are a traditional savory snack that are difficult to find these days, as very few vendors make them and even fewer make them well.

Rice flour–based dumpling dough is trickier to work with than its wheat-flour counterpart. Stretch the dough too thin and it tears; keep it nice and thick and it ends up tough and doughy. The dumplings should be as tiny as possible—no larger than what can be enjoyed comfortably in one bite—which calls for even more dexterity.

Do not confuse these with Chinese-style dumplings such as *har gow* (Cantonese shrimp dumplings), which have translucent wheat starch–based skins. They are similar in appearance but different in texture. The filling, though primarily salty, is also a bit sweet—a perfect foil for the fresh chiles that are served alongside. ⚜ **Makes 48 bite-size dumplings; serves 4 to 6**

To make the filling, in a mortar, grind together the garlic, cilantro roots, and peppercorns to a smooth paste. Transfer the paste to a 10-inch frying pan, add the lard and shallots, and set over medium-high heat. Fry until the shallots have softened, about 1 minute. Add the chicken, salt, and sugar and stir-fry, breaking up the chicken as finely as possible with the blunt end of a wooden spatula, until the chicken is opaque and all of the moisture has evaporated, about 5 minutes. Stir in the chopped peanuts and transfer the filling to a plate to cool, spreading it as thinly as possible to speed the process.

To make the dough, while the filling cools, in a small saucepan, bring the water to a boil over high heat. (You won't need all of the water, but it's better to have more than you need on hand.) Meanwhile, in a heatproof bowl, stir together the tapioca starch, rice flour, glutinous rice flour, salt, and oil until the oil is fully dispersed into the dry ingredients and becomes invisible. Get a sturdy wooden spoon ready. The moment the water is at a rolling boil, slowly pour it in a thin stream into the center of the flour mixture while simultaneously using the wooden spoon to stir everything together briskly. Stop adding the water the moment a stiff and shaggy ball of dough forms that cleans the bottom and sides of the bowl. If in doubt, err on the side of too little water, as you can always add more. With one hand, knead the dough lightly in the bowl, using your palm to gather the dough into a ball and your knuckles to push it down, just until the dough is smooth and supple, about 2 minutes. Shape the dough into a smooth ball, wrap it tightly in plastic wrap, and then invert the bowl over the dough. Let rest for 30 minutes.

continued

At this point, you should have a ball of dough that weighs about 1½ pounds and 2 cups (96 teaspoons) filling. The goal is to make 48 dumplings, each with 2 teaspoons filling. Do your best to divide the dough into 48 uniform pieces (a scale comes in handy here) and roll each piece into a smooth ball about 1 inch in diameter. Keep the balls under an overturned bowl. Line a steamer tier with parchment paper or a piece of banana leaf.

Have additional rice flour nearby for dipping your fingers as you assemble the dumplings, as the dough can get sticky. Use your fingers to flatten a dough ball into a round 2½ to 2¾ inches in diameter and of even thickness. Place the dough round in the center of your cupped palm and push the center down a bit so the wrapper looks like a flared bowl. Place 2 teaspoons of the filling in the center. Fold the wrapper over the filling to form a half-moon. Pinch the edges of the wrapper together—quite hard—to form a very flat seal from one end to the other.

You can stop at this point or you can give your dumpling a beautiful rope edge by using the tips of the fingers of your nondominant hand to grab a sealed dumpling by its "belly" and hold it vertically. Starting from the bottom end, use the thumb and index finger of your dominant hand to fold the seal upward and pinch it down on itself to secure the first pleat. Repeat, forming decorative pleats until you reach the top end. Tuck the end of the "rope" behind the top end and secure it with a light squeeze. If at any point the dough gets too sticky to fold, dip your fingers into the rice flour. Set the dumpling aside on a lightly floured surface and cover it with a kitchen towel. Repeat until you have used all of the dough and filling.

When all of the dumplings have been shaped, bring the water in the steamer pot to a rolling boil. Working in batches, arrange the dumplings in the prepared steamer tier, spacing them ½ inch apart. Set over the boiling water, cover, and steam the dumplings until the wrappers turn glossy and slightly translucent, 5 to 6 minutes. Meanwhile, brush a large platter with a thin coat of the garlic oil. When the dumplings are ready, use a spoon to gently transfer them one by one to the prepared platter and brush a little oil on them to keep them from sticking together. Steam the remaining dumplings in the same way.

Sprinkle the dumplings with the fried garlic and serve them while they are still warm by wrapping in half a leaf of lettuce along with a little bit of chile and a sprig of cilantro and enjoying it in one bite.

Fresh spring rolls

ปอเปี๊ยะสด ◆ PO PIA SOT

SPRING ROLLS

8 ounces bean sprouts

6 ounces extra-firm tofu, cut lengthwise into strips ¼ inch wide and thick and 4 inches long

½ teaspoon Chinese five-spice powder

2 star anise pods

2 (3-inch) cinnamon sticks

1 tablespoon plus 1 teaspoon Thai sweet dark soy sauce

1 tablespoon Thai thin soy sauce or Golden Mountain seasoning sauce

2 teaspoons crushed Chinese rock sugar or dark or light brown sugar

½ teaspoon ground white or black pepper

3 eggs

1 tablespoon homemade lard (page 28) or vegetable oil

4 ounces Chinese dried sweet sausage (lap cheong), cut lengthwise ¼ inch thick

12 fresh spring roll skins, 8 inches square, kept under a damp kitchen towel

1 small pickling cucumber, peeled and cut lengthwise ¼ inch thick and wide

6 ounces Chinese or mildly seasoned Western headcheese, cut lengthwise into strips ¼ inch wide and thick and 4 inches long

6 ounces fresh lump crabmeat, picked over for shell fragments and cartilage, plus 2 ounces, for garnish

If you order "fresh spring rolls" from the menu of most Thai restaurants in the United States, you will nearly always be served Vietnamese-style spring rolls wrapped in chewy, translucent rice wrappers. But if you say the same words to most Bangkokians, the first thing that leaps to their minds would be the Chinese-style spring rolls they grew up eating.

The rolls are wrapped in *paeng po pia*, diaphanous wheat flour–based spring roll wrappers found in the freezer section of most Asian stores. Don't confuse them with egg roll skins (basically supersized wonton skins) or the recipe will fail. To use frozen spring roll skins, thaw them in the unopened package overnight in the refrigerator, peel as many wrappers as you need off the stack, and refreeze the stack in a resealable plastic bag for future use.

You may have a hard time finding Chinese-style headcheese, which is similar in concept to European-style headcheeses but is denser, seasoned with soy sauce, and spiked with Chinese spices. If there is a Chinatown with well-stocked grocery stores where you live, you will likely find it in one of them. If not, any dense, minimally seasoned headcheese from the deli department will do. Make sure it is not pickled and ask for it in a single thick chunk, so you can cut it as needed at home. ⬧ **Makes 12 spring rolls; serves 6**

To make the spring rolls, fill a 1-quart saucepan three-fourths full with water and bring to a boil over high heat. Add the bean sprouts and blanch for 20 seconds. Remove the pan from the heat and, using a mesh skimmer, transfer the bean sprouts to a plate to cool. Put the pan back over high heat.

Gently drop the tofu strips into the water, then discard some of the water, leaving just enough to immerse the tofu. Add the five-spice powder, star anise, cinnamon, both soy sauces, rock sugar, and pepper and bring to a boil. Lower the heat to a simmer, cover, and cook for 10 minutes. Using the skimmer or a slotted spoon, transfer the tofu to a plate, shaking off any excess liquid over the pan. Strain the cooking liquid through a fine-mesh sieve. Measure ¾ cup of the liquid and transfer it to a small bowl to use for the sauce. Let the tofu strips and the cooking liquid cool to room temperature. Reserve the remaining liquid for another use or discard.

In a bowl, beat the eggs with a fork until well blended. Heat the lard in a 12-inch frying pan (preferably nonstick) over medium heat. When the lard is hot, pour in the eggs and immediately tilt the pan so they cover the entire bottom in a thin, even layer. Cook just until the bottom sets

continued

SAUCE

¾ cup liquid from cooking tofu

1 cup homemade
chicken stock (page 323),
store-bought sodium-free
chicken stock, or water

3 tablespoons cornstarch

¼ cup tamarind paste,
homemade (page 316)
or store-bought

3 tablespoons granulated
sugar

¼ teaspoon salt

SIDES

6 green onions, trimmed

3 or 4 fresh Thai long,
jalapeño, or serrano chiles,
thinly sliced crosswise on
the diagonal

6 tablespoons Chinese-style
prepared mustard or
Dijon mustard

(no need to brown it), 1 to 2 minutes, then use a wide rubber spatula to flip and cook the second side, 30 to 40 seconds. Transfer to a plate. When the egg crepe is cool enough to handle, halve it and roll up each half into a tight cylinder, starting from the short side. Using a sharp knife, cut each cylinder crosswise into ⅛-inch-wide ribbons. Set the ribbons aside.

Wipe out the frying pan and set it over medium heat. Add the Chinese sausage and stir until seared on all sides, taking care not to burn it (because it's sweet, it burns easily), about 2 minutes. Transfer to a plate and set aside.

To make the sauce, in a 1-quart saucepan, whisk together all of the ingredients until smooth, then place the pan over medium-high heat. Bring to a boil and cook, whisking constantly, until glossy and the consistency of ketchup, 2 to 3 minutes. If it's too thick, whisk in a little water. Remove from the heat; you should have about 2 cups. Cover the sauce and keep lukewarm— the perfect temperature to serve it.

Lay a spring roll skin flat on a work surface. Position about one-twelfth each of the tofu, egg ribbons, sausage, cucumber, headcheese, and 6 ounces crabmeat about ¼ inch from the edge of the skin closest to you, making sure the filling ingredients extend to the left and right edges of the skin. The filling ingredients should cover about 1½ inches of the spring roll skin. Fold the edge nearest you over the filling, then roll up as tightly as possible (the roll should be 1 to 1½ inches in diameter), leaving the ends open. Make a second roll the same way.

Line up 2 rolls next to each other on a cutting board and, using a very sharp knife, quarter them crosswise. Carefully transfer both rolls to a plate. Drizzle about one-sixth of the sauce along the length of the rolls and garnish with about one-sixth of the remaining crabmeat. Arrange a green onion and one-sixth of the pepper slices to one side of the rolls and 1 tablespoon of the mustard to the other side. This is one serving, repeat to make five more servings. Serve immediately.

Rice noodle parcels with chile-lime sauce

ก๋วยเตี๋ยวลุยสวน KUAI TIAO LUI SUAN

2 tablespoons homemade lard (page 28) or vegetable oil

8 dried shiitake mushrooms (1 inch in diameter), soaked in warm water until softened, squeezed dry, stems discarded, and caps cut into ¼-inch dice

1 pound fatty ground pork

8 ounces carrots (about 2 medium), peeled and cut into ¼-inch dice

1 tablespoon Thai thin soy sauce or Golden Mountain seasoning sauce

6 cilantro roots or ½ cup packed coarsely chopped cilantro stems

1 tablespoon granulated sugar

3 tablespoons fresh lime juice

¼ cup water, homemade chicken stock (page 323), or store-bought sodium-free chicken stock

5 large cloves garlic

5 or 6 fresh green bird's eye chiles, 2 green jalapeño chiles, or 3 green serrano chiles

¾ teaspoon salt

16 green lettuce leaves

16 fresh Thai sweet basil leaves, plus more for the platter (optional)

16 fresh mint leaves, plus more for the platter (optional)

½ cup packed cilantro leaves, coarsely chopped

16 rice noodle sheets, formula 1 (page 330), freshly made and kept covered with a kitchen towel

You can find these bite-size rice noodle packets that come with a spicy-sweet-tart dipping sauce anywhere in Bangkok, even in the prepared food section of most supermarkets. But no one makes this savory snack better than its birthplace, Khun Thip, a little stall inside the renowned market behind the headquarters of Thai Airways International. That's where I first discovered this dish many years ago, and I've been hooked on it ever since.

Two things are key to helping you achieve a result as close as possible to what you'd get at Khun Thip (and these are where the inferior copycats go wrong). The first is to use ground pork with 20 to 30 percent fat for a juicy, succulent filling. The other is to use high-quality fresh rice noodle sheets that are thin, translucent, and tender yet slightly chewy. Most of the commercial rice noodle sheets available in the United States are thicker and doughier than what you find in Bangkok, especially at Khun Thip. They lack elasticity and tear at the slightest pull. The solution is to make your own sheets (see page 330). Yes, making them is labor-intensive, but the result will take you right to the heart of Bangkok. ⬧ **Makes 16 parcels; serves 4**

Heat the lard in a 12-inch frying pan over medium-high heat. When the lard is hot, add the mushrooms and stir-fry until fragrant, 1 to 2 minutes. Add the pork, carrots, and soy sauce and stir-fry, breaking up the pork as finely as possible with the blunt end of a wooden spatula, until the pork has turned opaque, the carrot cubes have softened, and all of the moisture has evaporated, 7 to 8 minutes. Transfer the filling to a plate and let cool completely.

Meanwhile, to make a dipping sauce, in a blender, combine the cilantro roots, sugar, lime juice, water, garlic, chiles, and salt and process until the ingredients are the size of a match head. Transfer to a small serving bowl.

Arrange the lettuce leaves (and some basil and mint leaves) to one side of a serving platter. Place the bowl holding the dipping sauce in the center.

Stir the cilantro leaves into the cooled filling and divide the filling into 16 equal portions.

Place a rice noodle sheet on a clean work surface. Position a basil leaf in the middle of the lower one-third of the sheet, then place a mint leaf and a portion of the filling, respectively, on top of it. Starting from the edge closest to you, roll the noodle over the filling twice, tucking it in somewhat

continued

Rice noodle parcels with chile-lime sauce, continued

tightly as you go. Fold the two sides inward as tightly as possible without breaking the noodle and on a slight angle so the remaining rolling path is tapered. Continue to roll to the opposite edge. Place the parcel, seam side down, on the prepared serving platter and keep covered. Repeat until you have used all of the noodle sheets, filling, and herb leaves.

Serve the parcels immediately. Instruct diners to wrap each parcel with a piece of lettuce, to dip the whole thing into the dipping sauce, and then to consume the parcel in one satisfying bite, or perhaps two smaller bites if you're with company.

Brother Uan

Sitting alone at night in one of the areas in Bangkok known for nocturnal entertainment isn't an activity that I normally look forward to. But I will do anything to see this man. Once ten o'clock rolls around, I know, after just a few more minutes of swatting mosquitoes in this dark corner on Convent Road, one of my favorite individuals in the city will arrive, pushing a cart carrying a grill loaded with hot, glowing coals through the crowd—like a chariot of fire through a parted sea.

I've eaten the man's grilled pork (*mu ping*) since the days when he was known as simply *phi* Uan (Brother Uan), before the international food media discovered him and began calling him Owen. The global fame hasn't done any damage to the quality of Brother Uan's product, however. You can tell care is taken in how he alternates pieces of lean and fatty pork on the skewers and how he scrunches the pieces together tightly to form a compact body of bite-size meat so amply seasoned that it hardly needs a dipping sauce. Taking his time, Brother Uan grills his pork over hot ash-covered coals and trims off any overcharred bits with a pair of shears, one skewer at a time. The line is always long (that's why I like to arrive before he does so I can be the first), Brother Uan never seems to be in a hurry, and the people not familiar with how things work around this famous cart often grow impatient. But Brother Uan knows his customers will wait. They always do. When it's my turn, he looks up and our eyes meet. I nod. He nods. Then he proceeds to bag fifty skewers of grilled pork for me. Brother Uan remembers I make a trip out there to stock up for the next few weeks. *Mu ping* freezes and reheats well—especially his.

Grilled pork on skewers

หมูปิ้ง MU PING

MARINADE

6 large cloves garlic

¼ cup packed grated palm sugar

¼ cup oyster sauce

2 tablespoons Thai thin soy sauce or Golden Mountain seasoning sauce

2 tablespoons fish sauce

2 tablespoons finely chopped cilantro roots or stems

1 teaspoon white peppercorns

3 pounds boneless pork shoulder

DIPPING SAUCE

5 dried Thai long or guajillo chiles, stemmed

5 dried bird's eye chiles, stemmed

1 cup tamarind paste, homemade (page 316) or store-bought

⅓ cup packed grated palm sugar

3 tablespoons fresh lime juice

⅓ cup fish sauce

3 tablespoons finely chopped cilantro leaves

Vegetable oil, for greasing the grill grate

Steamed glutinous rice (page 18), for serving (optional)

These pork skewers are best enjoyed as a between-meal snack right out of the plastic bag, standing or walking. But you can serve them on a plate as an accompaniment to warm sticky rice and a bowl of dipping sauce on the side and call it a full-on meal. To get results as close to what you'd get on the streets of Bangkok, grill the pork over natural wood charcoal. ◆ **Makes 16 skewers; serves 4**

Soak 16 (10-inch) bamboo skewers in water overnight.

To make the marinade, in a blender, combine all of the ingredients and process until smooth. Transfer to a large bowl. Rinse out the blender.

Slice the pork against the grain on a 40-degree angle into pieces about 1½ inches wide, 2 inches long, and ¼ inch thick. Transfer the pieces to the marinade and mix well. Cover and refrigerate for 6 to 12 hours.

To make the sauce, meanwhile, toast all of the chiles in a 12-inch frying pan over medium heat, turning to color evenly on all sides, until fragrant and darkened, about 5 minutes. Transfer to the blender, add the tamarind, sugar, lime juice, and fish sauce, and process until smooth. Transfer to a 1-quart saucepan, place over medium heat, bring to a boil, and cook for 1 minute. Remove from the heat and let cool. Taste and adjust with more fish sauce if needed. The sauce should taste sour first and then equally sweet and salty. Stir in the cilantro and set aside. (The sauce can be made up to 3 days in advance and refrigerated in an airtight container.)

Divide the pork into 16 equal portions. Thread a portion onto each skewer, running the skewer through each piece as if you are sewing. Then, rather than stretch each piece taut, scrunch it together to form a round bundle that is as tight as possible. If there are any overhangs, tuck them in. The meat should occupy half of the length of each skewer, leaving the other half as a handle.

Light a chimney half full of natural wood charcoal. When all of the charcoal glows in the center and is covered with gray ash, scatter it onto the tray of a hibachi-style grill in a single layer. Position the cooking grate about 3 inches above the charcoal and allow to preheat for about 5 minutes. Oil the grate and arrange the pork skewers on the grate, spacing them about ¼ inch apart. Grill the skewers, flipping them often, until no pink remains and they are charred on the edges, 8 to 10 minutes.

Serve the skewers immediately with the dipping sauce as a snack. Add the sticky rice to make it a meal.

Memento Mori

The wind and the rain were pummeling us, and the boat was tossed about by unrelenting waves. It was only four in the afternoon, yet the sun was nowhere to be found. Lightning flashes revealed some passengers exchanging glances and others looking as if they were mentally comparing the number of lifesavers against the number of people on board. No words. Silent screams filled the air.

I was no stranger to the often-turbulent rainy season in Bangkok, and I'd commuted up and down the Chao Phraya thousands of times. But when the boat engine coughed and sputtered and eventually flatlined in the midst of a storm during high tide, even I let out a little whimper. We were stranded in the middle of the river waiting for the next boat, which wouldn't arrive for a while.

We'll die, said the older man next to me who had been quiet since he got on the boat at Sathon Pier. He came from the province of Nakhon Sawan, up north. It was the birthplace of the Chao Phraya itself, he reminded me, where the tributaries merge into this great river that runs through the center of Bangkok before dissolving into the Gulf of Thailand. Like the

Chao Phraya, he said, we come into existence under circumstances not of our own making. Like this river, we flow through life, trying our best to make ourselves useful while still alive. And someday, like this river, we will reach a point where we will be no more. We'll die, the philosopher reiterated, and if not today, then soon. There is no sense holding on to any earthly, corporeal things. In other words, had this been the *Titanic* and had there been romance between us, this Jack was telling this Rose not to bother—to just let go and embrace the end.

But not before he brought up the subject of pomelo, the fruit he loved so much that he'd eat it as his last meal on Earth.

Why Bangkokians are so crazy about pomelos from Nakhon Pathom was something he never understood, he said, shaking his head wearily and adding that supermarkets in the city always stocked up on them. But Nakhon Sawan pomelos were the best in the country, he insisted, especially the *Khao Taeng Kwa* (White Cucumber) cultivar that had just the right balance between firmness and juiciness. He believed it was the perfect cultivar for pomelo salad, which calls for crumbling the segments into small clusters of juice sacs. If the cultivar you use comes with juice sacs that are hard and not succulent enough, it's no good, he said. If you use a cultivar with soft flesh dripping with juices and perfect for eating out of hand, it will "weep" into the salad, diluting the dressing and making the dish sloppy and watery.

My fellow passenger was right on all counts. Different pomelo cultivars, much like apple cultivars, are good for different uses. If you live in Thailand, *Khao Nam Phueng* (White Honey) and *Khao Taeng Kwa* (White Cucumber) cultivars are best for salad. In the United States, my favorite pomelo cultivar has pink flesh. Its juice sacs aren't as crisp and voluptuous as those of the Thai cultivars, but it performs beautifully—especially if you let the fruit sit on the counter for two or three days, which tends to firm up the flesh and make it easier to remove the bitter white membranes.

He'd give anything to be back in Nakhon Sawan right now, sitting on the porch with his family and eating pomelo salad bites, the man soliloquized. He then proceeded to give me detailed instructions on how to make the salad his way. So for the next half hour, I forgot that, according to my fellow passenger, we would die, and instead I was listening to him share his recipe with great pleasure, until we were told the next boat was approaching.

Help's coming at last, I said to the sound of the other passengers clapping and cheering. The man turned to me and looked right into my eyes, his face as ominous as the thundering sky. And just as I was certain the pomelo-loving prophet of doom was about to remind me once again that we would all croak someday, he deadpanned, "When does help ever not come?"

Pomelo salad bites

เมี่ยงส้มโอ MIANG SOM O

½ cup unsalted roasted peanuts or cashews

1 heaping tablespoon unsweetened dried fine coconut flakes

6 large cloves garlic, sliced crosswise paper-thin

1 ounce shallots, halved lengthwise, placed cut side down, and cut lengthwise into paper-thin slices

¼ cup vegetable oil

8 ounces shrimp, peeled, deveined, and cut into ¼-inch dice

2 heaping tablespoons chile jam, homemade (page 22) or store-bought

2 cups (12 ounces) packed crumbled pomelo sections, kept chilled

Granulated sugar, for seasoning

Fresh lime juice, for seasoning

Salt

Dried red chile powder (page 323), for seasoning

Green or Bibb lettuce leaves, trimmed into 48 (3-inch-square) pieces

Make this recipe during the citrus season when pomelos are abundant in the market. In the United States, the best cultivar to use is the one with firm pink flesh that usually comes from Florida. Be prepared to improvise the seasoning, as you never know how sweet or tart each pomelo will be until you cut it open and taste it. ♦ **Makes 48 bites; serves 4 to 6**

Refresh the roasted peanuts by toasting them in an 8-inch frying pan over medium heat, stirring constantly, until fragrant and light brown, 8 to 10 minutes. Transfer to a plate and let cool. Wipe the pan clean. Add the coconut flakes to the pan and toast over medium heat, stirring constantly, until the color of light brown sugar, 1 to 2 minutes. Transfer to another small plate and let cool. Wipe the plan clean again. Add the garlic and shallot slices and the oil to the pan and fry over medium heat, stirring constantly, until both the garlic and the shallot slices are light brown and crisp, 8 to 10 minutes. Using a slotted spoon, transfer to a third small plate.

Pour off and discard all but 1½ teaspoons of the oil from the pan and return the pan to medium heat. Add the shrimp and stir-fry until opaque, about 2 minutes. Transfer to a bowl. Add the chile jam to the shrimp and stir to mix. Chop the toasted peanuts into match head–size pieces and add to the shrimp mixture along with the coconut flakes, garlic, and shallots. Add the pomelo and stir to mix well but gently to prevent the pomelo from "weeping." Taste the salad and season with the sugar, lime juice, salt, and chile powder. It should taste sweet and sour and then salty. You decide how hot you would like it to be. Regardless, the overall flavor should be pretty strong, as you will be eating this wrapped in bland lettuce.

Once the flavor suits you, spoon the salad into a serving bowl and place the bowl on a large platter. Arrange the lettuce pieces around the bowl. Invite diners to fill each lettuce piece with 1 tablespoon of the salad, then wrap and enjoy.

Grilled meatballs with spicy sweet-and-sour sauce

ลูกชิ้นปิ้ง **LUK CHIN PING**

5 large dried Thai long or guajillo chiles, cut into 1-inch pieces, soaked until softened, and squeezed dry

3 large cilantro roots, chopped, or 2 tablespoons finely chopped cilantro stems

6 large cloves garlic

⅓ cup canned tomato puree

2 tablespoons distilled white vinegar

1½ tablespoons tamarind paste, homemade (page 316) or store-bought

⅓ cup packed grated palm sugar

½ teaspoon salt

1 teaspoon cornstarch mixed with 3 tablespoons water

2 tablespoons finely chopped cilantro leaves

72 Asian-style beef, pork, or chicken meatballs, homemade (page 324) or store-bought

Vegetable oil, for greasing the grill gate

Grilled meatballs are a prime example of true street food. People seldom make them at home, preferring instead to buy them off the streets. When I was a child, we would buy ready-made meatballs from a noodle shop in the Si Yan neighborhood, famous for its supersmooth, superbouncy meatballs, which my mother would serve with her homemade sweet, sour, and glossy dipping sauce.

In the United States, Asian beef or pork balls come vacuum-packed and frozen. They're found at most Asian grocery stores, especially ones specializing in Southeast Asian ingredients (they're the same meatballs used in Thai noodle dishes and Vietnamese *phở*). You can also make your own. ♦ **Serves 4**

Soak 12 (10-inch) bamboo skewers in water overnight.

In a blender, combine the chiles, cilantro roots, garlic, tomato puree, and vinegar and process until the ingredients are the size of a match head. Transfer the puree to a 1-quart saucepan; add the tamarind, sugar, and salt; and bring to a boil over medium heat, stirring and scraping down the sides of the pan with a heat-resistant rubber spatula. Once the mixture boils, continue to cook, stirring and scraping, for 2 minutes longer. Stir in the cornstarch slurry and cook, stirring, for 1 minute longer. Remove from the heat and let cool completely, then stir in the cilantro leaves.

Light a chimney half full of natural wood charcoal. When all of the charcoal glows in the center and is covered with gray ash, scatter it onto the tray of a hibachi-style grill in a single layer. Position the grate about 3 inches above the charcoal and allow to preheat for about 5 minutes.

Thread 6 meatballs onto each skewer. Oil the grate and arrange the meatball skewers on the grate, spacing them about ¼ inch apart. Grill the meatballs, flipping the skewers often, until the surface appears dry and is slightly charred and blistered, 5 to 7 minutes. Remove the skewers from the heat and coat the meatballs, still on the skewers, with the sauce. Serve immediately and enjoy right off the skewers.

Rice crackers with pork-shrimp-coconut dip

ข้าวตังหน้าตั้ง **KHAO TANG NA TANG**

2 dried Thai long or guajillo chiles, cut into 1-inch pieces, soaked until softened, and squeezed dry

1 teaspoon white peppercorns

1 tablespoon finely chopped cilantro roots or stems

4 large cloves garlic

½ cup freshly extracted coconut cream, or ½ cup canned coconut cream plus 1 tablespoon extra-virgin coconut oil

1 tablespoon fresh river prawn tomalley or faux river prawn tomalley (page 29; optional)

2 ounces shallots, finely diced

1 cup coconut milk

8 ounces ground pork

8 ounces shrimp, peeled, deveined, and finely chopped

1½ tablespoons packed grated palm sugar

1 tablespoon tamarind paste, homemade (page 316) or store-bought

1 teaspoon salt

⅓ cup unsalted roasted peanuts, very finely chopped

2 tablespoons coconut cream, for garnish

3 or 4 fresh red chile slivers, for garnish

3 or 4 fresh cilantro leaves, for garnish

Fried rice crackers (page 20), for serving

Rice crackers, *khao tang*, are the traditional (and the best-tasting) vehicle for this creamy, flavorful dip. Together, they form this old-school dish that is still very much in demand, even though the city is flooded with all kinds of modern appetizers these days. The dip looks reddish but is not—should not be—hot. The color comes from river prawn tomalley, which also contributes extra creaminess and flavor.

Serves 4

In a mortar, grind together the chiles, peppercorns, cilantro roots, and garlic to a smooth paste. Transfer the paste to a 2-quart saucepan and add the coconut cream and tomalley. Place the pan over medium-high heat and stir constantly for 1 minute. Stir in the shallots, coconut milk, pork, shrimp, sugar, tamarind, and salt and adjust the heat to maintain a gentle boil. Cook, breaking up the pork and shrimp with the blunt end of a wooden spatula into fine crumbles, until they are opaque, 6 to 8 minutes. Taste for seasoning and adjust as needed; you want it to be salty first, then sweet, and finally ever so slightly tangy (keep in mind that you'll eat this with unseasoned rice crackers). Once the taste suits you, stir in the peanuts. Remove from the heat and let cool until just slightly warmer than room temperature.

Transfer the dip to a bowl and garnish with the coconut cream, red chile slivers, and cilantro leaves. Place the bowl on a large platter and arrange the rice crackers around it. Serve immediately.

Stuffed pancakes with beef filling and cucumber relish

มะตะบะเนื้อ MATABA NUEA

FILLING

2 teaspoons ghee, butter, or vegetable oil

1½ tablespoons mild curry powder

3 large cloves garlic, minced

12 ounces lean (10 percent fat) ground beef or lamb

1½ teaspoons salt

½ teaspoon granulated sugar

4 eggs

1 yellow or white onion, cut lengthwise into paper-thin slices

PANCAKES

1 recipe roti dough (page 335), aged in the refrigerator for 48 hours, then brought to room temperature

About 1 cup ghee or vegetable oil, for frying

SIDES

Cucumber relish (page 319), assembled just before serving

2 tablespoons peeled and julienned fresh ginger (the younger, the better)

This Thai Muslim specialty can be enjoyed as a between-meal snack or a one-plate meal. I've modeled my recipe for this panfried stuffed pancake after the one sold at my favorite *mataba* stand by the Chao Phraya, adjacent to Thammasat University. It boasts a fragrant beef filling and flaky crust.

Before you begin, read through the entire recipe to get a clear idea of what it entails. The entire process stretches over three consecutive days because the dough must rest for that long. *Mataba* is usually served with plain cucumber relish, but an addition of fresh ginger—inspired by another famous Thai Muslim shop in Old Town Bangkok—makes the whole ensemble even better. ♦ **Makes 4 pancakes; serves 4 to 6**

To make the filling, put the ghee in a 10-inch frying pan and set over medium-high heat. When the ghee is hot, add the curry powder and garlic and stir-fry until fragrant, about 1 minute. Add the beef, salt, and sugar and stir-fry, breaking up the beef as finely as possible with the blunt end of a wooden spatula, until no pink remains and all of the moisture has evaporated, 8 to 10 minutes. Remove the pan from the heat, transfer the filling to a plate, and let cool completely. Wash the pan and wipe it dry, then keep it handy.

Grab four bowls and crack an egg into each one; beat with a fork just until blended. Divide the beef and onion slices evenly among the four bowls; stir to mix.

To make the pancakes, place a ball of dough on a clean, smooth, shiny work surface and flatten it with the heels of your hands into an 8-inch round of even thickness, pressing it down so it sticks to the surface. With your hands palm up, reach under the dough and, starting from the center, gently pull the dough outward a little at a time until you have a round of even thickness 15 to 18 inches in diameter and so thin and translucent that you can read a magazine through it (if the edges are slightly thicker than the middle, don't sweat it). Lay the round on the work surface and, using your fingers, press down on the edges to secure it to the surface in the stretched position.

The pastry will curl up over itself around the very edge. Don't worry, as that's normal. Drag the tip of a knife around the perimeter of the round to trim off the curled edge, discarding the scraps. Spoon a bowl of the filling into the center of the dough and spread it out to form an 8-inch square. Gently lift up the bottom edge and fold it over the filling. Repeat with the top edge. Then fold the left and right "wings" over the filling, overlapping the top and bottom edges to form a sealed pouch (the dough is so sticky that it

continued

will seal itself). Repeat with the remaining dough and filling to make four filled pancakes.

Preheat the oven to 300°F. Have a sheet pan ready. Return the reserved frying pan to medium heat and add ¼ cup of the ghee. When the ghee is hot, use a flat plate or a large spatula to lift a filled pancake off of the work surface and place it, seam side down, in the center of the pan. Fry the pancake, pressing down on it lightly with a spatula as you go and adding more ghee as needed to keep the pancake half-submerged, until it feels firm—a sign that the filling is cooked through—and is golden brown, 6 to 8 minutes. Make sure the sides are browned, too. To do this, tilt the pan so the ghee forms a pool at its edge. Position the pancake to submerge one side of it in the pooled oil and then rotate the pancake until all of the sides are browned. Using a spatula, transfer the fried pancake to the sheet pan and place in the oven to keep warm. Fry the remaining three pancakes, one at a time, the same way, using about ¼ cup of the remaining ghee for each pancake.

Transfer the final pancake from the frying pan to a cutting board. Take the first three pancakes out of the oven. Cut all of the pancakes into 2-inch squares and arrange the pieces on a serving plate. Assemble the cucumber relish in a bowl and stir in the ginger. Serve the relish immediately alongside the pancakes.

On Bitter Oranges

The juice and rind of the green (immature) *som sa*, or bitter orange (*Citrus aurantium*), was routinely used to perfume many classic Thai dishes in the past. Known as the Seville orange in the Mediterranean, it can be found in abundance in some areas of the world but is astoundingly hard to find in and outside Bangkok—at least as of this writing. And if you do come upon bitter oranges in a market, you'll discover how expensive they are compared with other citrus fruits. This might be part of the reason the bitter orange fell into disuse among the general population. Today, many Thai cooks don't even know this sour fruit exists, much less that it once was an essential ingredient in Thai cooking.

Durian is widely regarded as the king of fruits in Asia, but in certain circles of Bangkok society, the bitter orange reigns above it. Many recipes from the early 1900s, the period when recipes began to be recorded and published, show bitter orange as an ingredient in dishes that are made today without it. *Mi krop* (page 55) is an example of a dish that most purists insist must contain bitter orange and that no other citrus will do. *Matsaman* curry (page 95) is another example.

My hunch is that growers will soon catch on and start producing this citrus commercially. And when that happens, the fruit will become—one can hope—just as common and affordable as *makrut* lime or regular lime. Until then, I and others will have to use something in its place. Many recipes in this book call for bitter oranges, and in every instance I've made navel oranges an option. That in no way suggests the two are interchangeable, as they're definitely not. But I've found that navel oranges are the sole type that not only performs adequately—quite impressively in some recipes—but can also be found regularly in supermarkets. If you have access to unripe navel oranges with green skin, that's even better.

If you live where the *som sa* is found in abundance, you're lucky. As you make the recipes in this book, that citrus will be your DeLorean, taking you back in time to the era when Bangkok was young.

Sweet-and-sour crispy angel hair rice noodles

หมี่กรอบทรงเครื่อง **MI KROP SONG KHRUEANG**

4 ounces Wai Wai brand dried angel hair rice noodles

1 tablespoon light salted soybeans, mashed to a coarse paste

1 tablespoon fresh shrimp tomalley or faux river prawn tomalley (page 29; optional)

1 tablespoon liquid from Thai pickled garlic

2 tablespoons fish sauce

1 tablespoon tamarind paste, homemade (page 316) or store-bought

1 tablespoon fresh lime juice

⅓ cup fresh bitter (Seville) orange juice or ½ cup fresh navel orange juice

½ cup packed soft, sticky, dark pure palm sugar from Thailand, or ¼ cup each packed grated light, hard palm sugar and packed dark brown sugar

Vegetable oil, for deep-frying

2 ounces extra-firm tofu, cut into ⅛ by ⅛ by 1-inch sticks

10 large shrimp, peeled and deveined

1 egg, beaten in a bowl with a fork just until blended

1 (1-ounce) shallot, finely minced

3 large cloves garlic, finely minced

1 tablespoon finely chopped bitter (Seville) orange rind, or 1½ teaspoons each finely chopped lime rind and navel orange rind

Whether this beloved classic should be classified as a savory between-meal snack, an hors d'oeuvre, a main rice accompaniment, or a one-plate meal depends on whom you ask. This dish of light, shatteringly crisp rice noodle straws held together by a sticky sweet-and-sour sauce can be anything you want it to be. I like to eat *mi krop* as a stand-alone snack—almost like an appetizer—so I'm including it in this chapter.

One thing I think everyone agrees on is that *mi krop* isn't the easiest dish to make. It's an advance-level recipe that offers little to no flexibility in terms of ingredients. You must use Thai dried angel hair rice noodles (*sen mi*), which are not to be confused with thin rice noodles or glass (cellophane) noodles made with mung beans. You must make a tricky caramel—if you add the fried noodles when the caramel is too runny, the noodles will be soggy and the dish ruined; if you add the noodles when the caramel has thickened too much, the caramel will be too sticky and there won't be enough of it to coat every noodle strand.

That said, a great reward awaits you at the end of this fun adventure. This version is fancier than what you'd find on the streets or at a casual eatery in Bangkok. Feel free to eliminate any of the add-ons, such as the fried egg drops or the pickled garlic. ⬧ **Serves 2 or 3**

Separate the noodles into eight bunches of equal size. Turn on the faucet and give the noodles a quick cold "shower" by running them through the water just long enough to moisten them (no more than 4 seconds). Shake off the excess water and spread the noodles out on the counter, keeping the bundles separate.

Combine the light salted soybeans, shrimp tomalley, pickled garlic liquid, fish sauce, tamarind, lime juice, orange juice, and sugar in a bowl and mix well. Set aside.

Pour the oil to a depth of 3 inches into a wok and heat to 350°F to 370°F. Line a sheet pan with paper towels and set it near the stove. When the oil is ready, gently drop a single noodle bunch into it (never fry more than one at a time). The noodles will puff up and form a raft immediately. Flip the raft so both sides are crispy. The noodles are done when the bubbling and sizzling substantially subside, with the entire process taking less than a minute. Using a mesh skimmer, transfer the noodles to the prepared sheet pan. Repeat with the remaining bunches.

continued

GARNISHES AND SIDES

1 head Thai pickled garlic, thinly sliced crosswise

2 fresh red bird's eye chiles, stemmed and sliced lengthwise

1 lime, cut into wedges

1 cup bean sprouts, refreshed in cold water for 5 minutes, then drained and patted dry

6 Chinese garlic chives

2 wedges trimmed banana blossom, 1 inch thick, soaked in acidulated water until serving, then drained and patted dry (optional)

Once all the noodles have been fried, don't turn off the heat. Using the skimmer, scoop out all of the sediment from the oil and discard it. Line two large dinner plates with paper towels and place them near the stove.

Drop the tofu sticks into the hot oil and fry them until golden brown, 1 to 2 minutes. Using the skimmer, transfer the sticks to one side of a towel-lined plate. Drop the shrimp into the hot oil and fry until opaque, about 1 minute, then transfer them to the other side of the tofu plate.

Next, hold the bowl of beaten egg over the wok with your nondominant hand. Dip the fingers of your other hand, one knuckle deep, into the egg, and, with your fingers pointed straight down, move your hand in a circular motion over the oil, letting the egg fall where it may. Do this no more than two or three times per batch to avoid crowding the pan. In less than 1 minute, the egg drops will be crisp and golden brown. Fish them out with the mesh skimmer and place them on the other towel-lined plate. Repeat until all of the egg is fried.

Pour off all but 2 tablespoons of the oil from the wok. Return the wok to medium-high heat, add the shallot and garlic, and stir-fry until fragrant, about 1 minute. With a rubber spatula, scrape every bit of the prepared sauce out of the bowl into the wok. Take note of the original level of the sauce when it bubbles, then boil, stirring constantly, until it has reduced by half. Working quickly, add the fried noodles, fried tofu, and fried shrimp to the wok and, using the blunt end of a wooden spatula, "chop" the noodles into little pieces while stirring to coat them thoroughly, about 30 seconds. Add the orange rind and give the mixture one last stir before turning off the heat.

Transfer the noodles to a large serving platter. Scatter the egg drops and the pickled garlic all over the noodles. Top it all with the chiles. Arrange the lime wedges, bean sprouts, chives, and banana blossom wedges on the side to eat along with the noodles. Serve immediately.

The Royal Thai Cuisine

Although debunked many times, one of the myths surrounding the food culture of Thailand that has never gone away is the notion that there exists a separate class of cuisine known as royal Thai cuisine. Worse still is the belief that the palace is where Thai food is closely guarded and codified and, therefore, represents the cuisine at its most "unadulterated."

Historical documents, whether the literature of the royal courts, the cookbooks written by aristocrats, eyewitness memoirs, or epistolary writings by the royals themselves, show that, in general, the food of the royal courts has never been markedly different from that of the ordinary citizen. What sets royal fare apart from that of the everyday table has more to do with the way it is composed and presented—refined and elegant. Attention is given to the scenting, the carving, and the decoration of food. A meal is always presented in a manner that ensures it can be eaten with ease—that it requires no cutting, slicing, boning, or seeding at the table. Highly spiced food or food with a strong odor is often avoided or dialed down. It's also not uncommon for a dish from the royal kitchen to be made up of many ingredients or require multiple long and laborious preparation steps—occasionally just to produce something as simple as a sweet that can be enjoyed in no more than a few bites. Not surprisingly, some recipes originating from a royal court have been devised with an assumption that you have a large kitchen crew doing all the prep work for you. Replicating such dishes in a modern-day kitchen can sometimes be tricky and time-consuming. The ones included in this book, however, fall on the easy end of the spectrum.

Beef satay with sweet-and-sour dipping sauce

สะเต๊ะเนื้อ ✦ SATE NUEA

Ma-ngum-ma-nga-ra is one of a few loanwords that have entered the Thai lexicon by way of Panji, a legendary Javanese prince known as Inao in the several Thai versions of the tales. The most widely circulated one was penned by Rama II, whose reign in the early years of Bangkok is referred to as the golden age of literature. Even though in the context of Inao this verb is used to depict wandering or roaming about for pleasure, in the present day it is used—archaized—colloquially to refer to moving slowly and awkwardly in confusion and disorientation. Look at the word. Say it out loud a few times, pronouncing the digraph *ng* with a little more feeling than what society expects, and you'll get a murmuring sense of someone, dazed and discombobulated, feeling his or her way around an unfamiliar place.

As with the word, this version of satay came to Thailand from Java. However, it isn't the type you normally see on the streets of Bangkok (or on the menus of Thai restaurants worldwide), where Chinese Thai–style pork satay dominates the scene. Instead of being served with the usual peanut sauce and cucumber relish, it has peanuts in the marinade, is more strongly spiced, and comes with a sweet-and-sour dipping sauce. A plate of toast is absent, making way for a bed of lettuce leaves and for crisp cucumber slices on the side.

This satay came out of the royal mansion of Princess Saisavali Bhiromya, a consort of King Chulalongkorn and the head of the royal kitchen in the late nineteenth century. The dish is said to have been introduced to the mansion through a Javanese teacher and later adapted to better suit the local palate. According to Mom Luang Nueang Nilrat, a renowned cook and author who lived in the mansion under the princess's patronage, the dish had become so popular among people who tasted it that the princess named it *sate lue,* literally "satay [that people] talk about"—famous satay, if you will.

Like most people, I have never tasted the original famous satay, but thanks to the detailed description of the dish and thorough instructions that M. L. Nueang included in her writings, I was not completely lost. Her list of ingredients provides no measurements, however, so I still had to *ma-ngum-ma-nga-ra* my way through trying to replicate this renowned satay for a few years until I came up with something that pleased me.

I have no way of knowing how close my adaptation is to the original. For what it's worth, this version has been pretty famous within my circle of friends. ✦ **Makes 16 skewers; serves 4**

continued

MARINADE

1 tablespoon coriander seeds

1 tablespoon cumin seeds

3 tablespoons unsalted roasted peanuts

1½ ounces shallots, cut into small cubes

¼ cup fish sauce

¼ cup sweetened condensed milk

2 teaspoons granulated sugar

1 tablespoon packed grated palm sugar

1 tablespoon ground turmeric

2 tablespoons brandy or dark rum

½ cup coconut cream

3 pounds trimmed well-marbled boneless rib-eye or chuck steak

DIPPING SAUCE

2 ounces shallots, cut into small cubes

4 fresh red Thai long, jalapeño, or serrano chiles

1 cup distilled white vinegar

1 tablespoon salt

½ cup granulated sugar

Vegetable oil, for greasing the grill grate

½ cup extra-virgin coconut oil, for brushing

SIDES

1 head green lettuce, separated into individual leaves and kept chilled

1 English cucumber, peeled, cut on the diagonal into ¼-inch-thick slices, and kept chilled

Soak 16 (10-inch) bamboo skewers in water overnight.

To make the marinade, toast the coriander and cumin seeds in a small frying pan over medium heat, stirring constantly, until fragrant, about 3 minutes. Transfer to a small blender or food processor, add the peanuts, shallots, fish sauce, condensed milk, both sugars, turmeric, brandy, and coconut cream, and blend until smooth. Transfer to a large bowl.

Thinly slice the beef against the grain on a slight diagonal into pieces about 1 inch wide and 3 inches long. Transfer the pieces to the marinade and, using your hands, massage the marinade into the meat. (According to M. L. Nueang Nilrat, it would be wise to remove any diamond rings you may be wearing at this point. The severe and chronic lack of diamonds in my life makes this a nonissue, but your situation may be different.) Once everything is well mixed, cover the bowl and refrigerate for 3 hours.

To make the sauce, meanwhile, combine all of the ingredients in a blender and process until a coarse puree forms. Transfer to a 1-quart saucepan, bring to a boil over medium heat, and boil for 2 minutes. Remove from the heat, transfer to heatproof bowl, and let cool.

Drain the beef and divide into 16 equal portions. Thread a portion onto each skewer, running the skewer through each piece as if you were sewing. Then, rather than stretching each piece taut, scrunch it together to form a round bundle that is as tight as possible. If there are any overhangs, tuck them in. The meat should occupy half the length of each skewer, leaving the other half as a handle.

Light a chimney half full of natural wood charcoal. When all of the charcoal glows in the center and is covered with gray ash, scatter it onto the tray of a hibachi-style grill in a single layer. Position the cooking grate about 3 inches above the charcoal and allow to preheat for about 5 minutes. Brush the grate with vegetable oil and arrange the beef skewers on the grate, spacing them about ¼ inch apart. Grill the skewers, flipping them often and brushing them with the coconut oil along the way, until no pink remains and they are charred on the edges, 8 to 10 minutes.

Serve the skewers immediately with the dipping sauce and with the lettuce and cucumbers alongside.

Egg net parcels with pork-peanut filling

ล่าเตียง **LA TIANG**

2 cilantro roots, chopped, or
2 tablespoons finely chopped
cilantro stems

½ teaspoon white peppercorns

2 large cloves garlic

1 (1-ounce) shallot, minced

1½ teaspoons homemade lard
(page 28) or vegetable oil,
plus more for greasing

2 ounces ground pork or
chicken

4 ounces shrimp, peeled,
deveined, and finely chopped

1½ tablespoons packed
grated palm sugar

½ teaspoon salt

2 tablespoons unsalted
roasted peanuts, finely
chopped

6 duck or chicken eggs

1 tablespoon water

24 cilantro leaves

24 thin slivers fresh red
Thai long, jalapeño,
or serrano chile

These bite-size parcels are fitting as a prelude to a special Thai meal when you have company or as a savory snack to be enjoyed with hot jasmine tea.

Although this dish is referred to as *rum* (หรุ่ม) in several sources, respected historical and modern-day documents confirm that *la tiang* is the correct name, and that *rum* is a similar appetizer that is wrapped in simple thin omelet sheets rather than the lacy, ethereal crisscrossed egg sheets used here.

Cooking the egg nets can be challenging, and it may take a few tries before you get the hang of it. This is a dish you want to make on a lazy weekend when you have time to spare. Having a few extra eggs on hand is a good idea, too. ◆ **Makes 24 pieces; serves 4 to 6**

In a mortar, grind together the cilantro roots, peppercorns, and garlic to a smooth paste. Put the paste, shallot, and lard in a 12-inch nonstick frying pan and set over medium heat. Stir-fry until the shallot is translucent and the paste is fragrant, about 2 minutes. Add the pork, shrimp, sugar, and salt and stir-fry, breaking up the pork and shrimp with the blunt end of a wooden spatula into fine crumbles, until the pork and shrimp are opaque and all of the moisture has evaporated, 5 to 6 minutes. Stir in the peanuts and fry for 1 minute longer, then transfer to a bowl and leave to cool completely. You should have 1 cup (48 teaspoons) filling. Wash the pan and wipe it dry, then keep it handy.

Crack the eggs into a bowl, add the water, and beat together with a fork until homogenous. Set the reserved pan over low heat. Brush a thin coat of lard on the bottom of the pan. With your third eye, imagine a 3-inch circle in the center of the pan. Now, dip your fingers into the beaten eggs and, with your fingers pointing straight down, move your hand back and forth so the egg drips off the tips of your fingers in thin strands onto the imaginary circle, forming a crisscross pattern about ¹⁄₁₆ inch thick. (If it helps, "draw" the circumference first with egg strands, then go all Jackson Pollock inside it.) Once the circle is adequately filled in, cover the pan and leave undisturbed until the surface of the net is no longer wet, about 10 seconds. Uncover the pan and, using a spatula, very gently transfer the net to a large platter. Keep the platter covered while you make more egg nets with the remaining beaten eggs, brushing the pan lightly with lard before cooking each net. You should have 24 nets.

continued

Now, picture a 1-inch square in the center of an egg net and spread 2 teaspoons of the filling in the square, covering the entire square and forming a mound of even height. Fold in all four sides of the circle to form a square parcel, then set the parcel on a serving platter, seam side down; the weight of the filling will help keep the parcel closed. Cover the platter. Repeat the process—don't hate me—twenty-three times. (The key to success is never to overcook the egg nets, as they will become dry and brittle and thus impossible to fold. If you mess up, move on; make a new circle. That's what the extra eggs are for.)

Once you have made all of the parcels and beautifully arranged them on the platter, top each one with a cilantro leaf and a red chile sliver. Serve at room temperature.

Fried taro dumplings with shrimp-coconut filling

ค้างคาวเผือก **KHANG KHAO PHUEAK**

DOUGH

1 pound taro roots or malanga roots

½ cup Thai rice flour

¼ teaspoon salt

FILLING

2 cloves garlic

½ teaspoon white peppercorns

2 tablespoons finely chopped cilantro roots or stems

1 tablespoon homemade lard (page 28) or vegetable oil

4 ounces shrimp, peeled, deveined, and finely chopped (not ground)

¼ cup unsweetened dried fine coconut flakes

2 heaping tablespoons coconut cream

1½ tablespoons packed grated palm sugar

½ teaspoon salt

2 tablespoons fresh shrimp tomalley or faux river prawn tomalley (page 29; optional)

1 teaspoon finely cut makrut lime leaves, in whisker-thin strips

Vegetable oil, for deep-frying

BATTER

1 cup Thai rice flour, plus more for dusting

¼ cup limestone solution (page 336)

¼ cup cold water

1 egg yolk

¼ teaspoon salt

Cucumber relish (page 319), for serving

By the time Bangkok was founded, this appetizer was already a favorite among the royals. That means it was likely enjoyed even when the Kingdom of Ayutthaya was in power and Bangkok was just a village by the Chao Phraya. Although how these dumplings were prepared in the old days is different from the way they're made in modern-day Bangkok, many similarities remain. My recipe reflects the contemporary version.

The word *phueak* in the name of this dish has two meanings, "taro root" and "albino," so I see *khang khao* (bat) *phueak* as a wordplay that can be read two ways: bats made with taro or albino bats. The dumplings are light beige and are traditionally shaped into a domed isosceles triangle that mimics the shape of a bat unfolding its wings, so both translations fit. The interpretation is up to you.

For best results, use mature taro roots, which are starchy—we need starch—and not as slimy as the smaller, younger ones. Because of the high starch content, malanga roots, taro's close cousin, are also ideal.

◈ **Makes 24 dumplings; serves 4 to 6**

To make the dough, peel the taro and cut into 1½-inch cubes. Put the cubes into a 2-quart saucepan, add water to cover, and bring to a simmer over medium heat. Simmer until fork-tender, about 15 minutes. Drain the taro well and spread it out on a sheet pan. Let stand until completely cooled and the surface is dry, 45 to 60 minutes.

To make the filling, while the taro is cooling, in a mortar, grind together the garlic, peppercorns, and cilantro roots to a smooth paste. Heat the lard in a 10-inch frying pan over medium-high heat. When the lard is hot, add the prepared paste and stir-fry nonstop until fragrant, about 1 minute. Add the shrimp, coconut flakes, coconut cream, sugar, salt, and shrimp tomalley and stir-fry until the shrimp turns opaque and all of the moisture has evaporated (it should seem like you are "toasting" the filling), 8 to 10 minutes. Remove the pan from the heat, stir in the lime leaves, and let cool completely. You should end up with ¾ cup (36 teaspoons) packed filling.

When the taro has cooled completely and is dry (be patient; it must be fully cooled), transfer it to a bowl and mash it with a potato masher or pass it through a ricer into a bowl. Add the rice flour and salt and, using your hands, mix the ingredients to create a homogenous mixture. You want a smooth dough that is soft and malleable but doesn't stick excessively to your fingers. Add a couple of spoonfuls of flour if needed to reduce the stickiness.

Divide the dough into four equal portions, roll each portion into a rope of equal thickness, and cut each rope into six equal pieces. (If you have a scale, divide the dough into 24 pieces of equal weight.) Roll each piece between your palms into a smooth ball and keep the formed balls under an overturned bowl. Put a ball of dough between two pieces of plastic wrap and flatten it with the heel of your palm into a round 3 inches in diameter and of even thickness. Remove the top piece of plastic wrap and place 1½ teaspoons filling in the center. Using the bottom piece of plastic wrap to help you, lift the sides of the dough to make a triangle and pinch the edges together to seal them. Use your fingers to adjust the dumpling so it looks symmetrical, making sure the seals are secure. (This is like forming hamantaschen, except the filling is not exposed.) The bottom of the dumpling is fragile, so be careful when you peel it off of the plastic wrap. Set the shaped dumpling aside on a lightly floured surface. Repeat until you have used all of the dough and filling.

When all of the dumplings have been shaped, pour the oil to a depth of 2 inches into a wok or Dutch oven and heat to 350°F.

To make the batter, while waiting for the oil to heat, in a small bowl, whisk together all the ingredients until smooth. Line a sheet pan with paper towels and place it near the stove. When the oil is hot, dip a "bat" into the batter, coating it on all sides and letting the excess drip back into the bowl, and then gently drop it into the oil. Repeat to add more dumplings to the oil, being careful not to crowd the pan. Fry until the batter crisps and the dumplings turn light brown, 5 to 7 minutes. Using a slotted spoon, transfer to the prepared sheet pan to drain. Fry the remaining dumplings in the same way. Serve at slightly warmer than room temperature with the cucumber relish.

Watermelon with fish dip

ปลาแห้ง-แตงโม PLA HAENG-TAENG MO

1 pound skinless trout, salmon, or tilapia fillets

1¼ teaspoons salt

1 (1-ounce) shallot, halved lengthwise, placed cut side down, and cut lengthwise into paper-thin slices

¼ cup homemade lard (page 28) or vegetable oil

6 tablespoons granulated sugar

1 (8- to 10-pound) watermelon

The Thai tradition of eating fruits with a meal—with rice at the center of the meal, of course—goes back centuries. It's a way of cooling down the palate when eating spicy dishes and of tempering the oppressive heat of the summer months.

Although it is historically an everyday dish, watermelon with a fish dip isn't something sold by street vendors in modern-day Bangkok. But you will see it in elegant restaurants serving old-style or royal Thai dishes and in homes where people still cook decades-old recipes from their grandmother's vault.

You can serve this dish in the traditional manner, as a rice accompaniment at a meal. But I've decided to put it in the snack and appetizer category, because that's the way it is most often served nowadays. ⬥ **Makes 2 cups dip; serves 4 to 6**

Preheat the oven to 375°F. Make a few cuts about three-fourths of the way into the flesh of the fish. Rub ¾ teaspoon of the salt all over the surface of the fish and deep into the cuts. Place the fish on a sheet pan.

Bake the fish until it flakes easily, about 30 minutes. Remove from the oven and immediately transfer to a food processor or mortar and grind into fine, cottony flakes. Set aside.

Line a small plate with a paper towel and place it near the stove. Put the shallot slices and lard in a 6- or 8-inch nonstick frying pan (or a well-seasoned wok), set over medium heat, and cook, stirring almost constantly, until the shallot slices are golden brown, 6 to 7 minutes. Using a slotted spoon, immediately transfer the fried shallots to the prepared plate, then transfer the lard to a 12- or 14-inch frying pan or a wok.

Stir the fish flakes and the remaining ½ teaspoon salt into the lard, set the pan over medium heat, and toast the fish flakes, stirring nearly constantly, until light, crisp, and golden brown, 30 to 35 minutes. Do not raise the heat in the hope of speeding up the process; the fish needs to be toasted slowly. Add the sugar and continue to stir for 2 minutes. Remove from the heat and leave the mixture in the pan to cool.

Meanwhile, cut the watermelon flesh into 1½-inch cubes or use a large melon baller to scoop out the flesh in bite-size balls. Cover and chill until serving.

Once the fish flakes have cooled, stir in the fried shallot slices. Serve the dip with the chilled watermelon.

Chicken curry puffs

กะหรี่ปั๊บไส้ไก่ KARI PAP SAI KAI

FILLING

1¼ pounds waxy potatoes, peeled and cut into ¼-inch dice

1 tablespoon vegetable oil

¼ cup mild curry powder

1 pound boneless, skinless chicken breasts or tenderloins, cut into ¼-inch dice

8 ounces yellow or white onions, cut into ¼-inch dice

1 tablespoon salt

⅓ cup granulated sugar

OUTER DOUGH

4 cups all-purpose flour, preferably King Arthur brand

2 teaspoons granulated sugar

1 teaspoon salt

¼ cup limestone solution (page 336)

About 1 cup water

INNER DOUGH

2¾ cups all-purpose flour, preferably King Arthur brand

1 cup vegetable oil

All-purpose flour, for dusting

Vegetable oil, for deep-frying

Consumed throughout Southeast Asia, curry puffs have long been popular with Bangkokians, who can't seem to get enough of these savory dumplings with flaky shells sporting a spiral design—a sign of properly prepared laminated pastry—and their richly spiced filling. They are usually about half the size of your palm, making them a handy snack easily enjoyed out of a paper bag as you walk away from a vendor's stand. At home or at a sit-down restaurant, they're served as an appetizer—sometimes with a side of sweet-and-tart cucumber relish (page 319), an option you may want to consider here.

A kitchen scale will serve you well for this recipe. Without it, it's nearly impossible to divide the dough and the filling into portions of equal weight, a step critical to ensuring a good ratio of dough and filling. ◆ **Makes 32 puffs; serves 8**

To make the filling, put the potatoes in a 2-quart saucepan, add water to cover, and set the pan over high heat. When the water is boiling, lower the heat to medium, cover the pan, and cook until the potatoes are barely fork-tender, about 10 minutes. Drain and reserve.

Heat the oil in a 12-inch frying pan over medium-high heat. Add the curry powder and stir until fragrant, 30 to 40 seconds. Add the potatoes, chicken, onions, salt, and sugar all at once, then turn the heat to medium and stir-fry until the chicken is opaque, the onions are translucent, and the potatoes are thoroughly softened, 15 to 20 minutes. Turn the heat to medium-high and cook, stirring constantly, to evaporate all of the visible moisture in the pan, about 2 minutes. Remove from the heat and let cool completely.

To make the outer dough, in a bowl, stir together the flour, sugar, and salt. Add the limestone solution and then begin adding the water, a little at a time, mixing with your hand. Continue adding the water until a shaggy ball of dough has formed that cleans the bottom and sides of the bowl. Turn the dough out onto a work surface, invert the bowl over it, and leave to hydrate for 20 minutes.

To make the inner dough, meanwhile, in a bowl, combine the flour and ¾ cup of the oil and mix with your hand, adding more of the oil, a couple of teaspoons at a time, until a smooth dough forms. (You may not need all of the oil.) Turn out the dough onto the work surface, invert the bowl over it, and leave to rest for 20 minutes.

continued

Knead the outer dough briefly until smooth and supple, about 1 minute. Divide it into 16 portions of equal weight and roll each portion into a ball. Invert the bowl over the dough balls and set them aside. Do the same with the inner dough.

Using your palm, flatten a portion of the outer dough into a 4-inch round of even thickness. Place a portion of the inner dough in the center of the round and gather the edges of the outer dough over the top of the inner dough, encasing the inner dough completely and creating a ball. Seal the outer dough, making sure no part of the inner dough peeks through. Cover with a large overturned bowl and leave to rest for 20 minutes. Repeat with the remaining portions, slipping them under the bowl as they are made.

While the dough is resting, divide the filling into 32 equal portions. With immaculately clean hands, squeeze each portion into an oblong lump about 3 inches long; set aside.

Lightly dust a work surface with flour. Remove a ball from under the bowl, leaving the others covered, and place it on the floured surface. Using a rolling pin, roll out the ball into an oval of even thickness about 10 inches long and 4 inches wide. Starting from a narrow end, use your fingers to roll up the oval as tightly as you would a yoga mat, being careful not to press down or squeeze the cylinder. Put the dough roll back under the overturned bowl and repeat with the remaining dough balls.

Using a very sharp knife (a dull knife will mess up the layers), make a swift and clean cut crosswise down the center of each dough roll. Arrange the pieces, cut side up, on your work surface and cover them with an overturned bowl.

Set a piece, cut side up, on the work surface. Use your palm to push it from the top slightly to one side, so that if you squat down and peer at it at eye level, it reminds you of the Leaning Tower of Pisa. (This step is important to ensure the spirals overlap ever so slightly when the dough is rolled out. If you don't do this, the spirals tend to unravel in the fryer—an irrevocable disaster.) With your downturned palm perfectly parallel with the surface of the counter, flatten the leaning tower just enough for it to be easy to roll. Then, using the rolling pin, roll it into a thin oval about 5 inches long and 4 inches wide, being careful not to disturb the spirals more than necessary. (The dough should not be at all sticky, but if it sticks to the counter, dust the counter lightly with flour.) Place a lump of filling in the middle of the oval, with the long side of the filling perpendicular to the long side of the oval. Fold the two sides of the dough over the filling. Seal the shell shut, pinching and pleating as you go (follow the crimping instructions for the steamed chicken dumplings on page 34), working from one end to the other end. (If you are

not feeling confident the seal is good, use fork tines to crimp the edges shut.) Set the dumpling aside (once the dumplings are formed, they do not need to be covered). Repeat the process until you run out of dough and filling.

Pour the oil to a depth of 4 inches into a wok or Dutch oven and heat to 325°F to 350°F. Set a cooling rack on a sheet pan and place it near the stove. When the oil is ready, working in batches to avoid crowding, gently lower the dumplings into the hot oil. Using a mesh skimmer or slotted spoon, flip the dumplings around almost constantly until they are golden all over, about 4 minutes. (The constant movement is necessary to keep the puffs from sinking and sitting at the bottom of the pan, which would cause their fattest part to darken and burn.) Using the skimmer or slotted spoon, transfer the puffs to the cooling rack and let cool. Repeat until all of the puffs are fried, then serve at, or slightly warmer than, room temperature.

Rice
Accompaniments

Young Warlord

Warlord cried a lot. And my dad, who'd never cooked, suddenly cooked.

Warlord was a fifteen-year-old boy who had left his hometown in rural northern Thailand to prepare himself for the police constable training center in Bangkok, a city in which he'd never set foot. Warlord's parents, two banana farmers, had known my grandfather during his short stint there in the police force, and they'd asked my dad to help host their son while he was getting acclimated to a new city. And just like that, Warlord showed up at the front gate of our house with a small bag of personal stuff. He moved into a room above the rear detached garage, where we could often hear him sobbing in solitude.

I was in first grade at the time, and when my parents told me someone was coming to stay whose name was Khun Suek, literally "Warlord" or "Chief Warrior"—a name as novel in Thai culture as it would be in American culture—the last thing I expected to see was a skinny, shy, soft-spoken teen who cried when anything reminded him of his hometown.

We did our best to make him feel as comfortable as possible. For Dad, it meant letting him tag along on our family outings around the city. For me, it meant sharing my snacks with him. For Mom, it meant learning to make new regional dishes from his hometown that she'd never made before.

Those efforts seemed to help until the day we found Warlord standing in the backyard, wiping away tears. It turned out that our voluptuous, fertile banana trees reminded him of a curry his mom made, a memory that triggered a major bout of homesickness. It was a red curry of freshwater eels and banana hearts. No one else in the world made it better than his mother. First, she'd scrub the slime off live eels with *bai khoi*, the sandpaper-like leaves of Siamese rough bush. Then, she'd chop up the eels into bite-size pieces and fry them with some curry paste and coconut cream. After that, she'd add banana hearts to the pot.

When Warlord mentioned the banana hearts, which weren't readily available at the market and would require cutting down one of our banana trees to get to the inner core of its trunk, Dad gently told him it wouldn't happen. Just as we'd feared, this promptly reactivated Warlord's lacrimal glands.

A negotiation ensued and finally things ended happily with Dad (who *never* cooked) making my grandmother's famous red curry of bone-in chicken, which we had in the fridge, and unripe *nam wa* bananas that we could pick off the tree. As Dad cooked, Warlord stopped crying and helped. I watched. We all enjoyed the curry. Eels and banana trees across the city lifted up their voices in jubilation.

Warlord moved out a few months later into his own place and eventually finished his training. My parents later told me he had become a junior police officer with young men reporting to him. And I never saw Warlord again until the night of my father's wake a couple of years after that news. He looked handsome, all grown up, and strong in his uniform. I saw him help the other officers drape the flag over Dad's casket before walking away to a dark corner, where he stood in solitude for a long time, sobbing.

Chicken–green banana curry

แกงไก่กับกล้วยดิบ **KAENG KAI KAP KLUAI DIP**

½ cup homemade red curry paste (page 317) or ¼ cup store-bought red curry paste

½ cup freshly extracted coconut cream, or ½ cup canned coconut cream plus 2 tablespoons extra-virgin coconut oil

1 cup coconut milk

2½ pounds skinless chicken thighs, each cut crosswise through the bones into thirds

2 teaspoons packed grated palm sugar

1 tablespoon fish sauce

6 green (unripe) nam wa bananas or Manzano bananas, 10 baby bananas, or 3 large Cavendish bananas

½ cup distilled white vinegar or fresh lime or lemon juice

3 fresh Thai long, jalapeño, or serrano chiles, each cut lengthwise on the diagonal into 4 strips

¾ cup packed fresh Thai sweet basil leaves

Even though Thai *nam wa* bananas, which are short, square, and stocky, are the traditional choice, nearly any type of banana you can find in the United States, including Cavendish (the regular supermarket banana), works here. ⬦ **Serves 6**

Combine the curry paste and coconut cream in a 4-quart saucepan and set over medium-high heat. Stir constantly until the paste is fragrant and the coconut fat separates, about 2 minutes. Stir in the coconut milk, chicken, sugar, fish sauce, and just enough water so the liquid is flush with the chicken. Turn the heat to high and bring to a boil. Lower the heat to a gentle simmer, cover, and cook for 30 minutes.

Meanwhile, using a paring knife or vegetable peeler, remove the thin layer of skin on the surface of the peel from each banana, leaving the fibrous peel that covers the flesh intact. (The peel helps keep the banana slices from disintegrating; it also becomes tender and sweet when cooked.) Cut the bananas crosswise on the diagonal into 1-inch-thick slices (2-inch-thick slices if using baby bananas) and place in a large bowl. Pour the vinegar over the bananas slices, then add water to cover. Place a plate or other weight on top of the bananas to keep them submerged in order to prevent them from turning brown.

When the chicken has cooked for 30 minutes, drain the bananas into a large sieve, rinse off any residual acidulated water under running cold water, and shake dry. Add the bananas and chiles to the chicken, then add water until the liquid is flush with the solid ingredients. Return the liquid to a gentle simmer, cover, and cook until the bananas are barely fork-tender, 6 to 8 minutes. Taste and add more fish sauce if needed.

Remove from the heat and stir in the basil. For the best flavor, let the curry stand, uncovered, for 2 to 3 hours, then reheat it briefly before serving with rice.

Beef and cucumber curry

แกงบุ่มไบ่เนื้อ **KAENG BUMBAI NUEA**

2 teaspoons coriander seeds

2 teaspoons cumin seeds

4 whole mace blades

1½ tablespoons finely chopped galangal

3-inch piece fresh turmeric, thinly sliced crosswise

1½ ounces shallots, cut into small cubes

2 teaspoons packed Thai shrimp paste

5 dried Thai long or guajillo chiles, cut into 1-inch pieces, soaked until softened, and squeezed dry

1 teaspoon white peppercorns

½ cup freshly extracted coconut cream, or ½ cup coconut cream plus 2 tablespoons extra-virgin coconut oil

2½ pounds boneless beef shank, cut into 2-inch cubes

1 cup coconut milk

5 tablespoons tamarind paste, homemade (page 316) or store-bought

3 tablespoons fish sauce, or as needed

2 teaspoons packed grated palm sugar

8 ounces yellow or white onions, cut lengthwise into ½-inch wedges

1½ pounds cucumbers, peeled, halved lengthwise, seeded, and cut crosswise into 1½-inch slices

This is a very old curry that, like *kaeng jin juan kai* (page 84) is heavier on dried spices than fresh herbs. But this one is believed to have followed the tradition of the Indian subcontinent rather than the Malay Archipelago (the name *bumbai* is thought to be the localized pronunciation of Bombay or Mumbai). You can find this curry today in some Thai restaurants specializing in traditional Thai dishes. Serve it with a side of cucumber relish (page 319) or a salty, acidic salad. ⚜ **Serves 6**

Put the coriander, cumin, mace, galangal, turmeric, and shallots in an 8-inch frying pan, set over medium heat, and toast, stirring constantly, until the shallots have softened and the dried spices are fragrant, about 3 minutes. Transfer to a mortar or food processor, add the shrimp paste, chiles, and peppercorns, and grind to a smooth paste.

Put the paste and coconut cream in a 4-quart saucepan, set over medium-high heat, and stir-fry until fragrant, about 2 minutes. Add the beef, coconut milk, tamarind, fish sauce, and sugar and stir to combine. Add just enough water so the liquid is flush with the beef and bring to a boil. Lower the heat to a gentle boil, cover, and cook until the beef is tender but still slightly chewy, about 2 hours. Check on the liquid level occasionally and replenish with more water as needed to keep the liquid flush with the beef at all times. Resume the simmer with each addition.

Taste the sauce and adjust the seasoning with fish sauce if needed, taking into account the onions and cucumbers you are about to add and the bland rice the curry will accompany. Once it tastes good, add the onions and cucumbers, pushing them down lightly to submerge them. Check on the liquid level and add more water if needed to keep the liquid flush with the solids. Return the mixture to a simmer, re-cover, and cook for 2 minutes.

Remove the curry from the heat and let stand, covered, for 15 minutes, before serving with rice. The residual heat will soften the onions and turn the cucumbers tender-crisp.

Sour curry of cha-om cakes and shrimp

แกงส้มชะอมไข่ใส่กุ้ง KAENG SOM CHA-OM KHAI SAI KUNG

4 cups fish stock, or 2 cups bottled clam juice plus 2 cups water

12 ounces skinless trout or tilapia fillets

3 dried Thai long or guajillo chiles, cut into 1-inch pieces, soaked until softened, and squeezed dry

2 dried bird's eye chiles, broken in half, seeded, soaked until softened, and squeezed dry

1 (1-ounce) shallot, cut into ½-inch cubes

1 tablespoon finely chopped galangal

2 large cloves garlic

1 tablespoon finely chopped fingerroot

2 teaspoons packed Thai shrimp paste

1½ tablespoons packed grated palm sugar

About ½ cup tamarind paste, homemade (page 316) or store-bought

1 tablespoon fish sauce, or as needed

12 ounces large shrimp, peeled and deveined

2 cha-om cakes (page 334), cut into 2-inch squares

The *cha-om* cakes, which also accompany Shrimp Paste Relish and Fried Mackerel (page 110), are the highlight of this curry. *Cha-om* (*Senegalia pennata*), also known as climbing wattle, is often grown in the home garden, as the shoots and leaves, prized for their distinctive scent and taste, are a common ingredient in everyday cooking. When mixed with beaten eggs and fried into flat cakes, the leaves soak up the curry broth like a sponge, creating a wonderful flavor. This is one of the most popular varieties of Central-style sour curry in Bangkok.

I usually serve sour curry and an omelet in the same meal. But because the *cha-om* cakes have eggs in them, a fried or roasted meat, such as Fried Chicken with Crispy Garlic (page 153) or Black Pepper Roasted Chicken (page 155), would complement this variant of sour curry better. ⚜ **Serves 4 to 6**

Bring the stock to a boil in a 4-quart saucepan over high heat. Add the fish, adjust the heat so the stock is boiling gently, and cook undisturbed until the fish flakes easily, about 10 minutes. Turn off the heat and use a mesh skimmer to transfer the fish to a plate to cool. Leave the stock in the pan.

Meanwhile, in a large mortar or a food processor, grind together the chiles, shallot, galangal, garlic, fingerroot, and shrimp paste until smooth. Add the cooked fish and grind to a smooth paste.

Put the fish stock back over high heat. When it is boiling, add the fish paste and stir as briefly as you can, just long enough to get the paste to disperse. When the liquid returns to a boil, lower the heat to a gentle simmer. Add the sugar, 6 tablespoons of the tamarind, and the fish sauce, stir well, and adjust the seasoning with more tamarind and fish sauce if needed. The sauce should taste sour first and then salty, with sweet trailing behind. When the sauce tastes good, add the shrimp and the *cha-om* cake pieces, pushing them down lightly to submerge them. Check on the liquid level and add more water if needed to keep the liquid flush with the solids. Cover and adjust the heat to maintain a gentle simmer and cook until the shrimp are cooked through, about 3 minutes.

Remove the curry from the heat and let stand, covered, for 10 minutes, before serving with rice.

Chicken and banana pepper curry with toasted peanuts

แกงจีนจ๊วนไก่ KAENG JIN JUAN KAI

½ cup unsalted roasted peanuts

2 teaspoons coriander seeds

2 teaspoons cumin seeds

1 teaspoon cardamom seeds

3 whole cloves

4 whole mace blades

3 large cloves garlic, halved crosswise

1 tablespoon finely chopped galangal

1 tablespoon thinly sliced lemongrass (with purple rings only)

5 dried Thai long or guajillo chiles, cut into 1-inch pieces, soaked until softened, and squeezed dry

1 teaspoon freshly grated nutmeg

1 teaspoon white peppercorns

2 teaspoons packed Thai shrimp paste

½ cup freshly extracted coconut cream, or ½ cup canned coconut cream plus 2 tablespoons extra-virgin coconut oil

1 cup coconut milk

2½ pounds skinless, boneless chicken thighs, cut into 2-inch cubes

2 tablespoons fish sauce, or as needed

2 teaspoons packed grated palm sugar

2 (3-inch) cinnamon sticks

12 ounces sweet banana peppers, cut crosswise into 1-inch pieces

2 tablespoons fresh bitter (Seville) orange juice or ¼ cup fresh navel orange juice

1½ teaspoons grated bitter (Seville) orange zest or 2 teaspoons grated navel orange zest

¾ cup coarsely chopped cilantro leaves and stems

This rich curry, heavy on dried spices and light on fresh herbs, goes by an odd name that has misled some into assuming it is Chinese (in other contexts the Thai word *jin* usually points to "Chinese" or "China"). It actually arrived in Siam from Java sometime in the late 1800s and was enjoyed by royals and aristocrats. Today, you'll find it in the kitchens of old Bangkokian families and restaurants that specialize in heirloom dishes.

I adapted this recipe from a version I found in a collection of recipes published in honor of Princess Yaovabha Bongsanid, a daughter of King Chulalongkorn. If you prefer something higher on the Scoville scale than banana peppers, substitute Anaheim chiles. ◆ **Serves 6**

For maximum flavor and aroma, toast the peanuts again. Put them in an 8-inch frying pan, set over medium heat, and toast, stirring constantly, until fragrant, 2 to 3 minutes. Transfer to a plate to cool; set aside.

Put the pan back over medium heat. Add the coriander, cumin, cardamom, cloves, mace, garlic, galangal, and lemongrass and toast, stirring constantly, until fragrant, about 3 minutes. Transfer to a mortar or food processor; add the chiles, nutmeg, peppercorns, and shrimp paste; and grind until smooth.

Put the ground spice mixture and coconut cream in a 4-quart saucepan, set over medium-high heat, and stir-fry until fragrant, about 2 minutes. Add the coconut milk, chicken, fish sauce, sugar, cinnamon, and just enough water so the liquid is flush with the chicken. Stir to combine and bring to a boil. Lower the heat to a simmer, cover, and cook until the chicken is tender but still holds its shape, about 20 minutes.

Taste and adjust the seasoning with more fish sauce if needed. When the sauce tastes good, add the banana peppers, pushing them down lightly to submerge them. Check on the liquid level and add more water if needed to keep the liquid flush with the solids. Turn the heat to high, bring to a rolling boil, and then turn off the heat immediately.

Stir in the orange juice and zest and the peanuts and let the curry stand, covered, for 15 minutes. The residual heat will cook the peppers tender-crisp. Remove and discard the cinnamon sticks. Plate the curry and top with the cilantro before serving with rice.

Sam Sen

Historically, few areas in Bangkok are more culturally diverse than the Ban Yuan neighborhood in Sam Sen District by the Chao Phraya, one of the oldest settlements in Bangkok and home to the National Library. This is the area where Portuguese mercenaries settled in Siam during the Ayutthaya period in the 1600s. A wave of Khmers arrived here in the late 1700s, followed by the Vietnamese in the early 1800s. In the midst of Thai Buddhist temples, we have the prominent Conception Church, founded in the mid-1800s by a French priest. The church's architecture is half Thai and half Dutch, and its bell tower was designed by an Austrian showcasing Renaissance features with Romanesque elements.

My maternal grandmother grew up in the Sam Sen area. She moved out to a suburb when Bangkok was bombed by the Allied forces during World War II, then returned to the area once the war ended, married a young military officer, and started a family.

A few years later, my mother and her three siblings came along, one by one. They all spent much of their childhood in that old, multicultural neighborhood, went to a Catholic school a few blocks from the house, hopped about the historical areas on both sides of the river, and enjoyed all sorts of food offered by members of the Ban Yuan community, descendants of the Portuguese, Vietnamese, and Khmer. I'm convinced my mother's and her siblings' childhood experience was responsible for their growing up to be culturally sensitive, open-minded individuals who also aren't afraid to try a broad range of food from a variety of cultures.

Eventually they all married and moved out of the area. My grandparents rented out their marital home and moved back into my great-grandparents house twenty miles away, and their lives no longer revolved around the neighborhood. But that changed when a family restaurant, Krua Apsorn, opened a few doors away from the National Library. My family checked it out and was immediately hooked on the traditional home-style dishes. We were once again back in the old neighborhood, reliving fun memories over meals at the restaurant, and it remains a special place for us. When I had a chance to interview its head chef a few years ago, I considered it a great privilege. The crabmeat dish on page 87 is my adaptation of one of the restaurant's most popular dishes.

Stir-fried lump crabmeat with long beans and hot yellow chiles

เนื้อปูผัดพริกเหลือง NUEA PU PHAT PHRIK LUEANG

5 fresh hot Thai yellow chiles, or 1 large (8- to 9-ounce) orange or yellow sweet bell pepper and 8 fresh red bird's eye chiles

¼ cup homemade lard (page 28) or vegetable oil

6 ounces long beans or green beans, trimmed and cut into ¼-inch pieces

5 or 6 makrut lime leaves, lightly bruised and torn into ½-inch pieces

12 ounces fresh jumbo lump crabmeat, picked over for shell fragments and cartilage

1 tablespoon fish sauce

1 tablespoon oyster sauce

1½ teaspoons granulated sugar

To replicate this famous dish successfully, you can't skimp on the crabmeat. It must be high-quality, firm, and very fresh. That means absolutely no shelf-stable can. It must also be jumbo lump meat. The claw meat won't work here, so if that's all that's available, you're better off using medium-sized shrimp or bay scallops. You also need what the Thais call "yellow chiles," which look like green or red Thai long chiles except they're orange and, though quite fiery, have a heady, sweet scent. In the United States, it's unlikely you'll find this chile in even the lushest of Asian fresh markets. This is something I used to grieve over until I figured out I could replace them with a combination of hot red bird's eye chiles and sweet, mild orange or yellow bell peppers, a stand-in that works better than simply using red long chiles. The joy of being able to bring my family's favorite neighborhood into my kitchen in Chicago is indescribable. ◈ **Serves 4**

If you are using the yellow chiles, remove and discard the stems and veins and cut the chiles into ½-inch pieces. Pound them in a mortar until some pieces are split up, some are reduced to about ¼-inch pieces, and all of them have released their juices; set aside. If you are going with the bell pepper option, trim away the skin with a paring knife, cutting about one-third of the way into the flesh. Chop the pepper skin by hand into ¼- to ½-inch pieces. Reserve the remainder of the pepper for another use. Stem the bird's eye chiles and pound them in a mortar, veins, seeds, and all, to a smooth paste. Mix the two together and reserve.

Heat the lard in a wok over medium-high heat. When it smokes, add the chiles, long beans, and lime leaves all at once and stir-fry until fragrant (you should cough a little) and the beans are tender-crisp, no more than 2 minutes.

Add the crabmeat, fish sauce, oyster sauce, and sugar; turn the heat to high; and stir-fry gently, being careful not to break up the crabmeat, until everything is heated through. Transfer to a plate, then serve immediately with rice.

Curry Pastes

Pastes are the foundation of Thai cuisine. Nearly every traditional dish is made with a paste of some type as its seasoning base, from the basic mix of cilantro root, garlic, and peppercorns—the trifecta of Thai aromatics—to the most complex curry paste. To make Thai food as a hobby, you should feel free to take advantage of store-bought curry pastes without guilt. After all, Thai cooks often buy their curry pastes, too. Nowadays, many Bangkokians live in a condo with a kitchen the size of a shoebox and where the sound of someone pounding a curry paste would get an exasperated neighbor knocking on the door. Just as many live far away from the city center and, after a long commute home from work, don't even want to think about making a curry paste from scratch.

But if the goal is to understand Thai food or to make Thai food at its best, knowing how to make curry pastes from scratch is imperative. The immediate benefit is also obvious; a curry prepared with a properly assembled homemade paste tastes exponentially better. This is particularly true with the classic green curry, one of the favorite rice accompaniments of Bangkokians. That's because, unlike nearly all of the other curries in the Central repertoire, green curry is made with fresh chiles rather than dried. So when a homemade paste is used, you experience green curry at its most fragrant and herbaceous. But green curry paste has more to lose, as well. The heating process that all commercial curry pastes undergo destroys much of what green curry has to offer. In contrast, red curry paste, which is made from dried chiles, has a higher tolerance for such treatment.

When I make a green curry paste from scratch, I can also customize it to my liking in terms of color and flavor. For example, if I want a vividly green curry instead of the greenish khaki curry that tends to be the norm—not that there's anything wrong with the latter—I use the deveined flesh of a lot of dark green Thai long chiles. If I want to raise the heat in addition to the color, I add whole green bird's eye chiles, which are hotter than the long chiles. If I want a gentler, mellower color—a small step in the chartreuse direction—I add a tiny bit of turmeric to the paste.

Regardless of what you may have been told, Thai cooks don't traditionally add green herbs, like cilantro or basil, to green curry paste. The herbs oxidize when bruised or pulverized and turn the paste brownish green—the opposite of what you want. Some cooks add chile leaves to the paste, but that's by no means the norm. (Fresh Thai basil is, however, reserved for adding to the curry right before you take it off the heat, so you get the most out of its essential oil. This is because its job is to provide fragrance and not color.)

If I make green curry with beef (or lamb, as I like to do in Chicago), I add more cumin seeds to the paste because cumin complements red meat. If I make a fish version, I add just a tiny bit of fingerroot to the paste (and more to the curry) for the same reason and also because fingerroot helps ameliorate any fishy smell.

With homemade paste, I don't need any more than just a tiny pinch of salt—enough to create a little friction to ease the grinding of the chiles and any hard herbs but not enough to flavor the paste. The low level of salt allows me to use as much or as little paste in my curry as I like. And this is where commercial curry pastes fall short. They need a high level of salt as a preservative. That means that if I use more paste in the hope of achieving a more intense flavor, I'll also be adding more salt to the curry, a problem I don't run into when I make my own paste.

Beef green curry

แกงเขียวหวานเนื้อ **KAENG KHIAO WAN NUEA**

CURRY PASTE

1 tablespoon coriander seeds

1 tablespoon cumin seeds

1 teaspoon white peppercorns

1 teaspoon coarse salt (omit if using a food processor)

1 tablespoon finely chopped galangal

1 tablespoon paper-thin lemongrass slices (with purple rings only)

1 teaspoon finely chopped makrut lime rind

½-inch piece turmeric root or ½ teaspoon ground turmeric

1 teaspoon packed Thai shrimp paste

5 fresh green Thai long chiles, deveined and coarsely chopped

7 fresh green bird's eye chiles

1 tablespoon finely chopped cilantro roots or stems

5 large cloves garlic

¼ cup sliced shallots, cut against the grain

CURRY

½ cup freshly extracted coconut cream, or ½ cup canned coconut cream plus ¼ cup coconut cream, for serving

½ cup coconut milk

2 pounds untrimmed boneless well-marbled chuck or rib-eye steak, thinly sliced against the grain on a 40-degree angle into bite-size pieces

2 teaspoons fish sauce

1 teaspoon packed grated palm sugar

4 makrut lime leaves, lightly bruised and torn into small pieces

Fresh green Thai long or bird's eye chiles, stemmed and halved lengthwise

¼ cup packed Thai sweet basil leaves

Here is the most satisfying and delicious beef green curry I've ever made. It's thicker than most versions, with just enough sauce to coat the meat—*khluk khlik*, as a Thai would say—and it is heavier on cumin. It has no vegetables—not even eggplants—allowing the beef to take center stage with the fragrance of the paste and the sweet, creamy coconut milk sharing the spotlight. Although the curry is intensely green, it isn't very hot, as the veins of the chiles have been removed. But then I top it with fresh green chiles, vibrant and fragrant, reinforcing the fresh chiles in the paste as well as ratcheting up the heat. Finally, I drizzle some fresh coconut cream on top. This is beef green curry at its best. ◆ **Serves 4**

To make the curry paste, in a small frying pan, toast the coriander and cumin over medium heat, stirring constantly, until fragrant, about 2 minutes. Transfer to a mortar, add the peppercorns, and grind to a fine powder. Add the salt, then, one at a time, add the galangal, lemongrass, lime rind, turmeric, shrimp paste, chiles, cilantro, garlic, and shallots, grinding to a smooth paste after each addition. Alternatively, combine all of the ingredients except the salt in a food processor and grind to a smooth paste.

To make the curry, put the paste and coconut cream in a 4-quart saucepan, set over medium-high heat, and stir until the fat separates and the paste is fragrant, 1 to 2 minutes. Add the coconut milk, beef, fish sauce, and sugar, stir well, cover, turn the heat to medium, and cook until the beef is no longer pink, 7 to 8 minutes. Taste and adjust the seasoning with more fish sauce and/or sugar if needed. For this curry, I like just enough sauce to coat the meat—like pot roast. Check the consistency and amount of the sauce and add water if needed. Stir in the lime leaves, fresh chiles, and basil leaves.

The curry can be transferred to a serving dish and served right away with rice, or it can be cooled, covered, and refrigerated overnight and then reheated the next day (the flavor will be even better). When you serve the curry, top it with the coconut cream.

Spicy beef tenderloin stir-fry with holy basil

เนื้อสันในผัดกะเพรา NUEA SAN NAI PHAT KA-PHRAO

With pad thai being not only one of Bangkok's signature dishes but also arguably the best-known Thai dish in the rest of the world, you would think Bangkokians would be up in arms if anyone alters it in any way. But it seems whenever that happens, they just shake their heads, roll their eyes, mumble and grunt under their breath, and move on.

But when it comes to the spicy basil stir-fry known as *phat ka-phrao*, heaven help the poor soul who dares mess with it. The Bangkokians' displeasure over vendors adding vegetables to their beloved dish had been simmering for years until it came to a head in 2013. That was when a Facebook page emerged demanding that the "unadulterated" *phat ka-phrao* be returned to the Thai people. Immediately. Or else. The dish, said the supporters of the page, should not contain any vegetables. It should be only meat, garlic, chiles, seasoning sauces, and the star of the show, holy basil. They saw the versions with baby corn, carrots, onions, and long beans that had cropped up all over the city as an abomination—a sly tactic many vendors used to widen the profit margin at the cost of integrity. The discussion has since died down (and vendors have quietly added those vegetables back into the dish). But when the topic first came up, the press reported it in the same way it does issues of national importance. Perhaps that's because it *is* an issue of national importance.

This recipe is inspired by the version served at Soei, a long-established family restaurant in the Sam Sen area. Soei's basil stir-fry is different from what you see elsewhere in the city—and is far different from what you find at Thai restaurants around the world. It's spicier and saucier than usual; it's made with boneless beef shank that is sliced thinly, then boiled for a long time until tender, and added to the stir-fry; it's perfumed with *makrut* lime leaves in addition to holy basil; it's served as a rice accompaniment on its own plate in a *samrap* rather than on top of a mound of rice along with a fried egg as a one-plate meal. My version uses beef tenderloin, which—to me—produces an equally delicious rendition of this Bangkokians' favorite in much less time. It calls for some thin soy sauce and oyster sauce, the flavors of which have come to characterize modern versions of this classic. The purists, however, will tell you to season it with nothing but fish sauce. If you'd like to go that route, simply omit the soy sauce and oyster sauce and add fish sauce to taste.

But if you decide to add vegetables to the stir-fry, you may want to make absolutely sure that there are no Bangkokians in the vicinity.

Serves 4

continued

1 tablespoon Thai thin soy sauce or Golden Mountain seasoning sauce

1 tablespoon oyster sauce

1 teaspoon fish sauce

¼ cup homemade chicken stock (page 323), store-bought sodium-free chicken stock, or water

1 teaspoon grated palm sugar

8 large cloves garlic

8 to 10 fresh bird's eye chiles

1½ tablespoons homemade lard (page 28) or vegetable oil

1½ pounds beef tenderloin, sliced against the grain on a 40-degree angle into small pieces about 2 inches long, 1 inch wide, and ¼ inch thick

3 or 4 makrut lime leaves, lightly bruised and torn into small pieces

1½ cups loosely packed fresh holy basil leaves

Stir together the soy sauce, oyster sauce, fish sauce, stock, and sugar in a small bowl. In a mortar or small chopper, grind together the garlic and chiles into a coarse paste.

Put the lard in a large wok or a 14-inch skillet and set over medium-high heat. Add the paste and stir until fragrant, about 1 minute (lower the heat a little bit, if the garlic turns brown). Add the beef and stir-fry to separate. With a rubber spatula, scrape every bit of the sauce into the wok and stir-fry until the beef is only barely pink, about 2 minutes. Stir in the lime leaves and continue to stir-fry until no pink remains on the beef, about 1 minute longer. Remove the wok from the heat and stir in the basil leaves, which will be wilted by the residual heat. If desired, pick out the lime leaves (which you won't be eating); transfer to a serving plate and serve with rice.

24-hour chicken matsaman curry

แกงมัสมั่นไก่ KAENG MATSAMAN KAI

CHICKEN

16 (6- to 8-ounce) skin-on, bone-in chicken thighs

1 tablespoon salt

CURRY PASTE

1 tablespoon cumin seeds

1 tablespoon coriander seeds

4 whole cloves

2 Siamese cardamom pods or 3 green cardamom pods

1 teaspoon white or black peppercorns

15 dried Thai long or guajillo chiles, cut into 1-inch pieces, soaked until softened, and squeezed dry

2 teaspoons salt

2 tablespoons finely chopped galangal

2 tablespoons thinly sliced lemongrass (with purple rings only)

2 teaspoons thinly sliced makrut lime rind

2 teaspoons packed Thai shrimp paste

2 tablespoons finely chopped cilantro roots or stems

10 cloves garlic

½ cup sliced shallots (cut against the grain)

¾ cup extra-virgin coconut oil or vegetable oil

SPICE SACHET

¼ cup whole mace blades

1 tablespoon coriander seeds

1 tablespoon cumin seeds

1 tablespoon fennel seeds

10 Siamese cardamom pods or 12 green cardamom pods

¼ cup coarsely crumbled bay leaves

Vegetable oil, for deep-frying

I often tell people that the only curry that tastes better than the best curry is the best curry that has been sitting for a day. My family's favorite chicken *matsaman* curry, which we intentionally make twenty-four hours in advance, is proof of this claim. The recipe calls for sixteen chicken thighs—*thirty-two* in the original recipe! I invested in a 15-quart enameled cast-iron Dutch oven for this reason, although a stockpot will also work here.

This recipe does not scale down well; piling chicken thighs high in a pot and stewing them long and slow yields a succulent, flavorful curry that you won't get if you cook a smaller portion. Deep-frying the skin side of the chicken thighs before they go into the big pot turns the skins almost spongy as they soak up the flavorful sauce.

Dishes of Muslim origin are often assumed to originate in southern Thailand, where a large number of Thai Muslims reside. However, history shows that the south is not the sole region from which many Thai Muslim dishes or dishes of South Asian origins currently enjoyed in Bangkok have emerged. Early visitors from South Asia—my Brahmin paternal ancestors among them—and the Middle East, especially Persia (Iran), came to the central plain and settled in the area that later became Bangkok, establishing communities and food traditions that are distinctly Bangkokian. This recipe follows one such tradition.

🔸 **Serves 16 in theory; serves 8 to 10 in reality**

To prepare the chicken, rub the chicken thighs with the salt, being careful to keep the skin intact. Cover and refrigerate for 1 to 2 hours.

To make the curry paste, meanwhile, toast the cumin seeds, coriander seeds, cloves, and cardamom pods in a small frying pan over medium heat, stirring constantly, until fragrant, about 3 minutes. Transfer to a mortar, add the peppercorns, and grind to a fine powder. (This step can also be done in a spice grinder or a coffee grinder reserved for spices.) One at a time, add the chiles, salt, galangal, lemongrass, lime rind, shrimp paste, cilantro roots, garlic, and shallots, grinding to a smooth paste after each addition. (Alternatively, you can grind everything all at once in a food processor.) Stir in the coconut oil and transfer the curry paste to a covered container and refrigerate for now.

To make the sachet, cut an 8-inch square of cheesecloth. Using the same small frying pan you used for the curry paste, toast all of the spices over medium-low heat, stirring constantly, until fragrant, about 3 minutes. Pour the spices onto the center of the cheesecloth square, bring up the corners to form a purse, and tie securely with kitchen string. Set aside.

continued

CURRY

4 cups coconut cream

4 cups coconut milk

½ cup packed grated palm sugar

5 tablespoons tamarind paste, homemade (page 316) or store-bought

½ cup fish sauce

7 (2-inch) cinnamon sticks

5 yellow or white onions, peeled

3 pounds Yukon gold or other waxy potatoes, peeled and cut into 2-inch cubes

1 tablespoon salt

½ cup fresh bitter (Seville) orange juice or ¾ cup fresh navel orange juice

¼ cup finely cut bitter (Seville) orange zest or ⅓ cup finely cut navel orange zest, in whisker-thin strips

¾ cup unsalted roasted peanuts

Place a large platter next to the stove. Pour the vegetable oil to a depth of 1 inch into a wok or Dutch oven and heat to 350°F. Working in batches to avoid crowding, lay the chicken, skin side down, into the hot oil and fry until the skin is medium brown, about 4 minutes, leaving the flesh side uncooked. Using tongs, transfer the chicken to the platter. Repeat until all of the chicken is fried.

To make the curry, put the curry paste and 2 cups of the coconut cream in a 15-quart Dutch oven (best) or stockpot (acceptable), place over medium-high heat, and stir until fragrant, about 1 minute. Layer the chicken in the pot, stir in the remaining 2 cups coconut cream along with the coconut milk, sugar, tamarind, and fish sauce, and then drop in the cinnamon sticks and spice sachet. If necessary, add water so the liquid is flush with the top of the chicken pile, making sure the spice sachet is fully submerged. Cover and bring to a boil, then immediately lower the heat to a gentle simmer and cook, undisturbed, for 2 hours.

During this time, quarter the onions lengthwise through the core, so the core holds the onion layers together; set aside. Put the potatoes in a 4-quart saucepan, add water to cover along with the salt, and bring to a boil over high heat. Immediately lower the heat to a simmer and cook the potatoes for only 5 minutes. Drain into a colander, rinse under cold running water to cool, shake off the excess water, and spread on a tray or sheet pan in a single layer to dry.

After 2 hours have passed, uncover the pot and add the onions and potatoes, pushing them down gently so they wedge themselves among the chicken pieces and are fully submerged. If they are not submerged, add just enough water to come flush with the solids. Turn off the heat, uncover the pot, and stir in the orange juice and orange zest. Taste for seasoning; aim for equally salty, sour, and sweet (all in all, strong enough to flavor the bland rice with which the curry will be eaten). Once everything tastes good, leave the curry to cool completely with the spice sachet and cinnamon in it, then refrigerate for 24 hours.

Take the pot straight from the refrigerator to the stove and set it on medium heat to bring it slowly to a boil undisturbed. Once the curry boils, the chicken will have become fork-tender yet juicy and firm, the onions soft and translucent, and the potatoes firm and tender. Turn off the heat and stir in the peanuts. Fish out and discard the spice sachet and cinnamon sticks before serving with rice.

Pork belly–green juice curry

แกงบวน **KAENG BUAN**

1 (3-pound) piece boneless pork belly

⅔ cup paper-thin lemongrass slices (with purple rings only)

3 tablespoons finely chopped cilantro roots or stems

2 teaspoons white peppercorns

2 tablespoons finely chopped galangal

2 tablespoons dried shrimp, soaked in hot water until softened and squeezed dry

2 teaspoons packed Thai shrimp paste

5 large cloves garlic

2 ounces shallots, thinly sliced against the grain

4 ounces (4 tightly packed cups) ya nang leaves, pumpkin leaves, zucchini leaves, or spinach (preferably curly leaf)

1½ cups water

2 tablespoons packed grated palm sugar

½ teaspoon salt

Fish sauce, for seasoning

2 tablespoons finely cut makrut lime leaves, in whisker-thin strips

This dish shows up in a few historical documents including in centuries-old literary works, the most famous of which is *Phra Aphai Mani*, a gem penned in the early 1800s by poet Sunthorn Phu, a Bangkokian who is often described as the Shakespeare of Siam. The protagonists of this epic poem are a prince who plays a mind-controlling flute, a mermaid, and an ogress, and together they are caught in a highly complicated love triangle that leads to a long saga. Indeed, the story is so fantastical that you will wonder how anyone could focus on a reference to curry.

This pork belly version is my adaptation of a recipe dated to early 1900s Bangkok. It calls for pork meat and all kinds of pork offal, as well as fresh green leaves, smashed in a mortar and their juice extracted to use in the curry to provide depth of flavor and camouflage the odor of the offal. The leaves of the *ya nang* plant (*Tiliacora triandra*) are what I recommend; they are available frozen at most well-stocked Thai stores. ◆ **Serves 4**

Trim the skin and some of the excess fat from the pork belly. If there is cartilage, it is fine to leave it. You should now have about 2½ pounds. Cut the pork belly into 1½-inch cubes and set aside.

One at a time, add the following ingredients to a mortar, grinding to a smooth paste after each addition: 2 tablespoons of the lemongrass, the cilantro roots, peppercorns, galangal, dried shrimp, shrimp paste, garlic, and shallots. (Alternatively, you can grind everything all at once to a smooth paste in a mini chopper.) Set aside.

Cut the *ya nang* leaves into narrow ribbons to facilitate blending, then transfer to a blender, add the water, and blend into a smooth puree. Strain the puree through a fine-mesh sieve placed over a bowl, pressing out every drop of juice with a rubber spatula. Discard the solids. Transfer the strained puree to a 4-quart saucepan, and set over high heat. When the liquid begins to boil, add the prepared paste, pork, sugar, salt, and just enough water so the liquid is flush with the pork. Return the liquid to a boil, then lower the heat to a gentle simmer, cover, and cook until the pork is tender but still has some bite, about 1¼ hours. As the curry cooks, check the liquid level occasionally and add water if needed to maintain the original level from the beginning to the end.

Taste for saltiness and add fish sauce to taste, taking into account the bland rice with which the curry will be served. Stir in the remaining lemongrass slices and *makrut* leaves, transfer to a serving dish, and serve with rice.

Mussel-pineapple curry

แกงคั่วสับปะรดใส่หอยแมลงภู่ KAENG KHUA SAPPAROT SAI HOI MALAENG PHU

1 (4-pound) unripe pineapple (green all over with absolutely no yellow)

¼ cup homemade red curry paste (page 317) or 2 tablespoons store-bought red curry paste

2 tablespoons dried shrimp, soaked in hot water until softened, squeezed dry, and ground into fine, cottony flakes

½ cup freshly extracted coconut cream, or ½ cup canned coconut cream plus 1 tablespoon extra-virgin coconut oil

1 cup coconut milk

1 tablespoon fish sauce, or as needed

Grated palm sugar, for seasoning

Tamarind paste, homemade (page 316) or store-bought, for seasoning

2 pounds live mussels, scrubbed and debearded

4 or 5 makrut lime leaves, lightly bruised and torn into small pieces

The curry broth is supposed to be somewhat thin and light and its flavor vibrant and refreshing from the fresh pineapple. The savoriness, however, relies on the juices released from live mussels, so, for the best results, don't use frozen mussels on the half shell. But if you must use them, add ½ cup bottled clam juice to the pan along with the thawed mussels. ⬧ **Serves 4 to 6**

Peel and core the pineapple, then cut the flesh into 1-inch cubes. Measure out 5 cups to use; save the rest for another use.

Put the curry paste, shrimp, and coconut cream in a 4-quart saucepan and set over medium-high heat. Stir-fry until the paste is fragrant and the coconut fat separates, about 1 minute. Add the pineapple cubes, coconut milk, and fish sauce, then bring to a boil, lower the heat to a gentle simmer, cover, and cook for 5 minutes.

By this time the pineapple will have released some of its juice and will have softened somewhat. Since it is impossible to know exactly how sour, sweet, or bland the pineapple is, taste the sauce along with a piece of pineapple to get a good idea of how the end result will be. Add the sugar, tamarind, and more fish sauce as needed to achieve a sauce that is primarily sweet and sour with salty trailing closely behind. Stir in the mussels (discard any that fail to close to the touch), add lime leaves, re-cover, and cook until all of the mussels have opened, 5 to 10 minutes, depending on their size. Remove from the heat and discard any mussels that failed to open. Transfer to a serving dish and serve with rice.

Sweet-and-sour curry of water spinach and fish

แกงเทโพ KAENG THE-PHO

½ cup homemade red curry paste (page 317) or ¼ cup store-bought red curry paste

2 tablespoons dried shrimp, soaked in hot water until softened and squeezed dry

2 tablespoons homemade lard (page 28) or extra-virgin coconut oil

½ cup coconut cream

1 cup coconut milk

3 tablespoons packed grated palm sugar, or as needed

3 tablespoons tamarind paste, homemade (page 316) or store-bought, or as needed

1 tablespoon fish sauce, or as needed

12 ounces trimmed water spinach, cut into 2-inch pieces

4 black cod steaks, each measuring 1 inch thick and weighing approximately 6 ounces

1 to 2 cups sodium-free fish stock, homemade chicken stock (page 323), store-bought sodium-free chicken stock, or water

2 teaspoons fresh makrut lime juice and 3 or 4 makrut lime slices, or ¼ cup fresh (bitter) Seville orange juice and 1 tablespoon grated zest, or ⅓ cup fresh navel orange juice and 1 tablespoon grated zest

3 or 4 makrut lime leaves, lightly bruised and torn into small pieces

Like most dishes in this book, this classic curry has been in Bangkok for a long time. Unlike some of the other old dishes, however, this curry is still commonly found in the city. The only difference between the old and the contemporary versions is that the former used the rich and delectable freshwater *the-pho*, or black-ear catfish, while pork belly is used today.

By the early 1900s, *the-pho* had already been a popular fish choice among Bangkokians. Records of state banquets in the reign of Rama V show *the-pho* prepared in the French manner and served as one of the main courses. These days, this fish is hard to find, which is why *kaeng the-pho* now nearly always calls for pork belly—the version pretty much all of the rice-curry shop vendors in the city offer. It is confusing how the name of the fish has stuck, but the protein has changed.

For old times' sake, I've decided to use fish instead of pork belly in this recipe. Black cod is a perfect stand-in for *the-pho*; so is salmon, especially the belly. Swai or halibut, though not very fatty, will work here, too. If you live in Thailand, use Siamese water spinach, *phak bung thai*, which is the type of water spinach traditionally used in this classic curry. ⬥ Serves 4

Combine the curry paste and dried shrimp in a mortar or mini chopper and grind until smooth. Transfer the mixture to a 4-quart saucepan, add the lard and coconut cream, and set over medium-high heat. Stir until the mixture is fragrant and the coconut fat separates, 1 to 2 minutes. Add the coconut milk, sugar, tamarind, and fish sauce and stir well. Arrange the water spinach on the bottom of the pan and top with the fish. Add the stock as needed to cover everything by ½ inch (you may not need all 2 cups). Re-cover the pan and simmer until the fish is opaque and firm, 5 to 7 minutes.

Stir in the *makrut* lime juice and slices. Taste the sauce and adjust with more fish sauce, sugar, or tamarind if needed. Aim for it to be equally sweet, sour, and salty. Once the curry tastes good, stir in the lime leaves, and turn off the heat. You can pick out and discard the lime slices and leaves, or you can leave them in to keep the curry fragrant but warn diners not to eat them. Serve with rice.

Braised chicken in coconut-galangal cream sauce

ต้มข่าไก่กลั่น  TOM KHA KAI KLAN

My maternal grandmother spent a few years of her childhood away from Bangkok during the time her father served as *jao mueang* (equivalent of modern-day governor) of a northeastern province during the reign of King Vajiravudh, the sixth king of the Chakri dynasty. By the time Grandma moved back to Bangkok, the food of the northeast (Isan) was more than just something for which she had an appetite. It had become part of her identity.

The way she cooked reflected that. My grandmother had a knack for creating dishes that fused some elements of Central Thai cooking with those of the northeastern plateau in a way that not only honored both traditions but also elevated a familiar dish to great, unfamiliar heights. This recipe is an example. The Central Thai coconut-galangal chicken soup, or *tom kha kai*, needs no introduction, as it is one of the most popular Thai dishes around the globe. But this is my maternal grandmother's version, which incorporates an obscure cooking method she discovered while living in Isan (even though historical records show that it had also been used for at least a century in Bangkok to make rice porridge). It involves a MacGyver-esque contraption that first struck me as a reverse double boiler.

You begin by putting bone-in chicken chunks that have been mixed with an herb paste into a tall, narrow pot until it is half full. Then you put ice-cold water (or ice cubes) in a round-bottomed pan until it is half full as well and position the pan like a tight-fitting lid on the rim of the pot. The chicken is cooked undisturbed on the lowest heat, with the ice-cold water replaced as soon as it becomes lukewarm. About three changes of water later, you end up with tender chicken in a pool of deeply flavorful and intensely herbaceous sauce. My grandmother insisted that no matter how many times she made the dish, the aroma that wafted up from the chicken pot the moment she removed the water pan never got old.

This dish has several aliases. *Kai tai nam*, "chicken [cooked] underneath water," is by far the most common. *Kai sam nam*, "three-water chicken," referring to the three changes of water, is also in circulation. But my grandmother went with the least attested one: *kai klan*, literally "distilled chicken," which initially led me to believe some sort of distillation was going on.

Not so, says food scientist Harold McGee, author of the seminal *On Food and Cooking*, because this method doesn't collect or separate the vapors from their source. Why, then, does it coax the flavor and aroma out of food so effectively? What exactly happens underneath

continued

4 (6-ounce) skinless, bone-in chicken thighs

4 (6-ounce) skin-on chicken drumsticks

2 to 3 tablespoons fish sauce

⅓ cup paper-thin slices of young galangal

½ cup paper-thin slices of trimmed lemongrass (with purple rings only)

6 makrut lime leaves, thinly sliced

About 6 quarts ice cubes

2 cups coconut cream, or 1 cup each coconut cream and coconut milk

2 to 3 tablespoons fresh lime juice

Fresh bird's eye chiles, as many as you like, coarsely chopped

½ cup tightly packed cilantro leaves

the ice pan? McGee explained to me that while any well-sealed lid will help keep food aromas from escaping, the advantage of cooling with ice water is that the volatile aromas are not heated as much, which means they will persist longer in their original form. The French *doufeu* braising pot, which features a recessed lid designed to hold ice, works on the same idea. In the case of "distilled chicken," as the moisture inside the chicken pot starts to evaporate, the water pan on top causes it to condense, and the condensation falls back down onto the chicken. In short, it's a self-basting effect that keeps the food moist and preserves the aroma that would have deteriorated at higher heat.

It's hard to imagine how a globally adored dish such as *tom kha kai* could be improved on, but this cooking method does just that. It produces the same soup you already know and crave but makes it more concentrated and infinitely more flavorful and aromatic. I call for skinless chicken thighs because I've found that if the skins are left on, the dish is too oily. But the drumsticks are not as fatty, so I usually leave the skins on. ♦ **Serves 4**

Arrange the chicken on the bottom of a 4-quart Dutch oven. Drizzle 1 tablespoon of the fish sauce over the chicken, then scatter the galangal, lemongrass, and *makrut* leaves on top. Put the pot over low heat. Put 2 quarts of the ice cubes in a round-bottomed braising pan and place it on top of the Dutch oven, making sure the bottom of the pan doesn't touch the chicken. Cook undisturbed until the ice cubes have melted and the water is lukewarm. Empty the braising pan and repeat the process another two times.

When the last batch of ice cubes has turned into lukewarm water, the chicken should be tender and swimming in its own juices. Check to see how much liquid there is in the Dutch oven and add enough of the coconut cream so the liquid is flush with the chicken (you may not need all 2 cups). Stir in 1 tablespoon of the lime juice, then taste and add the remaining 1 to 2 tablespoons fish sauce and remaining 1 to 2 tablespoons lime juice if needed. Aim for equally salty and sour with subdued natural sweetness coming from the chicken juices and the coconut cream. Stir in the chiles to taste.

Spoon the chicken and sauce into a serving bowl and top with the cilantro. (If your galangal is on the mature side, you may want to pick it out and discard it. There's no need to remove the lemongrass or lime leaves; you can eat them along with the chicken, as I usually do.) Serve with rice.

Hot and sour fish soup

ต้มยำปลา TOM YAM PLA

¼ cup raw long-grain white rice, preferably Thai jasmine

8 cups homemade chicken stock (page 323) or store-bought sodium-free chicken stock

3 pounds snakehead fish steaks, about 3 inches thick

2 voluptuous lemongrass stalks, cut into 1-inch pieces and smashed until split

6 or 7 makrut lime leaves, lightly bruised and torn into small pieces

2 (2-inch) pieces galangal, smashed until split

2 tablespoons fish sauce, or as needed

About ¼ cup fresh lime juice

1 cup loosely packed julienned sour green mango

½ cup packed fresh mint leaves

6 fresh sawtooth coriander leaves, cut crosswise into ¼-inch-wide pieces, or ½ cup packed cilantro leaves

Plump fresh bird's eye chiles, as many as you like, smashed until split

The *tom yam* soup that's found at most restaurants in Bangkok and overseas is somewhat different from the *tom yam* I grew up eating at home. This is a recipe for the *tom yam* of my childhood. The use of rice (or rice rinsing water in some cases) in the broth, which turns it slightly cloudy, may seem odd even to Bangkokians who are familiar with the clear version of the soup. But this practice reflects what I've discovered from my studies of historical records. I've also found that fresh fish cooked in boiling water that has been slightly thickened with rice is less prone to developing a fishy smell.

The traditional choice of fish to use in this recipe is snakehead fish (*pla chon*). But trout, lake pike, black cod, halibut, and even salmon are all great choices. ⬩ **Serves 4 to 6**

Combine the rice and stock in a 4-quart saucepan, stir once to loosen up the rice grains, cover, and bring to a boil over high heat. Turn down the heat so the liquid bubbles gently and cook, stirring occasionally, until the rice has softened and the liquid has become cloudy and slightly starchy, about 30 minutes. Using a mesh skimmer, scoop out every bit of the rice and its sediments and discard or save it for another use. Lower the fish steaks into the pan and add water if needed to submerge the fish by 1 inch. Adjust the heat to maintain a gentle boil, cover, and cook the fish, undisturbed, for 20 minutes.

Add the lemongrass, lime leaves, galangal, and fish sauce, re-cover, and continue to cook, undisturbed, until the fish is done but not falling apart. The timing depends on the type of fish, so use your judgment. For fish steaks of this thickness, it will take 15 minutes from the point at which the herbs are added. Add more liquid if needed to keep the fish covered by 1 inch.

Using a slotted spoon, transfer the fish to a large bowl and then cover the bowl. Using a fine-mesh skimmer, lift out and discard the solids. Turn the heat to the lowest setting so the liquid is steaming but not bubbling. Taste the liquid and season with more fish sauce and with the lime juice, 1 tablespoon at a time, until the broth tastes primarily tart then salty. Don't be afraid to use a heavier hand; this is a soup that, when sipped steaming hot, should make beads of perspiration form on your forehead on a warm day. Once the flavors are in place, put the cover back on and continue to keep the liquid hot over low heat.

Skin and debone the fish, then separate it into hearty, beautiful chunks. Arrange the fish in individual soup bowls or a large tureen. Remove the broth from the heat, discarding the herbs, and ladle the steaming broth over the fish. Top with the sour mango, mint, sawtooth coriander, and chiles. Serve piping hot with rice.

On Relishes

Many English words are used to render what the Thai call *nam phrik*. They range from *chile dip* to *chile sauce* to *chile paste* to simply *dip*. Although none of these terms is inaccurate, each one is deficient in one way or another, so I prefer the umbrella term *relish*. It's specific enough that in no way can it be applied to other dishes outside this category, yet generic enough to cover all sorts of *nam phrik* without alienating any one type.

The terms *chile dip* and *dip* both imply a dippable liquid, with the former identifying chiles as an ingredient. But a *nam phrik* is neither always liquid nor always made with chiles (think of the ancient ones, from before the time chiles were introduced to our shores, when peppercorns were used). Chile *sauce* is just as misleading, if not more so. The word *sauce* gives a faulty impression of something served alongside a main dish to complement or enhance it. But if you observe how a relish functions in a Thai *samrap* (meal ensemble) you'll see that *nam phrik* is no sidekick.

What would the Thai people do without their relishes? We are intertwined with them in such a way that life without them is simply unimaginable. This is true not only of Bangkokians but also of people in every part of the country.

Nam phrik also represents the vastest category of Thai dishes, and no one demonstrates this fact better than M. R. Kukrit Pramoj, who wrote the excellent book *Nam Phrik*. It opens with the parody of the classic *One Thousand and One Nights* in which the Thai version of Scheherazade was a young consort of a fictional Siamese king from an unspecified ancient era who she knew was seeking to have her executed. Not a fan of dying young, the brainy girl came up with a plan to delay the event for as long as she could. After having successfully piqued the king's interest on various types of *nam phrik*, she had his promise not to kill her until she was done telling him about all the Thai relishes she knew. So she did just that—telling him about one *nam phrik* each night. When the woman died at a ripe old age several decades later, wrote Pramoj, she hadn't even reached the coconut relish category.

Salted soybean-coconut relish

หลนเต้าเจี้ยว LON TAO JIAO

½ cup coconut cream

½ cup coconut milk

¼ cup rinsed and drained light salted soybeans, ground to a smooth paste

4 ounces ground pork

8 ounces shrimp, peeled, deveined, and finely chopped

1½ ounces shallots, halved lengthwise and then thinly sliced crosswise

1 tablespoon tamarind paste, homemade (page 316) or store-bought

2 teaspoons fish sauce, or as needed

3 tablespoons packed grated palm sugar

2 fresh red and/or green Thai long, jalapeño, or serrano chiles, cut crosswise into ½-inch-wide pieces

RAW VEGETABLES

Thai round eggplants, quartered lengthwise

Pea eggplants

Pickling, Persian, or English cucumbers, trimmed and sliced crosswise ¼ inch thick

Long beans, green beans, or winged beans, trimmed and cut into 3-inch sticks

Green or napa cabbage, cut into thin wedges or bite-size pieces, respectively

Any mild, crunchy vegetables you like

Also commonly known as *tao jiao lon*, this relish represents a happy marriage of a Central Thai cooking tradition (*lon*) and a Chinese ingredient (salted soybeans) that is typical of Bangkok cuisine. Unlike other relishes that are often fiery and strongly seasoned, this one, like most of its friends in the *lon* category, is mild and creamy, containing no ingredients that could be considered "challenging." This is a perfect entry-level relish for *nam phrik* novices.

Be sure to use the correct type of salted soybeans, which are mild and pale yellow, rather than the intensely salty dark reddish brown soybean paste used in some recipes. In the United States, light salted soybeans are sold in glass jars in most well-stocked grocery stores specializing in Southeast Asian (especially Thai) ingredients.

Makes 2 cups; serves 2

Combine the coconut cream and coconut milk in a 2-quart saucepan and bring to a boil over medium-high heat. Add the soybeans, pork, and shrimp, then adjust the heat to a gentle simmer and stir, breaking up the meats as finely as possible with the blunt end of a wooden spatula, until they are opaque, 7 to 8 minutes. Stir in the shallots, tamarind, fish sauce, and sugar and cook, stirring, until the shallots have softened, 1 to 2 minutes. Taste and add more fish sauce if needed. Aim for salty and sweet at the forefront with sour trailing a few steps behind and take into account the rice and fresh vegetables you will be eating with the relish. Once the taste is good, stir in the chiles, cook for 1 minute, and then remove from the heat and let cool down to only slightly warmer than room temperature.

Arrange the vegetables on a platter and serve with the relish and with rice. As you eat, compose each bite with equal amounts of rice, relish, and vegetable.

Shrimp paste relish and fried mackerel

น้ำพริกกะปิ-ปลาทูทอด NAM PHRIK KAPI-PLA THU THOT

¾ cup vegetable oil

4 (5- to 6-ounce) Thai short-bodied mackerel, steamed until cooked through and patted dry

¾ cup shrimp paste relish (page 316)

2 cha-om cakes (page 334)

Cucumber

Raw or steamed green or napa cabbage

Canned whole bamboo shoots, rinsed well, drained, and patted dry

Raw or blanched long beans

Raw or blanched winged beans

Raw Thai round eggplants or pea eggplants

The preeminence of shrimp paste relish in Central Thailand, especially Bangkok, cannot be overstated. It's in our soul; if you cut us open, we may even bleed it. When paired with Thai short-bodied mackerel (*pla thu*), one of the types of fish most loved by Central Thais and Bangkokians, the duo form a canonized set, an enduring classic that the whole city never tires of. You can find it anywhere in the city, from the poshest restaurant to the most-humble street cart. I have yet to meet a born and bred Bangkokian who didn't grow up on *nam phrik kapi* and *pla thu*.

When Bangkokians visit Thailand after having lived overseas for a few years, their friends and family often ask them, in jest, if they have forgotten shrimp paste relish and fried mackerel. How, of all the edibles, this particular dish is singled out to be used as a synecdoche representing the entirety of the food of Bangkok and Central Thailand is telling of how important it is.

Traditionally, Thai short-bodied mackerel are steamed first before being fried. Cooked this way, the fish have crisp exteriors and tender and cottony interiors—just where we want them. In Thailand, short-bodied mackerel are nearly always sold already steamed and arranged in small bamboo baskets. Short-bodied mackerel from Thailand— what I strongly recommend you use—are sold in the United States already steamed, too. You can find them in the freezer section of most well-stocked Asian stores specializing in Southeast Asian ingredients. You need to thaw the steamed fish and pat them dry before frying them. ♦ Serves 4

Put the oil in a 12-inch nonstick frying pan and set over medium-high heat. Meanwhile, line a plate with paper towels. When the oil is hot, carefully lower the mackerel into the pan and fry just until the skin is golden brown, about 5 minutes. Flip them once to fry the other side, about 5 minutes longer. Transfer to the towel-lined plate to drain briefly.

Arrange the fish on a large serving platter. Place the relish bowl to one side. Cut the *cha-om* cakes and vegetables into bite-size pieces and arrange them around the fish, then serve with rice. Since the relish is heavily seasoned, it's best to enjoy it in small amounts along with generous bites of rice, fish, and side vegetables.

Grilled river prawn relish

แสร้งว่า SAENG WA

8 ounces head-on, shell-on river prawns or jumbo shrimp

3 tablespoons paper-thin lemongrass slices (with purple rings only)

¼ cup paper-thin shallot slices (cut lengthwise)

2 tablespoons peeled and finely cut young, tender ginger, in whisker-thin strips

2 tablespoons tamarind paste, homemade (page 316) or store-bought

1 tablespoon fresh lime juice

1 tablespoon fresh bitter (Seville) or navel orange juice

2 teaspoons very finely cut bitter (Seville) or navel orange zest, in ½-inch-long strips

½ teaspoon packed grated palm sugar

3 or 4 fresh bird's eye chiles, thinly sliced crosswise

Fish sauce, for seasoning

RAW VEGETABLES

Thai round eggplants, quartered lengthwise

Pea eggplants

Pickling, Persian, or English cucumbers, trimmed and sliced crosswise ¼ inch thick

Long beans, green beans, or winged beans, trimmed and cut into 3-inch sticks

Green or napa cabbage, cut into thin wedges or bite-size pieces, respectively

Any mild, crunchy vegetables you like

Often dubbed a "salad" in English, this dish has characteristics that are more consistent with those of a relish: intensely seasoned, served like a dip in a small bowl as part of a *samrap*, and consumed along with vegetable crudités.

The name of this recipe roughly translates as "to pretend" or "to disguise," which points to its origin as a royal court dish that has been adapted from an existing preparation deemed too harsh, too intense, too pungent, and too pedestrian. Written records differ on which dish this relish is pretending to be. Some say it is fermented fish innards relish, while others suggest the base is pickled blood cockles or mussels. Either way, grilled river prawns or shrimp represent a milder, sweeter, but just as delicious—if not more—disguise.

The key is to cook the prawns as quickly as possible over high heat. This ensures the flesh won't become tough and rubbery. In a traditional Thai kitchen, the cook would have thrown the prawns right into the charcoal embers in the clay stove that every household had. If grilling directly on hot charcoal as I have done here is not an option, you can use tongs to hold the prawns over an open flame on the stove top.

⬦ **Makes about 1½ cups; serves 3 or 4**

Light a chimney half full of natural wood charcoal. When all of the charcoal glows hot but is not covered with white ash, scatter it onto the tray of a hibachi-style grill. Lay the prawns directly on the hot coals and grill, turning them a few times, until the legs are singed and the shells are thoroughly opaque and blackened in spots. Set the prawns aside, covered (to keep the meat from drying), and leave until cool enough to handle.

Peel the prawns, then tear the flesh into ½-inch chunks and place in a bowl along with their tomalley or any juices they may have released. Add the lemongrass, shallot, ginger, tamarind, lime juice, orange juice, orange zest, sugar, and chiles and toss lightly. Add fish sauce, starting with 2 teaspoons, and then taste and continue to add more until you have a bold-flavored relish with very strong sour and salty flavors and with the faint natural sweetness of the prawns and the tiny amount of palm sugar (remember, this is not a salad but a relish).

Arrange the vegetables (pick what appeals to you from the list) on a platter and serve with the relish and with rice.

One Home Garden and the Two Grandmothers

In a world of unpredictability, one thing I always know is that I have the love of my family. As noted earlier, my father died when I was just a little kid, and my grandparents and my uncles and aunts from both sides stepped in to help fill any void I might be feeling in my life. My two grandmothers, especially, were never far from me.

The two women were drastically different, however—so different that sometimes it was hilarious to see them talking to each other in a courteous but awkward way. And being equally influenced by them as a child sometimes confused me. Only after I became an adult and looked back did I realize what a blessing it was to have them both in my life.

My paternal grandmother was an industrious housewife and mother who adhered fiercely to tradition. Being around her meant that I learned how to play Thai musical instruments and read the major works of Thai literature. During school breaks at her house, I would help her cook a lot. It didn't even matter that she had kitchen workers, as she wanted me to do everything. We would slice the herbs, one by one, into tiny pieces, and I would pound them in a mortar to make a curry paste. I would grate fresh coconut with a traditional Thai coconut grater and extract the milk (a job I hated passionately).

My maternal grandmother, in contrast, was a bit of a rebel, even though she, too, came from a very traditional Thai family. Marrying for love was one of those rebellious acts. She was hardworking, strong, extremely independent, self-reliant, opinionated, and unwilling to accept anything at face value. She kept only those traditions that had proved themselves noble, practical, and timeless and denounced the rest. Her level of tolerance for nonsense, superstition, and dogmatism was notoriously low.

My paternal grandmother wanted me to learn how to play a Thai dulcimer; my maternal grandmother bought me a Gibson electric guitar. My paternal grandmother served visitors ice water with fresh jasmine flowers from her garden in an heirloom silver bowl. My maternal grandmother had four brands of beer in the fridge. My paternal grandmother would wake up before the rooster to prepare food to offer to the monks on their morning alms round. My maternal grandmother would wake up before dawn, put on a headband, and power walk to U2. You get the idea.

But their differences came out most clearly in the way they took me out to the vegetable garden for a talk. Even today, I still don't know for sure why the vegetable garden was our "talking place" when something needed to be said, but I believe a cultural factor was at work: a side-by-side talk in which the eyes of the two primary parties focused on a third party—an inanimate object—made discussing something significant less awkward than a face-to-face talk would. What I do know for sure is that I was pulled aside for such a talk on the same subject on two separate occasions, one with my paternal grandmother and the other with my maternal grandmother.

As my paternal grandmother and I waded through the garden together just after my father had died, she said she didn't know what would happen to me in the future, but she wanted me to remember that I was the daughter of a great man who loved me and who had laid a firm foundation to which I could always return if I ever got lost in life. Know your roots, she said, remember where you come from. Remember your truth. Let that be your anchor. Then she sent me to the far side of the garden with a basket in hand with instructions to pick various vegetables and herbs. Go get the eggplants and the basil for the curry, she said. Not the basil with the hairy stems—those are for the stir-fry. And while you're out there, get some *cha-om* leaves to make a side for a relish, too. Be careful of the thorns.

Then she put me through the curry-making process just as she had done so many times before. Remember how we make the paste? she asked. We start by toasting and grinding the dried spices in the mortar, then all the dry, hard herbs go in, followed by their soft, watery friends at the very end. Then she had me stick my face over the curry pot in the initial frying stage. Look and then take a whiff of it, she said. When you fry the paste, things go in reverse. See that? The paste releases the scent of the last things you add to the mortar first, followed by the second last. Then it keeps going backward until the last things you smell are the dried spices you put in the mortar before anything else. That, darling, is when you know it's ready. It works like this every time. Some things never change, you see.

When my father died, my maternal grandmother was the first to comfort me and the last to let me dwell on how "unfair" my lot in life was. A master of parable, she asked me to look at an ivy gourd plant that clung onto the cement fence of the house. That *tam lueng* plant had been around for months, and we would pick its shoots and leaves to blanch and eat with relishes. She then asked me to look for its roots. To my astonishment, the lush ivy gourd didn't grow out of the ground; it grew out of a small crack in the cement fence, with the roots firmly embedded in a patch of dirt lodged inside it. Any moisture trapped in the crack became its source of sustenance.

How the seed got in there was literally crappy, she pointed out, most likely by way of bird droppings. But what mattered was that the seed clung on to what little was available to it. It wanted to live and grow and nothing could get in its way. Then it became not only a self-sustaining plant but also one that gave of itself to nourish others. Your dad died, she said to me, and that was unfortunate. But remember, she went on, if things ever get difficult, be like the ivy gourd that grows out of the little crack in the fence. Be resilient. Look for abundance even amid scarcity.

Sweet pork–shrimp paste relish (boat relish)

น้ำพริกลงเรือ **NAM PHRIK LONG RUEA**

CRISPY FISH FLAKES

18 ounces skinless catfish
or tilapia fillets

½ teaspoon salt

Vegetable oil, for deep-frying

CARAMEL-GLAZED PORK BELLY

8 ounces boneless meaty
pork belly with skin intact

½ teaspoon salt

¼ cup packed grated
palm sugar

RELISH

1 tablespoon homemade lard
(page 28) or vegetable oil

¾ cup shrimp paste relish
(page 316)

2 hard-boiled salted duck
eggs, peeled and quartered

3 tablespoons thinly sliced
Thai pickled garlic

FRESH VEGETABLES

Thai round eggplants,
quartered lengthwise

Pea eggplants

Pickling, Persian, or English
cucumbers, trimmed and
sliced crosswise ¼ inch thick

Long beans, green beans,
or winged beans, trimmed
and cut into 3-inch sticks

Green or napa cabbage,
cut into thin wedges or
bite-size pieces, respectively

Any mild, crunchy vegetables
you like

Knowing the history of this classic relish set is key to understanding—and hopefully making peace with—why it requires as many items as it does. This is another royal court dish that, like Spicy Shrimp Paste–Beef Soup (page 132), originated from leftovers.

Although different accounts—all usually reliable—give conflicting details about the genesis of this relish, what we know for sure is that the dish was created by Mom Rajawongse Sadab Ladawan, a consort of King Chulalongkorn, the fifth king of the House of Chakri, whose reign marked a peak period in the creation and documentation of traditional Central Thai and Bangkokian dishes. All accounts agree that it happened on the day during which a royal outing on a boat took place, and M. R. Sadab was given the task of putting together a meal for the occasion in a hurry. She walked into the kitchen, found miscellaneous leftovers, and mixed them together into this relish. Everyone loved it and asked her to make it again. The so-called boat relish has continued to be made in the royal court since then and gradually made its way into the homes and eventually the restaurants—and even the food courts—of Bangkok over the past century.

This explains why the relish is made up of so many components, each of which is a dish unto its own. But instead of being daunted, perhaps you'll be encouraged to know that by learning to make this delicious relish, you'll have acquired the skill to make three separate classic Thai dishes, namely crispy fish flakes, a streamlined version of caramel-glazed pork belly, and shrimp paste relish, all in one go.

Boat relish is sweet, salty, and sour. Expect absolutely no subtlety in flavors. ⬇ **Serves 2**

To make the fish flakes, broil or grill the fish fillets until they flake easily. Transfer to a mortar or food processor, add the salt, and grind into fine, cottony flakes. Spread the flakes out on a sheet pan and leave them to dry on the counter for 1 to 2 hours.

To make the pork belly, trim off the skin and some of the excess fat. You should now have about 6 ounces; cut into ½-inch cubes. Place the pork and salt in a 1-quart saucepan, add water so the liquid is flush with the pork, then bring to a boil over high heat. Lower the heat to a gentle simmer, cover, and cook until tender yet firm, about 30 minutes.

When the pork is done, using a slotted spoon, transfer it to a bowl. Pour the pork liquid into a 12-inch frying pan, set over high heat, and bring to

continued

a rolling boil. Reduce the liquid until it barely covers the bottom of the pan. Add the sugar and the pork, lower the heat to medium, and stir until the sauce becomes a glossy, tight glaze that coats the pork, 2 to 3 minutes. Remove from the heat and leave to cool.

Turn your attention back to the fish. Pour the oil to a depth of 1 inch into a wok and heat to 380°F to 400°F. Line a sheet pan with paper towels and place it near the stove. When the oil is hot, grab half of the fish flakes and sprinkle them evenly over the surface of the oil. Use two spatulas to manipulate the flakes so they form a single "raft." Once the raft sets, flip it around until golden brown on all sides, no more than 2 minutes. Transfer to the prepared sheet pan. Repeat with the remaining fish flakes.

To make the relish, put the lard in a 12-inch frying pan and set over medium-high heat. When the lard is hot, add the shrimp paste relish and stir-fry just until it sizzles and releases an aroma, 30 to 40 seconds. Add the prepared pork belly and one-fourth of the fish flakes and stir-fry until heated through and a loose paste forms, less than 1 minute. (The relish should be the consistency of thick oatmeal; stir in some water as needed, if it's too dry.) Transfer to a bowl. Spoon the pickled garlic to one side of the relish bowl, if using.

Serve the relish with rice and with the remaining fried fish flakes, the salted eggs, and the vegetables alongside. It's best to make the relish part of a larger meal ensemble comprising other complementary rice accompaniments. Since the relish is heavily seasoned, it's also best to enjoy it in small bites along with generous bites of rice and fresh vegetables.

Spicy fish flakes (hell relish)

น้ำพริกนรก  NAM PHRIK NAROK

12 ounces skinless trout or tilapia fillets

¼ cup dried shrimp, soaked in hot water until softened and then squeezed dry

4 dried Thai long or guajillo chiles, cut into 1-inch pieces, soaked until softened, and then squeezed dry

1 ounce (about 30) dried bird's eye chiles, stemmed, soaked whole until softened, and then squeezed dry

6 large cloves garlic

2 ounces shallots, cut into small cubes

2 tablespoons packed grated palm sugar

1 tablespoon fish sauce

1 teaspoon salt

3 tablespoons tamarind paste, homemade (page 316) or store-bought

1 tablespoon homemade lard (page 28) or vegetable oil

2 tablespoons fresh shrimp tomalley or faux river prawn tomalley (page 29; optional)

This relish is different from the other ones in this book because it is granular rather than sauce-like. The name "hell relish" or "hellish relish" gives you an idea of how red hot and spicy these flakes are supposed to be. Indeed, this could very well be Dante's tenth circle—the center of hell. That said, you can lower the heat level a few notches without compromising the quality.

There are many ways you can enjoy hellish relish. Mix some into warm jasmine rice and eat the rice with fried chicken (page 148), roasted chicken (page 155), a Thai omelet (pages 143 and 147), or a hard-boiled or fried egg. You can simply sprinkle some on top of plain rice much like the Japanese seasoning *furikake*, or you can spoon some into a small bowl, add some fish sauce and lime juice to make a loose paste the consistency of ketchup, and then enjoy it the way you would other pasty relishes or as a seasoning paste for making fried rice. One of my favorite ways to use the flakes is to create a saucy relish by mixing them with some chopped tomato, finely diced shallot, fish sauce, lime juice, and chopped cilantro—somewhat like pico de gallo, except very Thai and oh-so-hellish. **Makes 2 cups**

Broil or grill the fish fillets until they flake easily. Transfer to a mortar or food processor; add the dried shrimp, chiles, garlic, and shallots; and grind to a smooth paste.

Put the paste in a 12- or 14-inch frying pan (the wider and shallower the pan, the less time it takes) and set over medium heat. Add the sugar, fish sauce, salt, and tamarind and, using two wooden spatulas with blunt ends, stir and chop the paste nonstop for 30 minutes (you'll sweat and cough—possibly also cuss). Unless you use a nonstick pan, some of the paste will form a thin, dry film on the bottom of the pan. Don't let the crust build; scrape it up and mix it back into the paste along the way.

After 30 minutes, the paste will have become visibly drier. Add the lard and shrimp tomalley and continue to toast the paste. Continue to use the blunt ends of the spatulas to chop the paste into tiny granules and scrape the pan along the way. You know the relish is ready when the granules are as small as Grape-Nuts and feel dry to the touch, 15 to 20 minutes. Remove from the heat and let cool completely.

The relish will keep in an airtight container at room temperature for 1 week, in the refrigerator for 5 to 6 months, and in the freezer for a year.

Fire-roasted river prawns with tamarind sauce and blanched neem

กุ้งเผา-สะเดาลวก-น้ำปลาหวาน KUNG PHAO-SADAO LUAK-NAM PLA WAN

2 cups raw Thai jasmine rice

2 tablespoons homemade lard (page 28) or vegetable oil

4 dried bird's eye chiles, stemmed

½ cup packed soft, sticky, dark pure palm sugar from Thailand, or ¼ cup each packed grated light, hard palm sugar and packed dark brown sugar

¼ cup tamarind paste, homemade (page 316) or store-bought

¼ cup fish sauce, or as needed

About 6 pounds head-on, shell-on giant river prawns or 2 pounds head-on, shell-on colossal shrimp (U8 size)

1 tablespoon salt

8 ounces fresh or frozen neem shoots and buds (see Note, page 122)

1½ tablespoons fried garlic (page 322)

1½ tablespoons fried shallots (page 322)

3 or 4 cilantro sprigs (optional)

During the transition from the rainy season to the cold season, Bangkokians who live near the little canals, offshoots of the Chao Phraya, rejoice. They know that soon the water around the stilts of their houses will turn a faint red from a large gathering of river prawns in a state of discombobulation during high tide. When the prawns are in that condition, catching them is as easy as spreading chile jam on toast.

As if divinely predetermined, it is also the time of year when neem (*sadao*) plants compete with one another over who is the most fertile. Just one look out the window makes the decision on what to do with the prawns an easy one. One family member will start boiling a pot of rice. One will go out to the canal with a handheld fish net and bucket. One will start frying up some garlic and shallots and get a sauce of palm sugar, fish sauce, and tamarind going. An unlucky member will be assigned to climb up on one of the neem trees and pick a basketful of young shoots and buds. The person making the rice will pour the milky rice water—still hot and bubbling—right into a large bowl holding the neem, which will instantly blanch the herb and reduce its bitterness. Another family member will get the charcoal going, so that when the person who went to fetch the prawns returns with a bucket filled to the brim, the shellfish will be thrown right into the fire, where they will rest directly on the burning coals, blackening and cooking in minutes.

This is wintertime feasting, Bangkok style: a classic meal ensemble that represents the flavors associated with the region and also tells a story of life in the city with its broad, fertile river. There may be a hundred ways to prepare river prawns, but this one is more special than any other—the one the sight of which will make a homesick Bangkokian cry. ♦ **Serves 4**

Put the rice in a fine-mesh sieve or colander and rinse under cold running water until the water runs clear, capturing the rinsing water. Measure 8 cups of the whitest, cloudiest rinsing water and put it in a 4-quart saucepan; set the pan aside for now. Cook the rice on the stove top or in a rice cooker.

Put the lard and chiles in a 6- or 8-inch frying pan and set over medium heat. Stir until the chiles crisp up and turn dark red, less than 2 minutes. Transfer to a plate.

continued

Put the palm sugar, tamarind paste, and fish sauce in a 1-quart saucepan, set over medium heat, and bring to a boil, stirring constantly. Turn the heat to medium-low and boil gently, stirring often, for 2 minutes. Taste and add more fish sauce if needed, aiming for sweet first with salty trailing close behind. Scrape the sauce into a heatproof bowl that can hold twice its volume. Leave to cool.

If using river prawns, leave them whole to keep the tomalley inside the shells. If using colossal shrimp, leave the shell on but cut through it along the back of each shrimp and lift out the dark vein. Light natural wood charcoal until it glows hot but is not covered with white ash, scatter it onto the tray of a hibachi-style grill, and put the prawns or shrimp directly on the hot coals. The idea is to get the shellfish charred and blackened in spots on the outside and cooked on the inside as quickly as possible, so the flesh is firm and sweet and the tomalley is soft and oozing. Cooking time varies depending on the overall size and thickness of the shellfish, so play it by ear. Set the cooked shellfish aside, keeping them covered.

Bring the reserved rice rinsing water to a boil over high heat. Fill a large bowl half full with ice-cold water and set it near the stove. When the water boils, stir in the salt and turn down the heat so it bubbles gently. Lower the neem into the water. Don't stir. If using fresh neem, blanch for 1 minute; if using frozen neem, blanch for 30 seconds. Using a slotted spoon, transfer the neem to the ice water, to room temperature, then drain and gently blot dry with a clean kitchen towel.

Arrange the neem on one side of a large platter and the shellfish on the other side. Check the consistency of the cooled sauce, and if it has become too sticky, stir in some hot water until it has the consistency of maple syrup. Top the sauce with the fried chiles, garlic, shallots, and cilantro. Put the bowl in the middle of the platter, then serve with rice.

To enjoy, pinch the stem of the neem with your thumb and index finger and pull down the leaves to release them. Peel the prawns or shrimp and tear off a bite-size piece with your hand. Dunk the shellfish meat in the sauce and eat it in one perfect bite with some rice and a few neem leaves and buds. If you want some heat, take a fried chile, crumble it on your plate, and incorporate it into each bite, too. Expect all of the flavors in that one bite: salty, sweet, sour, bitter, and spicy. This is traditional Central Thai food of the Chao Phraya basin at its most glorious.

Note: In the United States, neem leaves and buds can be found vacuum-packed in the freezer of any well-stocked grocery store specializing in Thai ingredients.

Crispy green papaya salad

ส้มตำทอด SOM TAM THOT

Vegetable oil, for deep-frying

½ teaspoon salt

¼ cup limestone solution (page 336), or ¼ cup water mixed with ½ teaspoon baking soda

2 cups tightly packed grated green papaya (6 ounces), with shreds about 3 inches long

½ cup Thai tapioca starch or cornstarch

¼ cup Thai rice flour

4 cloves garlic

2 fresh bird's eye chiles, or to taste

2 tablespoons dried shrimp

4 ounces long beans or green beans, trimmed and cut into 1-inch sticks

2 tablespoons unsalted roasted peanuts

4 ounces cherry tomatoes (¾ cup), halved crosswise

2 tablespoons packed grated palm sugar, or to taste

2 tablespoons fish sauce, or to taste

3 tablespoons lime juice, or to taste

In this modern version of *som tam*, green papaya strands are either dredged in flour or dipped in a light batter and then fried until golden brown and crisp. To preserve the crispiness of the papaya for as long as possible, the dish usually comes to the table with the chunky dressing sitting atop the crispy papaya or the dressing and papaya arranged separately on a platter. This way, diners can toss them together just before they're ready to eat the salad—much the same way as Crispy Water Spinach Salad (page 127).

Som tam thot can be enjoyed with rice as part of a typical multidish meal or as a stand-alone between-meal snack. ⚘ **Serves 2**

Pour the oil to a depth of 2 inches into a wok or Dutch oven and heat to 350°F. Line a sheet pan with paper towels and place it near the stove.

While the oil is heating, combine the salt and limestone solution in a bowl and stir until the salt dissolves. Add the papaya to the bowl and mix until every piece is coated with the liquid. In another bowl, stir together the tapioca starch and rice flour. Grab the wet papaya, shaking off some of the excess liquid, and drop it into the flour mixture, then mix with your hands until every piece is coated with the flour.

When the oil is hot, drop half of the papaya pieces into it and spread them evenly, doing your best to keep them separate. Fry, stirring constantly, until the papaya sticks are golden brown, 3 to 4 minutes. Using a slotted spoon, transfer the papaya to the prepared sheet pan. Repeat with the remaining papaya. Leave the fried papaya to cool to only slightly warmer than room temperature, the perfect serving temperature, while you prepare the dressing.

In a mortar, grind the garlic to a smooth paste. Add the chiles and dried shrimp and pound them until they break open. Add the beans and peanuts and pound until the beans split open and the peanuts break into small pieces. Add the tomatoes and pound until they break open and release some juices. Add the sugar, fish sauce, and lime juice (start with slightly less of each amount if you think the seasoning will be too potent for you) and stir until the sugar dissolves. Taste and adjust the seasoning as needed.

Transfer the fried papaya to a serving platter. The moment you are ready to eat, spoon the dressing over the papaya, toss well, and enjoy immediately.

Spicy corn salad

ส้มตำข้าวโพด SOM TAM KHAO PHOT

4 ears corn, husks and silk removed

1 teaspoon salt

4 cups ice cubes

2 large cloves garlic

2 or 3 fresh bird eye's chiles

1½ tablespoons dried shrimp

¼ cup unsalted roasted peanuts

3 ounces long beans or 16 green beans, trimmed and cut crosswise into 2-inch pieces

10 cherry tomatoes, halved lengthwise

½ cup peeled and grated carrot (optional)

1 tablespoon fish sauce, or as needed

1½ tablespoons fresh lime juice, or as needed

Grated palm sugar, for seasoning

My mother was a corn fanatic who lived through the period in the 1970s when Bangkok-based Kasetsart University, the country's premier agricultural college, first introduced Super Sweet corn to the city. She, along with all of Bangkok, quickly pushed aside the local corn, bland, sticky, and chewy, in favor of this new cultivar with sweet, tender, juicy kernels. Before then, the most common form of sweet corn consumed, at least in our family, was canned creamed corn, a once-popular ice cream topping that you can still experience at some old ice-cream parlors in the city.

When Mom was alive, the excellent corn of the Midwest was one of the things she looked forward to when she visited me in Chicago. We would drive to the farm areas outside the city, buy more corn than we could eat, and make this modern variety of *som tam* over and over and over. ◆ **Serves 3 to 4**

Place the corn in a 4-quart saucepan, add water to cover barely, and stir in the salt. Bring to a boil over high heat. While the water is heating, put the ice cubes in a large bowl and add water to cover. The moment the water boils, cook the corn for 2 minutes, then immediately transfer it to the ice bath and let cool to room temperature. Drain well and pat dry with paper towels or a kitchen towel.

Stand an ear of corn on its stem end on a work surface and, using a sharp knife, cut from the top downward in a sawing motion, cutting as deeply into the kernels as possible, and rotating the ear a quarter turn after each cut. Transfer the kernels to a bowl. Repeat with the remaining ears.

In a mortar, grind the garlic to a paste. Add the chiles and smash them into small pieces. Add the dried shrimp and pound until they break up. Add 2 tablespoons of the peanuts and pound them into small pieces about the size of a match head. Add the beans and smash them until they split open, then do the same with the tomato halves. Transfer the contents of the mortar to the corn bowl and add the carrot.

Add the fish sauce, lime juice, and a pinch of sugar to the corn mixture and toss well. Taste and adjust the seasoning with fish sauce, lime juice, and sugar if needed. If your tomatoes and corn aren't very sweet, more sugar will be in order. I like my corn salad equally salty, sweet, and sour, but you do what you like.

Plate the salad, sprinkle the remaining 2 tablespoons peanuts over the top, and then serve right away with rice or alone as a mid-meal snack.

Crispy water spinach salad

ยำผักบุ้งกรอบ YAM PHAK BUNG KROP

CRISPY WATER SPINACH

8 ounces water spinach

1½ cups Thai rice flour

½ teaspoon table salt

½ cup ice-cold water

½ cup limestone solution (page 336), or ½ cup water mixed with ½ teaspoon baking soda

Vegetable oil, for deep-frying

3 or 4 dried bird's eye chiles, stemmed

¼ cup roasted cashews

DRESSING

12 ounces shrimp, peeled, deveined, and cut into ½-inch pieces

2 ounces shallots, halved lengthwise, placed cut side down, and sliced lengthwise paper-thin

3 tablespoons chile jam, homemade (page 22) or store-bought

2 to 3 tablespoons fresh lime juice

1 to 2 tablespoons fish sauce

2 teaspoons packed grated palm sugar

3 or 4 fresh red bird's eye chiles, cut crosswise into ⅛-inch-thick slices

This salad, popular in Bangkok and in a few Thai restaurants in large cities in the United States, can be enjoyed as a stand-alone appetizer with cold beer or as a rice accompaniment. To keep the water spinach fritters from becoming soggy, serve the salad unassembled, which is how Thais usually serve it. Then, just before you are about to take the first bite, pour the wet part over the dry part. ⬥ **Serves 4**

To make the water spinach, keep the top 8 or 9 inches of each stem for this dish and save the remainder for a stir-fry or other use. Cut the water spinach into 3-inch pieces. In a large bowl, whisk together the rice flour, salt, water, and limestone solution. Add the spinach to the batter and mix well with your hands, making sure every piece is coated. Let stand for 15 minutes.

To begin the dressing, meanwhile, fill a 1-quart saucepan halfway with water and bring to a boil over high heat. Lower the heat so the water is only steaming and not bubbling. Add the shrimp and stir until they turn pink, less than 2 minutes. Using a slotted spoon, transfer the shrimp to a small bowl and let cool.

Line a sheet pan with paper towels and set it near the stove. Pour the oil to a depth of 1 inch into a wok or Dutch oven and heat to 350°F. Mix the batter-coated water spinach again so the batter that has fallen to the bottom of the bowl won't feel left out. When the oil is hot, grab a handful of the water spinach and scatter it evenly over the surface of the oil, doing your best to keep the pieces as separate as possible. Deep-fry the water spinach, flipping it around, until thoroughly crisp and golden brown, about 2 minutes. Using a mesh skimmer, transfer the spinach to the prepared sheet pan to drain. Repeat. Once the last batch leaves the wok, throw the dried chiles into the wok and fry just until they turn maroon, 15 to 20 seconds, then transfer to a corner of the sheet pan.

To finish the dressing, add the shallots to the shrimp bowl, followed by the chile jam, 2 tablespoons of the lime juice, 1 tablespoon of the fish sauce, and the palm sugar and mix well. Taste and adjust the seasoning with more lime juice and/or fish sauce as needed. Aim for sour first and then equally salty and sweet; the fritters are bland, so don't be afraid to employ a heavy hand. Stir in the fresh chiles and transfer to a serving bowl.

Place the dressing bowl in the middle of a large platter, arrange the crispy water spinach around the bowl, and scatter the cashews and fried chiles over the water spinach. The moment you are ready to dig in, pour the chunky dressing over the water spinach. The fried dried chiles are there for you to crumble over the salad if you need more heat.

Winged bean salad

ยำถั่วพู YAM THUA PHU

2 ounces shallots

½ cup plus 1 tablespoon unsweetened dried fine coconut flakes

½ cup vegetable oil

4 or 5 dried bird's eye chiles, stemmed

1 pound winged beans

2 teaspoons salt

8 ounces shrimp, peeled and deveined

4 ounces ground pork

½ cup coconut cream

2 tablespoons chile jam, homemade (page 22) or store-bought

2 or 3 fresh bird's eye chiles, thinly sliced crosswise

2 tablespoons fresh lime juice

1 tablespoon fish sauce

2 teaspoons packed grated palm sugar

¼ cup roasted cashews or peanuts, coarsely chopped

2 medium- or hard-boiled eggs, quartered lengthwise

Regardless of the many forms Thai salads take, the common theme is dressing made from the juice (or flesh) of a sour fruit, fish sauce, and sometimes sugar. This classic features a delicious yet rarer *creamy* dressing. The creaminess comes from a combination of coconut cream and chopped or ground roasted nuts. ◆ **Serves 4**

Cut the shallots in half lengthwise, then place the halves cut side down and thinly slice lengthwise. Divide the slices into two equal portions and set aside.

In a 6- or 8-inch frying pan, toast the coconut over medium heat, stirring often, until golden brown, 7 to 8 minutes. Transfer the coconut to a plate, wipe the pan clean, and return it to medium heat. Line a plate with paper towels and set it near the stove. Put the oil and one portion of the shallots into the pan and stir until medium brown, 7 to 8 minutes. Add the dried chiles and continue to cook until the shallots are golden brown and the chiles get darker and crisp, about 1 minute. Using a mesh skimmer, transfer the shallots and chiles to the prepared plate.

Fill a 2-quart saucepan halfway with water and bring to a boil over high heat. Meanwhile, trim the stems and bottom ends off the winged beans and cut the beans crosswise on a 40-degree angle into ⅛-inch-thick slices. Fill a bowl halfway with cold water and set it near the stove. When the water boils, stir in the salt and the sliced beans and blanch, stirring often, for 40 to 50 seconds. Using the skimmer, transfer the beans to the cold water. Turn down the heat so the water is gently bubbling. Add the shrimp and stir until they turn opaque, about 1 minute. Use the skimmer to transfer them to a plate. Add the pork to the pan and cook, stirring to break it up into small pieces, until opaque, 1 to 2 minutes. Using the skimmer, transfer the pork to the shrimp plate.

Drain the beans, blot them dry with a kitchen towel, and put them in a large bowl. Add the toasted coconut, shrimp, ground pork, reserved fresh shallot slices, coconut cream, chile jam, fresh chiles, lime juice, fish sauce, and sugar and mix well. Taste a spoonful of the salad to make sure it is a perfect bite with all of the components and add more lime juice, fish sauce, and/or sugar if needed. Aim for a taste that is equally sweet, salty, and tart (and don't forget to account for the bland rice that the salad will accompany).

Plate the salad and top it with the fried shallots, dried chiles, and cashews. Arrange the egg quarters on the side and then serve with rice. Diners who prefer additional heat—the smoky kind—can crumble the fried chiles over their portion.

Egg sausage soup

แกงจืดลูกรอก **KAENG JUET LUK ROK**

8 eggs, preferably duck eggs

¼ cup water

½ teaspoon salt

2 (20-inch-long) natural hog casings, 1½ inches in diameter, soaked in cold water for 15 minutes

2 cloves garlic

¼ teaspoon white peppercorns

1 tablespoon finely chopped cilantro roots or stems

4 ounces ground pork or chicken

2 teaspoons Thai thin soy sauce or Golden Mountain seasoning sauce

8 cups homemade chicken or pork stock (page 323) or store-bought sodium-free chicken stock

Fish sauce, for seasoning

¾ cup packed coarsely chopped Chinese or regular celery leaves

1 tablespoon fried garlic and 1 tablespoon fried garlic oil (page 322)

Ground white pepper, for dusting

This soup got its name from the appearance of its featured component: twice-cooked egg sausage slices that resemble a pulley, or *luk rok*. Beaten eggs are funneled into natural pork casings to form bratwurst-size sausage links that are then poached until firm and cut into thick coins. When the sausage coins are cooked once more in broth, the casings shrink slightly and recede in the middle while the egg filling protrudes from both openings.

The cooked coins are reminiscent of little pulley wheels—at least that's what people from my parents' generation see. On the other hand, I see a yo-yo. But if you ask my young nieces and nephews, they insist this dish should be called *macaron* soup. Although the French sandwich cookies are a new phenomenon for people of my generation, my young relatives have seen them at most of the malls and bakeshops throughout the city since they were babies. These differences aside, this is an old-fashioned home-style soup that has been enjoyed in our family for decades. Sadly, although it is both fun to look at and good to eat, you can rarely find it in the city these days. ⬩ **Serves 4**

Crack the eggs into a bowl and add the water and salt. Using a fork, beat as gently as possible just until no whites remain. Tie a tight double knot on one end of a hog casing. Insert a funnel about 1 inch deep into the other opening, then firmly grab the part of the funnel that is covered with the casing and gently pour half of the egg mixture through the funnel into the casing until you have a sausage link about 1 foot long. Use the remaining unfilled casing to tie a double knot to close the casing, positioning the knot as close to the filling as possible. A snug fit will prevent large air pockets from forming that will result in holey or misshapen pulleys. Repeat with the remaining egg mixture and casing.

Gently put the links in a wide, shallow saucepan (to keep them as straight as possible) and add water to cover. Set the pan over medium heat. When the water is just about to boil, turn the heat to medium-low or low to prevent it from boiling. Keep the temperature in the 150°F to 170°F range. Poach the sausage links until they float to the surface, feel firm to the touch, and no liquid oozes out when you prick them with a toothpick, about 30 minutes. Using a mesh skimmer, transfer to a plate and let cool.

While the sausage links are cooling, put the garlic, peppercorns, and cilantro roots into a mortar and grind to a smooth paste. Transfer to a small bowl, add the pork and soy sauce, and mix thoroughly. Cover and refrigerate until needed.

When the links are cool enough to handle, use a very sharp knife to cut them gently and carefully into coins ¾ inch thick. Gently transfer the coins to a 4-quart saucepan, add the stock and enough water just to cover, and bring to a very, very gentle boil over medium heat. Drop the pork mixture into the liquid by the teaspoonful, then turn up the heat slightly to maintain a gentle simmer. By the time the pork floats to the surface, it is ready and the sausage coins will have turned into little pulleys. Taste for seasoning and add fish sauce as needed.

Stir in the celery leaves, fried garlic, and fried garlic oil, dust with the pepper, and serve with rice.

Spicy shrimp paste–beef soup

แกงรัญจวน   KAENG RANJUAN

1 pound boneless beef chuck steak, sirloin, or tenderloin

2 (1-ounce) shallots

3 large cloves garlic

2 large or 3 medium lemongrass stalks

6 cups homemade chicken stock (page 323) or store-bought sodium-free chicken stock

¼ cup shrimp paste relish (page 316)

Fish sauce, for seasoning

Fresh lime juice, for seasoning

½ cup packed fresh Thai basil leaves

½ cup packed fresh holy basil leaves

This intensely robust soup is another dish that has come out of a royal court. Its origin is spoken of in *Recipes from a Royal Mansion*, a recipe collection and an interview of author and memoirist Mom Luang Nueang Nilrat. According to her, the kitchen staff of the royal court in which she lived made a large pan of beef stir-fry to feed the workers who came to arrange the flowers at the mansion, and much of the stir-fry was returned to the kitchen untouched. To avoid waste, the kitchen staff (who, I imagine, must have been a little brokenhearted) picked out the beef and simmered it in a pot of plain broth. Then some leftover shrimp paste relish went in along with some fresh herbs and aromatics. With that, a new dish was born. It was served at dinner on the same day—and the whole pot was devoured. The guests came into the kitchen to ask the cooks for the recipe.

Spicy, pungent *kaeng ranjuan* has since become an elegant dish, now found in the homes of old Bangkokian families or at refined restaurants that serve retro-traditional Thai dishes. Its poetic name *ranjuan*, which means "to pine for" or "to yearn for," only adds to the air of romanticism that surrounds it.

This soup is salty, very tart, and very spicy. The scent of the shrimp paste is also unapologetically front and center—there's no subtlety here. Familiarity with and appreciation for these characteristics in traditional Thai dishes are prerequisites to understanding why the soup, as the name suggests, makes many of us pine for it. ◆ **Serves 2**

Slice the beef against the grain on the diagonal (30- to 40-degree angle) into very thin bite-size pieces. Cover and refrigerate until needed.

Halve the shallots lengthwise and crush them with the side of a cleaver, then crush the garlic. Trim off the root end of each lemongrass stalk. Then, starting from the root end, cut into *razor*-thin slices (they will be eaten), stopping when the purple rings disappear.

Pour the stock into a 2-quart saucepan, cover, and bring to a boil over high heat. Stir in the relish, shallots, garlic, and lemongrass, then lower the heat so the stock is boiling very gently. Taste and add the fish sauce and lime juice as needed to achieve an equally salty and sour flavor (and keeping in mind that the soup will accompany bland rice).

When the taste suits you, stir in the beef, adjust the heat to maintain a gentle simmer, cover, and cook until the beef is cooked medium-well, about 2 minutes. Stir in the basil leaves. Remove from the heat and serve while still steaming hot with rice.

Some Like It Bouncy

Just as different cultures have different standards for what constitutes beauty, they have different standards for what constitutes properly prepared food. When you enter into the realm of another food culture, you are wise to leave all of your preconceived notions at the door and adopt the senses of the new culture.

As odd as it may sound, in Thai food, chewiness and bounciness are desirable in certain food items; chewy rice cakes and tapioca pearls, meatballs so bouncy you can dribble them, squid and cuttlefish cooked quickly to retain a chewy—almost gummy-bear-like—texture, fish balls and fish cakes so firm and bouncy that they fight back when you bite into them. All of these describe what Thais consider good and righteous. Outsiders often wonder why they see Western frankfurters in one form or another at nearly every convenience store and corner shop in Bangkok. Given the locals' affinity for the firm, bouncy emulsified forcemeat of their own cuisine, the reason has always been clear to me.

Caramel-braised eggs with pork belly

ไข่พะโล้ KHAI PHALO

6 large cloves garlic

1 teaspoon white peppercorns

2 tablespoons finely chopped cilantro roots or cilantro stems

1 tablespoon homemade lard (page 28) or vegetable oil

¼ cup packed soft, sticky dark pure palm sugar from Thailand (the best kind to use in this particular dish), or 3 tablespoons packed grated light, hard palm sugar plus 1 tablespoon packed dark brown sugar

½ cup water, or as needed

1 tablespoon fish sauce, or more as needed

1½ pounds boneless, skin-on pork belly or fatty pork shoulder, cut into 2-inch cubes

8 hard-boiled duck or chicken eggs

3 tablespoons Thai dark soy sauce (optional)

2 star anise pods (optional)

2 (3-inch) cinnamon sticks (optional)

4 or 5 cilantro sprigs

Whole boiled eggs—almost always the fattier, heartier duck eggs—stewed in sweet and salty broth redolent of Chinese dried spices, are found nearly everywhere in Bangkok where home-style dishes are served. But the best *khai phalo* was always my maternal grandmother's. Not satisfied with the version featuring pale eggs in thin, mildly seasoned broth found at the average rice-curry shop in the city, Grandma went to town with the aromatic paste of cilantro roots, garlic, and white peppercorns (most modern versions call for Chinese spices and soy sauce, an option I've offered here). She also made sure the fish sauce–palm sugar base caramelized and developed a deep, complex flavor, which she said predestined the quality of the final product.

You know how conventional wisdom teaches us never to overcook eggs? Well, in our household, conventional wisdom was often found fanning itself between fainting fits while Grandma stewed the eggs for hours until they—forget soft and tender—turned the color of dark brown sugar and *shrank*. Grandma also insisted on allowing the finished stew to rest overnight before reheating and serving it the next day. When you finally split open one of the eggs, you could see that the stewing liquid had seeped all the way to the yolk, deepening both its color and its flavor. The white, saturated with the flavor of the broth, had condensed and taken on the bouncy texture that fights back when you bite into it. As off-putting as this may sound, let's not forget that Thais love this firm, bouncy texture (see page 133), so this is a description of something good.

I used to think we were the only egg shrinkers. Then I discovered that some well-loved old-school restaurants in Bangkok, such as Sanguan Sri in the Phloen Chit area and OV Kitchen inside the compound of the famed all-boys Vajiravudh College, make their *khai phalo* exactly the same way. Sometimes when I mentioned the way my family made this dish to others from a similar family background, they got excited and confessed that they, too, thought they were the only ones who made it that way. I'm now convinced that the underground society of egg shrinkers is much larger than I previously thought. ⬧ **Serves 4**

In a mortar, grind together the garlic, peppercorns, and cilantro roots to a smooth paste. Put the paste and lard into a 4-quart saucepan and set over medium-high heat. Stir just until fragrant—no need to brown the paste—about 1 minute. Add the sugar and water and boil, stirring, until the sugar dissolves. Add the fish sauce, turn down the heat so the mixture bubbles enthusiastically but not so much that it scorches, and stir nonstop for 3 minutes.

continued

Add the pork belly to the caramel and stir to coat. Once the outside of the pork turns opaque, after 2 to 3 minutes, add the eggs, soy sauce, star anise, and cinnamon, if using (if not, add more fish sauce to taste). Add enough water so the liquid is flush with the top of the eggs. Turn the heat to high and bring the mixture to a boil. Lower the heat so the liquid is simmering gently, cover, and cook until the pork is fully cooked but not yet tender, 10 to 12 minutes.

Add water to return the liquid to the original level if needed, then taste the liquid and adjust with fish sauce and sugar if needed, keeping in mind that you will be serving this with bland rice. My ideal version is slightly saltier than it is sweet; your palate may vary from mine. Once the taste suits you, continue to stew, covered, for 30 minutes more if using pork shoulder and 1 hour more if using pork belly, replenishing the water and resuming the simmer along the way as needed.

And here's where "two roads [diverge] in a yellow wood." Decide if you want to make the popular version most commonly found on the streets of Bangkok or the egg shrinkers' version.

If you're going with the former (which is quite good!), stew the eggs and the pork in the same manner for 1 hour longer. Before taking the pan off the heat and declaring your dish finished, make sure the level of the liquid is the same as it was when you started. Garnish with the cilantro sprigs and serve with rice.

But if you decide that this is the day you will shrink some eggs, do the following. With the sounds of the jubilantly choiring cherubim in the background, stew the eggs and the pork for 1 hour longer in the same manner, then fish out the pork and cover and refrigerate until needed. Stew the eggs, replenishing the water along the way as needed to maintain the original level, for another 5 hours, returning the pork to the pan during the last 10 minutes (don't forget to adjust the liquid level). Once that is done, you can garnish the stew with the cilantro and serve it with rice. Alternatively, you can let the stew stand uncovered overnight to deepen the flavor even more (refrigerate the pan if you like), then replenish the liquid as needed, reheat the stew, and take it off the heat. Finally, add the garnish and enjoy the stew with rice, recognizing that you—you "took [the road] less traveled by, and that has made all the difference."

Spicy beef soup with sweet potatoes and basil

ต้มจิ๋ว ❖ TOM JIO

2 pounds boneless beef shank, cut into 1½-inch cubes

4 cups sodium-free beef stock

1 tablespoon fish sauce, or as needed

1 pound Asian sweet potatoes, Yukon gold potatoes, or kabocha squash, peeled and cut into 1½-inch cubes

2 ounces shallots

2 tablespoons tamarind paste, homemade (page 316) or store-bought

2 tablespoons fresh lime juice

½ cup packed fresh holy basil leaves

½ cup packed fresh Thai sweet basil leaves

Coarsely chopped fresh bird's eye chiles, for seasoning

This soup from the early 1900s is believed to have been invented by Princess Yaovabha Bongsanid, who is said to have taken an active role in providing healthful dishes for her father, King Chulalongkorn (Rama V). If you're wondering whether this is simply a Western-style beef and potato soup, note the use of fish sauce, tamarind, lime, chiles, and two kinds of basil—Thai flavors through and through.

The best type of sweet potato to use here is the so-called Asian sweet potato with purple skin and pale yellow flesh that is starchy, firm, and only mildly sweet. But if you can't find Asian sweet potatoes, use regular potatoes or kabocha squash instead of the regular supermarket orange-colored sweet potatoes, as they are too sweet. ❖ **Serves 4 to 6**

Put the beef, stock, and fish sauce into a 4-quart saucepan and add water to cover the beef by 1½ inches. Set the pan over high heat and bring to a boil. Lower the heat so the liquid is simmering, cover, and cook until the beef cubes are fork-tender but still hold their shape, about 2 hours. As the beef cooks, uncover the pan occasionally and skim off and discard any fat and scum from the surface and add water as needed to maintain the original level.

Add the sweet potatoes and more water, if necessary, to cover, and continue to simmer until the sweet potatoes are fork-tender but still firm, 5 to 7 minutes longer. Meanwhile, halve the shallots lengthwise, place the halves cut side down, and cut lengthwise into paper-thin slices. When the potatoes are ready, add the shallots to the pan and heat through. Remove from the heat and stir in the tamarind, lime juice, holy basil, sweet basil, and the chiles to taste.

Taste a spoonful of the broth and adjust the seasoning with more fish sauce if needed. The broth should be equally sour and salty and be strong and spicy. You should detect a heady scent of the basil with every sip. Serve steaming hot with rice.

On Cook Shops

No one can write a book on the food of Bangkok without mentioning cook shops, the pioneers of the restaurant industry in the city. These are the restaurants our parents went to on dates. They are also the family restaurants of our childhood—the places our parents took us on the weekends. When I think of the Bangkok I know and love, images of cook shops never fail to pop into my mind: old restaurants in the middle of a modern business district with their decor and ambience unchanged since the 1950s—ceiling fans, old-fashioned dinnerware on the table and enamelware spittoons on the floor, older servers talking to one another in a peculiar blend of Thai and Chinese while setting soft white sandwich bread, butter, ketchup, and Worcestershire sauce before customers. These images of almost irreconcilable contrasts and multiple worlds colliding somehow make sense, and they have always captivated me.

Sadly, cook shops have been steadily dwindling in number over the last half century. Back in their heyday, however, they were the epitome of fine dining for upper-middle-class Bangkokians in the years after World War II. These were the places where the locals gathered to enjoy a wide variety of Western dishes prepared the Chinese way with a Thai flair—a whole repertoire you wouldn't find anywhere else.

The history of the so-called cook shops in Bangkok goes back to the turn of the twentieth century, when several Hainanese immigrants, known for their culinary skills, were employed as personal cooks to Western diplomats and businessmen who came to work in the city. The employment gave these men an opportunity to learn how to make several Western dishes and get acquainted with the various ingredients they wouldn't normally use in Chinese cooking, such as butter or Worcestershire sauce. In turn, they incorporated some Chinese ingredients into Western dishes that folks in those days never associated with Western food, such as soy sauce.

Chinese cooking techniques were also applied to the making of Western dishes. A meat stew, for example, when done the Western way, would have started off with dusting the meat with flour and searing it before it was braised. In the hands of these cooks, the meat was marinated first, with soy sauce and Chinese rice wine as part of the marinade, and then deep-fried before braising. Gravies and sauces were thickened with tapioca starch rather than with wheat flour or with cream or butter, making them look more like what you'd see in a Chinese restaurant than a French bistro.

Once their jobs ended, many of these Chinese cooks struck out on their own and opened restaurants in the well-established neighborhoods of Bangkok, offering a whole new category of hybrid dishes. They weren't totally Western, they weren't entirely Chinese, and they definitely weren't Thai. They were served with rice or with thickly sliced fluffy white bread and a generous pat of butter. Salt and pepper shakers, a bottle of Worcestershire, some yellow mustard, and, of course, ketchup were always on the table.

Bangkokians went nuts over these creations. And cook shops, that is, shops run by former personal cooks, became a Bangkok institution.

These restaurants—the ones that are still in business—serve different things. But nearly all of them offer some core dishes; beef steak accompanied by lettuce, tomatoes, onions, and cucumbers dressed in a simple vinaigrette is one example, and a stew of beef tongue or chicken is another. And this is the reason the cook shops were often colloquially referred to as *sitek-situ* restaurants, a nickname assembled from the localized pronunciations of the English words *steak* and *stew*, respectively.

Pork chops, cook shop style

ซี่โครงหมูอบแบบกุ๊กชอป SI KHRONG MU OP

PORK CHOPS

4 bone-in center-cut pork chops, ¾ to 1 inch thick

2 tablespoons Thai thin soy sauce or Golden Mountain seasoning sauce or Maggi seasoning sauce

1 tablespoon oyster sauce

1 teaspoon ground white pepper

Vegetable oil, for frying

½ cup Thai rice flour or all-purpose flour

2 eggs

1½ cups unseasoned fine dried bread crumbs (not Japanese panko)

GRAVY

1 tablespoon plus 1 teaspoon cornstarch

1½ cups homemade chicken stock (page 323) or store-bought sodium-free chicken stock

2 tablespoons tomato sauce or ketchup

1 tablespoon Thai thin soy sauce or Golden Mountain seasoning sauce or Maggi seasoning sauce

1 tablespoon oyster sauce

1 teaspoon granulated sugar

½ teaspoon ground white pepper

1 tablespoon unsalted butter or vegetable oil

1 small yellow or white onion, very finely diced

2 teaspoons Chinese rice wine (shaoxing)

½ cup fresh or thawed, frozen shelled English peas

SIDES

Thick slices of soft white bread

Softened butter

Worcestershire sauce

Warm cooked jasmine rice (optional)

These pork chops are dredged in eggs, breaded, panfried until golden brown, sliced to make it easy to eat with a spoon and a fork, and served under a blanket of light, glossy, pea-studded gravy. Although the pork chops are usually served with rice, a thick slice of soft white bread with butter is often offered to those who wish to enjoy their meal in a more Western manner (see page 139).

Canned peas have always been used in this dish, even now when plump, sweet fresh peas are available everywhere in the city. You can use either type or even frozen peas, though I suspect nostalgic Bangkokians will gravitate toward the soft, starchy canned ones. ⚬ **Serves 4**

To prepare the pork chops, using a meat mallet or the side of a large cleaver, flatten the pork chops to half their original thickness and then place the chops in a bowl. Add the soy sauce, oyster sauce, and pepper and mix well to coat the chops evenly. Cover and refrigerate for at least 6 hours or up to 12 hours.

Pour the oil to a depth of ½ inch into a 12-inch frying pan and set over medium heat. Put the flour, eggs, and bread crumbs in three separate shallow bowls, then beat the eggs until blended. One at a time, dredge the pork chops in the flour, coating both sides and shaking off the excess. Next, dip them in the egg, allowing the excess to drip off. Then, coat them thoroughly and liberally with the bread crumbs. When the oil is hot, place two chops in the pan and fry, turning once, until golden brown on both sides, 5 to 6 minutes. Transfer to a large plate and leave uncovered. Repeat with the remaining chops.

To make the gravy, while the chops are cooking, in a small bowl, whisk together the cornstarch, stock, tomato sauce, soy sauce, oyster sauce, sugar, and pepper.

Pour off and discard most of the oil and all of the bread crumb sediment from the pan, leaving only a thin film of oil. Add the butter to the pan and put it back on the stove over medium-high heat. When the butter sizzles but hasn't turned brown, add the onion and wine and cook, stirring, until the onion has softened (do not let it brown) and the wine has evaporated, about 1 minute. Give the stock mixture a quick stir, pour it into the pan, and cook, stirring constantly, until the gravy becomes thick and glossy, about 1 minute. Stir in the peas and heat through. Remove from the heat.

Cut the flesh part of the pork chops against the grain into ½-inch-wide strips, keeping the bones intact for presentation. Reassemble the pork chops on a platter, pour the gravy over them, and serve right away with the bread, butter, Worcestershire sauce, and warm jasmine rice.

On Omelet

When I speak of an omelet, I'm referring to a Thai-style omelet (*khai jiao*), which is very different from a French-style omelet. A Thai omelet can be plain or studded with various add-ins; it can be thin and soft, rotund and springy, or puffy and crispy around the edges; and it can be rolled, folded, or formed into a half sphere. But two things hold fast: a Thai omelet is typically seasoned with fish sauce and is meant to be eaten with rice.

The omelet is a favorite food of Bangkok locals, too—morning, noon, and night. It's certainly not a breakfast-only food. Let me put it this way: You're playing *Family Feud*. You're asked to name a comfort food served atop rice. If you are from Bangkok, omelet will be one of your answers. And if the people the show has polled are Bangkokians, omelet will be one of the answers on the board.

It is easy to see why. *Khai jiao* is the humble dish you make when you're broke and have only eggs in the refrigerator. It's also the dish you must add to the meal, even when you already have an abundance of foods on the table. And although sometimes more elaborate forms of omelet are seen at upscale restaurants, most Bangkokians prefer to make it at home or rely on street vendors who will customize their order with a requested add-in.

But the love of omelet is by no means limited to the streets. At the beginning of the 1900s, a Bangkok resident embarked on a ship to Europe. During the nearly yearlong voyage, there was never a shortage of skillfully prepared Western food for him to eat on and off the ship. But one night in 1908, he woke up with hunger pangs. "Ghosts" of all the delicious Thai dishes he loved to eat back home floated around the room, refusing to let him go back to sleep. He wrote humorously of the whole episode in a letter to one of his daughters. Despite a delightfully amusing account, the writer's yearning is palpable to anyone who reads that letter and who has known what it's like to pine for the taste of home.

The letter writer was King Chulalongkorn, whose reign saw the proliferation of food-related publications and whose royal kitchen was run by some of the most renowned cooks in the history of Thailand. This is a king who dined well at home and abroad. Yet one of the "ghosts" that kept him up that night? You guessed it—*khai jiao*.

Omelet roll with crabmeat filling

ไข่เจียวปู KHAI JIAO PU

Homemade lard (page 28) or vegetable oil, for deep-frying

3 eggs, preferably duck eggs

1 tablespoon Thai rice flour or all-purpose flour

1 teaspoon fish sauce

½ teaspoon ground white pepper

12 ounces fresh lump crabmeat, picked over for shell fragments and cartilage

Cilantro sprigs, for garnish

Thai Sriracha sauce, homemade (page 319) or store-bought (Shark or Sriraja Panich brand), for serving

The best protein to pair with a Thai omelet is crabmeat, as the popularity of crabmeat-filled omelets in Bangkok attests. Local cooks can always find plenty of fresh, sweet, voluptuous lump crabmeat in the city (being close to the ocean has its advantages), which is not to suggest that it is inexpensive. It is as costly here as it is everywhere in the world, but people don't seem to mind paying an outrageous amount of money for a crabmeat-stuffed omelet.

Restaurant cooks in Bangkok know that, and they never seem to run out of ideas on how to present a crabmeat omelet creatively. EAT, a respectable restaurant offering old-school family dishes, shapes its omelet into a half sphere, a style that goes by the euphemistic *khai yok song* (bra omelet). Another famous shop, Je Fai, whose walls are lined with photographs of celebrities such as Martha Stewart, goes boobless with its omelets, instead opting for a scroll-shape roll that packs in what seems like the meat from half of the crab population of the Gulf of Thailand. Even though this famous omelet roll is priced at 800 baht a serving (to give you some perspective, at the time of writing, a bowl of noodles is about 40 baht), the people of Bangkok can't get enough of it.

Not having that kind of money, I've been making my own version. Be sure to use a large wok and to have two wide, sturdy metal spatulas, as you can't form a proper omelet roll without them. ♦ **Serves 2**

Melt lard to a depth of 4 inches in a large wok over high heat. In a bowl, using a fork, beat together the eggs, flour, fish sauce, and pepper until no lumps remain. Gather the crab into a loose ball and gently drop it into the middle of the egg bowl; don't stir the crab.

When the lard is smoking, imagine a 4-inch circle in the center of the lard pool. Then, holding the egg bowl no higher than 1 inch above the surface of the pool, pour the egg mixture directly into the imaginary circle. Pull your hand up right away, as the egg mixture will puff up and spread over the hot surface. Using two large spatulas, immediately squeeze the omelet from both sides into a long rectangle in the middle of the wok and hold it still for 8 to 10 seconds. Repeat this two or three times. The omelet will be unruly—it just won't stay in place—but within 20 seconds of squeezing and holding, you will see a scroll taking shape. Don't worry about the position of the crab at this point; it will take care of itself. With the help of the spatulas, peek at the bottom of the scroll. When it is golden brown, use both spatulas to flip the scroll over. The uncooked eggs on the top will

continued

spread out and get unruly again, so you will need to show them who's boss with those spatulas. Continue to squeeze and hold, this time from both the long sides and the short sides, until the scroll is sealed and golden brown all over, about 1 minute longer. The whole cooking process should take no more than 3 minutes.

Transfer the omelet roll to a serving platter and garnish with the cilantro. Serve the omelet immediately with rice and Sriracha. When you cut the scroll open, you should see the crabmeat huddled together in the center and enveloped by a thin shell of omelet. Congratulations.

Preserved radish omelet with crispy basil

ไข่เจียวหัวใช้โป๊กะเพรากรอบ ◆ KHAI JIAO HUA CHAI PO KA-PHRAO KROP

Vegetable oil, for deep-frying

1 cup packed fresh holy basil or Thai sweet basil leaves

⅔ cup packed fine-matchstick-cut sweet preserved radishes (see page 344)

4 eggs

1 teaspoon fish sauce

2 tablespoons homemade lard (page 28) or vegetable oil

Thai Sriracha sauce, homemade (page 319) or store-bought (Shark or Sriraja Panich brand), for serving

Preserved radish is an underrated and underused ingredient. Even when it's used sparingly—almost like a condiment—as in pad thai, its absence would be acutely felt by anyone familiar with how pad thai is traditionally made in the city. But preserved radish can be so much more than a sideshow. For example, it goes famously well with eggs, as this dish demonstrates. The omelet, which is studded with soft, chewy preserved radish slivers, is panfried, but the basil leaves are deep-fried—a perfect interplay of flavors and textures. Preserved radishes are sold both salted and sweet. Be sure to get the latter for this dish.

◆ **Serves 2**

Pour the oil to a depth of ½ inch into a wok or Dutch oven and heat to 375°F. Line a sheet pan with paper towels and set near the stove. While the oil is heating, rinse the basil leaves, shake off any excess water, and then use a kitchen towel to pat them as dry as possible without bruising them. When the oil is hot, drop in the basil and step back right away. There will be some splattering, but it will subside in just a few seconds. Stir the leaves around until the bubbling subsides and the leaves look somewhat translucent. Using a mesh skimmer, transfer the leaves to the prepared pan. (To minimize the splattering, you can skip the rinsing, but the fried leaves will turn dark green and brown rather than be a beautiful bright green.)

Rinse the preserved radishes under cold running water for just a few seconds, then squeeze bone-dry. Crack the eggs into a bowl, add the fish sauce, and beat with a fork until frothy. Stir in the radishes.

Heat 1 tablespoon of the lard in a 10-inch frying pan (preferably nonstick) over medium-high heat. When the lard is hot, pour in the egg mixture, spreading it evenly over the bottom of the pan. Turn the heat to medium and cook until the bottom of the omelet is golden brown, 2 to 3 minutes. Using a wide spatula, lift up the omelet just enough to allow you to slip the remaining 1 tablespoon lard underneath it. Then, instead of lowering the omelet back into the pan, flip it over and cook the other side, pressing down lightly along the way, until golden brown, 2 to 3 minutes longer.

Slide the omelet onto a serving platter, top with the crispy basil, and serve immediately with Sriracha and rice. Another popular way to serve this omelet is to incorporate it into a set meal with plain rice porridge (page 185), omitting the sauce.

Fried chicken in pandan leaves

ไก่ห่อใบเตย KAI HO BAI TOEI

CHICKEN

3 tablespoons finely chopped cilantro roots or stems

5 large cloves garlic

1 teaspoon white peppercorns

2 tablespoons Thai Sriracha sauce, homemade (page 319) or store-bought (Shark or Sriraja Panich brand)

1 tablespoon packed grated palm sugar

1½ tablespoons Thai thin soy sauce or Golden Mountain seasoning sauce

2 tablespoons whole milk, heavy cream, or coconut milk

6 large skin-on, boneless chicken thighs (1½ pounds total weight)

DIPPING SAUCE

5 tablespoons honey

3 tablespoons packed grated palm sugar

2 teaspoons Thai Sriracha sauce, homemade (page 319) or store-bought (Shark or Sriraja Panich brand)

3 tablespoons Thai thin soy sauce or Golden Mountain seasoning sauce

2 tablespoons Thai sweet dark soy sauce

3 coins peeled fresh ginger, ¼ inch thick

2 teaspoons white sesame seeds, toasted

16 pandan leaves (about 7 ounces if purchasing frozen leaves)

Vegetable oil, for deep-frying

D'Jit Pochana, a famous family restaurant in Bangkok that my generation grew up eating in, originated this dish of marinated chicken wrapped in pandan leaves. It was once so popular that countless restaurants in the city copied it, and by the 1980s, it had become a menu staple at many Thai restaurants around the world. This is my version of the ubiquitous pandan chicken, which I've often made for friends in Chicago. ♦ **Makes 16 pieces; serves 4**

To make the chicken, in a mortar, grind together the cilantro roots, garlic, and peppercorns to a smooth paste. Transfer to a large bowl, add the Sriracha sauce, sugar, soy sauce, and milk, and mix well to form a marinade. Cut each chicken thigh into three equal cubes, add to the marinade, and mix well. Cover and place in the back of the refrigerator, where it is coldest, for 24 to 48 hours.

To make the dipping sauce, about 10 minutes before you are ready to wrap the chicken, combine the honey, sugar, Sriracha sauce, thin and dark soy sauces, and ginger in a saucepan and bring to a boil over medium heat, stirring to dissolve the sugar. Turn the heat to medium-low so the sauce bubbles gently, then stir and scrape down the sides of the pan constantly for 3 minutes. Scrape the sauce into a small serving bowl and sprinkle the sesame seeds on top. Leave to cool.

Hold up a pandan leaf horizontally, shiny side facing you. Bend the leaf backward at the center to form a loose cup, resembling an inverted triangle in the front and an X with one end of the leaf pointing in the two o'clock position and the other in the ten o'clock position. Put a piece of chicken in the cup. Grab the end of the leaf that is in the very back and fold it over the chicken and thread it through the opening at the bottom of the cup. Do the same with the other end. Extend both ends in opposite directions to tighten the pocket and secure the chicken. Trim off the ends, leaving about 2 inches. Repeat with the remaining chicken pieces and leaves.

Pour the oil to a depth of 3 inches into a wok or Dutch oven and heat to 350°F. Line a large sheet pan with paper towels. When the oil is hot, working in batches to avoid crowding, deep-fry the chicken packets until golden brown, about 10 minutes. Using tongs or a slotted spoon, transfer the chicken packets to the prepared pan to drain. Repeat until all of the chicken is cooked.

Arrange the chicken on a platter and serve warm with the dipping sauce and with rice. Advise diners to unwrap the chicken just before they're about to dip it in the sauce and enjoy it.

Lumphini Park

Bangkok is known for a lot of things, but green, shady areas in the city center aren't among them. And this is one of the many reasons Bangkokians love Lumphini Park, the inner city's haven of tranquility and fresh, cooler air. Our collective lungs depend on it.

People go to this 142-acre park at different times of the day for different things. When the sun isn't too hot, there might be an outdoor concert on the lawn and people on pedal boats in the lake. Before sunrise, older folks arrive in droves for their group tai chi exercise. Late afternoon is when office workers from the nearby business district of Si Lom change into their workout clothes and run laps around the park. Just before sunset, a large crowd forms near the main gate for a group aerobic workout during which they dance to upbeat country music. When it's dark, people gather in a yet another area to learn ballroom dancing.

I often go to Lumphini Park around midmorning, but for none of the mentioned reasons. My usual routine is a subway ride from my condo to the main gate on the west side of the park and then a power walk to the opposite side—the best way to avoid traffic. My gaze is determined, my pace quick and steady. I'm not exercising, however. After two triathlons, I've discovered my heart just isn't in it. My heart is in fried chicken, and that fried chicken is in the alleyway across the street from the east gate.

Polo Fried Chicken is one of the city's most popular fried-chicken joints, and the opportunity to eat the famed chicken with crispy skin, topped with a generous sprinkling of crispy garlic, is worth a brisk walk in the city's sweltering heat, especially if I can get there before the lunch crowd descends. At midmorning, the chicken is still fresh out of the wok, yet has had time to cool to warmer than room temperature—the sweet, sweet spot of fried chicken. The thought of it quickens my steps.

The chicken at Polo isn't batter-fried, which means more skill is required to get the skin to brown and crisp properly without overcooking the meat—a secret I'm sure the Polo kitchen staff will carry to the grave. But I've observed the cooks at Polo enough times to pick up ideas that will help me clone the fried chicken in my kitchen.

They cut whole chickens in half, marinate the halves, and then fry the halves whole, which keeps the chicken meat juicier than if you cut the bird into smaller pieces. Frying chicken halves is impractical for the home kitchen without a giant wok, however, so going with leg quarters is a good compromise.

Frying the chicken at moderate heat initially before turning up the heat toward the end of cooking is another Polo kitchen trick. The final hot blast—brief and intense—turns the skin, which has had much of the fat rendered out of it by that time, golden brown and shatteringly crisp.

Fried chicken with crispy garlic

ไก่ทอดกระเทียมกรอบ KAI THOT KRA-THIAM KROP

2 heads garlic

½ teaspoon white peppercorns

2 tablespoons finely chopped cilantro roots or stems

1 tablespoon salt

4 large skin-on, bone-in chicken leg quarters, 1 to 1¼ pounds each

Vegetable oil, for deep-frying

Warm steamed glutinous rice (page 18), for serving

¾ to 1 cup Thai sweet chile sauce, homemade (page 318) or store-bought

This home version of the chicken at Polo Fried Chicken (see page 151), which I top with crispy fried garlic just as the cooks at Polo do, is more than enough to tide me over until my next trip to the city. The Thai-style marinade is naturally pulpy, so be sure to wipe off all of the paste before the chicken goes into the wok or it will burn and turn bitter.

Serves 4

Remove the outer translucent, papery sheaths from the garlic heads and separate the cloves. Peel the skin off 4 cloves and put the cloves in a mortar or mini chopper. Set the remaining unpeeled cloves aside for now. Add the peppercorns and cilantro roots to the peeled garlic and grind to a smooth paste. Stir in the salt and mix well.

Rub the paste over the chicken quarters, covering them completely and taking care not to tear the skin or separate the skin from the meat. Put the leg quarters in a gallon-size resealable plastic bag, press the air from the bag, and seal the bag closed. Place the bag in the back of the refrigerator, where it is coldest, for 12 to 24 hours.

Take the chicken out of the refrigerator, wipe off all the tiny bits of aromatic paste with a paper towel, and allow the chicken to come to room temperature. Meanwhile, put the reserved unpeeled garlic cloves in a mortar or mini chopper (I don't recommend chopping them by hand) and grind until the pulp is in coarse shards. Don't worry if you can't break down the skins into pieces that small. Set the garlic aside.

Pour the oil to a depth of 3 inches into a large wok of Dutch oven and heat to 300°F. Line a sheet pan with paper towels and set near the stove. When the oil is hot, working in batches if needed to prevent crowding, gently lower the chicken pieces, flesh side down, into the oil, making sure they are fully submerged. When all of the chicken pieces are in the oil, the temperature will drop slightly; adjust the heat as needed to keep it between 260°F and 280°F. Deep-fry the chicken, undisturbed, until the pieces feel firm and the skin has turned light brown all over and dark brown around the edges, about 10 minutes. Turn the heat to the highest setting, turn the chicken, skin side down, and keep frying until the skin on each piece is golden brown and small cracks are visible at the "ankles" of the chicken, about 10 minutes. Transfer the chicken pieces, skin side up, to the prepared pan and leave to cool. If frying in batches, lower the heat to bring the oil temperature back down to 300°F and repeat the process.

continued

After the last batch of chicken has been removed from the oil, keeping the heat at the highest setting, sprinkle the pounded garlic evenly over the surface of the hot oil. Be careful, as the oil will foam up 2 to 3 inches high. Once that happens, stir down the oil promptly and swiftly with a mesh skimmer to prevent an overflow. Deep-fry the garlic, stirring constantly, until it turns the color of honey and is thoroughly crisp, less than 20 seconds. Turn off the heat and scoop every bit of the garlic out of the oil onto the prepared pan. You will need to work quickly before the residual heat burns the garlic and turns it bitter.

You can leave the leg quarters whole or separate the thighs from the drumsticks at the joint. If you'd like to serve the chicken the way they do it at Polo, separate the thighs from the drumsticks at the joint and cut each thigh and each drumstick in half across the bones. (In order to avoid crushing the bones and creating dangerous shards, you need to use a large, sturdy cleaver and swift, decisive blows. Do it unthinkingly, unblinkingly, like a robot.) By cutting the pieces crosswise, the muscles are shortened, which makes the meat easier to eat with a spoon and fork as the Thais do.

Arrange the slightly-warmer-than-room-temperature chicken on a platter, sprinkle the crispy garlic all over the top, and serve immediately with the sticky rice and sweet chile sauce.

Black pepper roasted chicken

ไก่อบพริกไทยดำ **KAI OP PHRIK THAI DAM**

2 teaspoons salt

2 tablespoons oyster sauce

2 tablespoons Thai thin soy sauce or Golden Mountain seasoning sauce

2 tablespoons honey or light or dark brown sugar

1 whole chicken, preferably free-range, between 2½ and 3½ pounds

6 large cloves garlic

¼ cup finely chopped cilantro roots or stems

1½ tablespoons black peppercorns

2 tablespoons vegetable oil

Thai sweet chile sauce, homemade (page 318) or store-bought, for serving

Warm steamed glutinous rice (page 18), for serving

No matter where you stand in the city, there's bound to be a *kai yang ha dao* (five-star grilled chicken) kiosk within a one-mile radius selling affordable grilled whole chickens, sweet chile sauce, and warm sticky rice ready for you to grab and go. The fact that this franchise has dominated—no, monopolized—the rotisserie chicken market for more than thirty years says a lot. I used to go nuts over their extraordinarily juicy, expertly seasoned chicken, especially the very peppery black pepper version. This is my copycat version. **Serves 4 to 6**

In a large bowl, combine the salt, oyster sauce, soy sauce, and honey and mix well to make a marinade. Pat the chicken dry with paper towels and put it in the marinade bowl. Rub the marinade on the chicken, going into every nook and cranny, inside and outside, and over and under the skin. Transfer the chicken to a gallon-size resealable plastic bag. Scrape every bit of the marinade into the bag, too. Seal the bag, and place it in the back of the refrigerator, where it is coldest, for 12 to 24 hours, flipping the bag a few times to make sure the marinade gets to every part of the bird.

When you are about to roast the chicken, take it out of the refrigerator and let it come to room temperature. Position an oven rack at the very bottom of the oven, then preheat the oven to 400°F.

In a mortar or small chopper, grind together the garlic, cilantro roots, and peppercorns to a smooth paste. Rub the paste all over the chicken the same way you did the marinade. Tuck the wings behind the bird's back and tie the legs together at the ankles with kitchen string. Rub the outside of the chicken with the oil. Place the chicken on its side in a shallow baking pan (preferably fitted with a rack).

Roast the chicken for 30 minutes. Turn down the temperature to 375°F, turn the chicken onto its other side, and continue to roast until the juices run clear when you pierce the inside of a thigh with the tip of a knife, 20 to 30 minutes longer. (If some parts of the chicken brown too soon during the baking, you can cover it loosely with an aluminum-foil tent.)

Let the chicken rest in the pan for 30 minutes (no less than that) before separating into bone-in breast quarters, thighs, and drumsticks. Serve with sweet chile sauce and rice. If you'd like a spicier, smokier sauce, the dried chile–tamarind dipping sauce that I pair with Grilled Pork on Skewers (page 42) would be a perfect choice.

Steamed stuffed squid in lime-chile-garlic dressing

ปลาหมึกสอดไส้นึ่งมะนาว   PLA MUEK SOT SAI NUENG MANAO

2 ounces glass noodles,
soaked in room-temperature
water for 15 minutes, drained,
cut into 1-inch lengths,
and blotted dry

1 pound ground pork

¾ teaspoon salt

8 large squid, each about
8 inches long and about
2½ ounces

4 large cloves garlic,
chopped into pieces the
size of a match head

4 fresh bird's eye chiles,
chopped into pieces
the size of a match head

3 tablespoons fresh lime juice

2 tablespoons fish sauce

½ teaspoon granulated sugar

4 or 5 thin lime slices

½ cup packed cilantro leaves

In Thailand, squid are cooked quickly rather than braised until tender, which is common in some other cultures. Thais like their chewy texture the same way they like bouncy meatballs. **Makes 8 pieces; serves 4**

In a bowl, combine the noodles, pork, and salt and mix well. Set aside.

Grasp the head of one squid and pull it from the body. Using a sharp knife, and positioning it between the tentacles and the eyes, cut off and discard the head. Press against the base of the tentacles to release the hard beak, discard the beak, and set the tentacles aside. Remove and discard the quill-like cartilage from the body, then peel away the mottled skin covering the body, leaving the fins on. Rinse the body well inside and out and set aside with the tentacles. Repeat with the remaining squid. Fill the steamer pot with water and bring to a rolling boil.

While the water is heating, fill each squid three-fourths full with the pork mixture. Arrange the filled squid and the tentacles in a single layer on a large heatproof plate that fits inside the steamer tier. In a small bowl, stir together the garlic, chiles, lime juice, fish sauce, and sugar, dissolving the sugar, and pour over the squid. Scatter the lime slices on top.

Set the steamer tier over the vigorously boiling water and steam until the squid turn opaque and firm up, releasing clear juices, 10 to 12 minutes. Remove the squid from the steamer and let cool slightly. Top with the cilantro leaves, then serve with rice. You can also slice the squid into bite-size pieces for serving.

Salted fish–pork patties

หมูสับปลาเค็มทอด MU SAP PLA KHEM THOT

1 recipe Panfried Salted Fish Steak (page 327)

3 tablespoons finely chopped cilantro roots or stems

½ teaspoon white peppercorns

6 large cloves garlic

1 pound ground pork (not too lean)

1 egg

1 to 2 tablespoons homemade lard (page 28) or vegetable oil

2 limes, halved lengthwise

2 (1-ounce) shallots, halved, and thinly sliced lengthwise

4 or 5 fresh bird's eye chiles, thinly sliced crosswise

Dried salted fish is usually served fried as a rice accompaniment. But because of its deep, umamic saltiness, it is sometimes used, as it is here, as a seasoning. Various types of fish—king mackerel and threadfin are among the more common choices—are salted, dried, and often sold whole on the eastern seaboard and in the seaside provinces immediately east and west of Bangkok. These salted fish are prized souvenirs I always buy for myself and for loved ones on the way back home from a beach vacation. In the United States, salted king mackerel steaks come vacuum-packed and frozen or packed in oil in a jar and are found at most well-stocked East Asian and Southeast Asian markets. However, I've found their quality to often be so bad—too salty and smelly—that I make my own (see page 327). I suggest you do the same.

Squeeze the limes over the patties just before you're about to serve them with rice, slip a few shallot and chile slices into each bite, and you'll understand why whenever you mention this dish to homesick Bangkokians, their eyes glaze over in rapturous yearning. ♦ **Serves 4**

Remove the skin and bones from the fish steak. Put the meat in a mortar or mini chopper and grind to fine, cottony flakes. Set aside.

Grind together the cilantro roots, peppercorns, and garlic in the mortar or mini chopper to a smooth paste and transfer to a bowl. Add the pork, egg, and salted fish flakes and, using your hand—no other tool will do—combine everything together until the mixture is sticky and homogeneous, making sure the salted fish is thoroughly dispersed. Cook a teaspoonful of the meat in a small frying pan, taste for seasoning, and adjust with salt or fish sauce if needed.

With damp hands, divide the mixture into four equal portions. Shape each portion into a very flat disk of even thickness and 6 inches in diameter.

Heat 1 tablespoon of the lard in a 10- or 12-inch frying pan over medium-high heat. One at a time, fry the patties, turning once, until golden brown on both sides, about 3 minutes on each side. Along the way, press the patties down quite hard with a sturdy spatula to maintain their shape, thickness, and size. This also helps them brown more evenly on both sides. Add the remaining 1 tablespoon lard if needed to prevent sticking.

Transfer the patties to a serving platter. Arrange the limes, shallots, and chiles on the side and serve with rice. Just before you're about to eat the patties, squeeze some lime juice over them, then eat the shallots and chiles along with the rice and the patties, treating them like you would flavor-enhancing condiments.

Shrimp and glass noodles in clay pot

กุ้งอบวุ้นเส้น KUNG OP WUN SEN

2 cups homemade chicken or pork stock (see page 323) or store-bought sodium-free chicken stock

1 tablespoon Chinese rice wine (shaoxing)

1 tablespoon Thai thin soy sauce or Golden Mountain seasoning sauce

2 teaspoons Thai sweet dark soy sauce

1 teaspoon toasted sesame oil

6 large cloves garlic

3 tablespoons finely chopped cilantro roots or stems

1 teaspoon white peppercorns

1 teaspoon Sichuan peppercorns

2 tablespoons peeled and coarsely chopped fresh ginger (the older and woodier, the better), plus 6 thin slices fresh ginger, about 1 inch in diameter

2 tablespoons homemade lard (page 28) or vegetable oil

3 ounces salt pork or thick-cut bacon, cut into quarter-size pieces about ⅛ inch thick

¾ cup coarsely chopped Chinese celery leaves or tender leaves and stalks of regular (Pascal) celery heart

6 ounces glass noodles, soaked in room-temperature water for 15 minutes, drained, cut into 6-inch lengths, and blotted dry

1 pound head-on, shell-on colossal shrimp (U8 size)

6 to 8 green onions, trimmed to 6 inches

Store-bought Thai seafood sauce, for serving (optional)

This recipe is inspired by Somsak Pu Op, a small street cart on the west side of Bangkok where people are willing to line up for a long time just to get a table where they then sit and wait for as long as an hour after they've placed their order. One wildly popular item on the menu is glass noodles and colossal shrimp cooked in a two-serving-size pot.

When choosing glass noodles, if you see any starch other than mung bean starch in the ingredients—tapioca, for example—steer clear of the brand. You want pure mung bean noodles. If you can find a Thai product, that's even better. Kaset brand is my favorite.

Don't be shy about eating with your hands. The shrimp are cooked with the shell on to keep them moist, which makes this a peel-and-eat affair. The green onions are also intentionally left whole and arranged on top of the noodles—the way they do it at Somsak Pu Op—so you'll eat those with your hands, too. ⚜ **Serves 2**

In a bowl, combine the stock, rice wine, thin and dark soy sauces, and sesame oil and mix well. Set aside.

In a mortar, grind together the garlic, cilantro roots, white and Sichuan peppercorns, and the chopped ginger to a smooth paste.

Put 1 tablespoon of the lard in a 2-quart shallow, heavy braising pan with a tight-fitting lid and set over medium-high heat. Add the paste and stir until sizzling and fragrant, about 1 minute. Add the remaining 1 tablespoon lard, the ginger slices, and the salt pork and stir until some of the salt pork is browned around the edges and renders some fat, about 2 minutes.

Turn the heat to the high end of the medium-low range. Layer the celery on the bottom of the pan and spread the noodles in an even layer on top of it. Pour the stock mixture over the noodles and arrange the shrimp in a single layer on top of the noodles. Cover and cook, undisturbed, until the noodles have absorbed nearly all of the liquid, about 15 minutes.

Arrange the green onions on top of everything, re-cover, and turn the heat to medium-high to dry out any residual moisture and crisp the bottom slightly. This part of the process is somewhat risky, as you can go from nice and smoky to burnt in just a few seconds, so keep your eyes and nose on high alert. Within 2 minutes, the dish should be ready—the noodles will have absorbed all the liquid and softened, the shrimp will be cooked, the good stuff at the bottom of the pan will have browned slightly, and the green onions will be bright green but soft and sweet. Serve immediately with rice and the seafood sauce, if desired. Let diners know that they should not eat the ginger slices at the bottom of the pan.

Set Meals

and One-Plate Meals

Songkran

When Bangkokians think of Songkran, the Thai New Year that rolls around every April, the first thing that comes to mind is usually the tradition of pouring water over one another, a practice that has evolved—or devolved—into a citywide water fight. Bangkok pretty much shuts down for three days for this crazy water-throwing festival. For me, however, the most thrilling event of Songkran doesn't happen on the streets; it happens in the firmament, in a dimension invisible to you and me. There, seven beautiful women float in the air with a severed head in tow.

According to legend, Kabinla Phrom, the four-faced god-king, lost a bet with a human that resulted in him having to cut off his own head. The story isn't clear on how that deal was struck or how the puzzling and potentially awkward act of self-decapitation was done. But the legend does go to great lengths to tell us what an environmental hazard Kabinla Phrom's head is.

In short, if his severed head dropped to the ground, it would set the whole earth on fire. If it was left bobbling about in the air, it would produce a drought so severe that all earthlings would die. If it was thrown into the ocean, all of the oceans would instantly dry up. The head clearly required careful handling, and any mistake would see a result similar to what supposedly happened to the dinosaurs when a giant asteroid or comet struck the earth.

Important details are often left out of ancient stories, and the legend of Songkran is no different. For example, it doesn't tell us who came up with the solution to this head-related problem. All we're told is that the only way to protect the earth is to put Kabinla Phrom's severed head on a plate and then once every year his seven daughters, with plate in hand, must circumambulate one sacred mythical mountain before making their way to a second mountain, where the head is kept until they return the following year to take it on a new journey. Why the head cannot just stay put somewhere, rather than go on what appears to be an unnecessarily risky annual trip, is a mystery to me.

Aside from this otherworldly tale, the most exciting thing about the holiday is the arrival of *khao chae*—rice in flower-scented ice water—in Bangkok. This New Year's special helps cool down Bangkokians just when they need it.

Khao chae came to us from the Mon people, who settled in various parts of Thailand, including Bangkok and its environs. Royal courtiers of Mon descent in the early nineteenth century elevated this down-home Mon meal into something worthy of the royals. Princess consort Sonklin, who lived during the reign of King Mongkut (Rama IV, the monarch whom the fictional *The King and I* attempts to portray correctly but fails), is believed by scholars, such as Ong Bunjoon, author of *Khang Samrap Mon* (At the

Mon Table), to be among those who popularized *khao chae* in the palace. The changes reflected the royal setting: Instead of plain water, flower-scented water was used. The accompaniments were more elaborate, the side vegetables were intricately carved, and the overall presentation was more refined and exquisite. It is this elegant version of *khao chae* that you now see all over the city around Thai New Year and throughout the hot season.

Rice in flower-scented water with accompaniments

ข้าวแช่ KHAO CHAE

1 recipe Sweet Shredded Beef (page 329)

GLAZED PRESERVED RADISHES

8 ounces whole sweet preserved radishes (see page 344)

3 tablespoons packed grated palm sugar

2 teaspoons homemade lard (page 28) or vegetable oil

Fish sauce or salt, for seasoning

SHRIMP PASTE DUMPLINGS

2 tablespoons finely chopped galangal

2 tablespoons finely chopped fingerroot

2 tablespoons finely sliced lemongrass (with purple rings only)

1 ounce shallots, diced

3 large cloves garlic

2 teaspoons packed Thai shrimp paste

6 ounces skinless trout fillet, grilled or broiled until it flakes easily

1½ tablespoons packed grated palm sugar

¾ cup coconut milk

Fish sauce, for seasoning

1 egg, beaten

STUFFED SHALLOTS

12 large (1-ounce) shallots or red or white pearl onions

¼ cup Thai rice flour

2 tablespoons coconut milk

2 tablespoons limestone solution (page 336)

Vegetable oil, for deep-frying

In the distant past, there didn't seem to be any rules on the accompaniments; anything that went well with rice in ice-cold water would work. Over time, however, a set pattern has formed and a codified—and refined—version emerged. Now, *khao chae* is so routinely served at homes of old Bangkokian families and at old-school restaurants with the accompaniments listed here that if just one of them is absent, the meal will appear incomplete. The rice is always served ice-cold and the accompaniments are usually at room temperature.

To those new to the ultratraditional cuisine of Bangkok, this set meal will be an adventure into an unfamiliar territory in terms of both taste and dining etiquette. This is certainly not Thai Cooking 101. But as a Bangkokian and a lifelong fan of *khao chae*, I cannot in my conscience leave this iconic set meal out of this book. ♦ **Serves 4**

Make the shredded beef as directed, then plate and set aside to cool.

To make the glazed radishes, cut the radishes into very fine matchsticks, then transfer to a fine-mesh sieve or colander. Rinse under cold running water two or three times to remove the excess salt, making it easier to control the salinity of the finished dish (even though the preserved radishes are the sweet kind, they still contain quite a bit of salt). Squeeze the radishes bone-dry, transfer to a 12-inch frying pan, and add the sugar and lard. Set the pan over medium heat and stir-fry until the sugar melts and all of the moisture has evaporated, leaving only radish strands that look glossy or candied. Some brands of preserved radish are saltier than others, so taste the glazed radishes now to see if they need any fish sauce or salt. You want the primary flavor to be sweet followed by salty. Once that is achieved, plate the radishes and leave to cool.

To make the dumplings, in a mortar, grind together the galangal, fingerroot, lemongrass, shallots, garlic, and shrimp paste to a fine paste. Add the fish and grind until smooth. Transfer the paste to a 12-inch frying pan, add the sugar and coconut milk, and set over medium heat. Stir-fry until all of the moisture has evaporated and the mixture becomes thick and sticky, 10 to 15 minutes. Taste for seasoning and add more fish sauce as needed. Aim for salty with a faint hint of sweet.

Remove from the heat, let cool, and then divide into 6 equal portions. Split each portion into 6 equal portions, then roll each portion into a tight, smooth round ball. You will have 36 dumplings. Set aside 24 dumplings. Use the remaining 12 balls for stuffing the shallots.

STUFFED BANANA PEPPERS

2 large cloves garlic

¼ teaspoon white peppercorns

1 tablespoon finely chopped cilantro roots or stems

6 ounces ground pork, or 3 ounces each ground pork and peeled shrimp, finely chopped

2 teaspoons fish sauce

4 sweet banana peppers or Anaheim chiles (which would be hotter) with stems on, each about 5 inches long (excluding stem) and about 2 ounces

3 or 4 eggs

1 to 2 tablespoons homemade lard (page 28) or vegetable oil

RICE

4 cups cooked Thai jasmine rice

Filtered or natural spring water, for rinsing

12 cups flower-scented water (page 23) or filtered or natural spring water

4 to 5 cups ice cubes

SIDE VEGETABLES AND HERBS

8 lengthwise slices sour green mango

8 spears pickling cucumber

4 sticks fresh fingerroot, quartered lengthwise three-fourths of the way, soaked in cold water to bloom, and wiped dry

4 green onions, trimmed to 5 inches

To make the stuffed shallots, peel the shallots, then, using a paring knife, slice off the root ends, creating a flat surface. Using the tip of the knife, dig through the flat surface into the center of each shallot and scoop out all but the outer two layers, keeping the shallot flesh for other uses. When all of the shallots are hollowed out, stuff each shallot with a shrimp paste dumpling, packing it in as best as you can and smoothing the top. Grab a bowl and whisk together the rice flour, coconut milk, and limestone solution until smooth to form a batter.

Pour the oil to a depth of 1 inch into a wok and heat to 350°F. Line a sheet pan with paper towels and set it near the stove. When the oil is hot, coat the stuffed shallots with the batter, letting the excess drip off, and, working in batches to avoid crowding, deep-fry until golden brown, 2 to 3 minutes. Using a slotted spoon, transfer the shallots to one side of the prepared pan.

When the last batch of shallots has been fried, don't turn off the heat. Grab the reserved 24 dumplings and the bowl of beaten egg. Working in batches to avoid crowding, dip the dumplings into the beaten egg, allowing the excess to drip off, and drop them into the oil. Fry until golden brown, 1 to 2 minutes. Using the slotted spoon, transfer them to the other side of the sheet pan. Repeat until all of the dumplings are fried.

To make the stuffed peppers, in a mortar, grind together the garlic, peppercorns, and cilantro roots to a smooth paste. Transfer the paste to a bowl, add the pork and fish sauce, and mix well. Divide the mixture into four equal portions. Lay a banana pepper on the counter with the pointed end toward you. Position a paring knife at the top of the pepper about ¼ inch from the base of the stem and make a straight, horizontal cut that goes halfway deep into the pepper. Now position the tip of the knife at the center of the horizontal cut and make a vertical cut along the length of the pepper, stopping 1 inch from the end. (When you look at the pepper from the top down, the cuts should from a *T*.)

Gently dig your fingers into the core of the pepper and remove and discard all of the seeds and veins. Fill the pepper cavity with one portion of the pork mixture, using a chopstick to push the filling down to the pointed end if necessary. Cut and fill the remaining 3 peppers the same way. Arrange the peppers on a plate in a steamer tier and steam over boiling water until they are soft and the filling that peeks through the slits is opaque and releases clear juices, about 15 minutes. Let cool until warm, then wipe any moisture from the surface.

continued

Crack 3 of the eggs into a bowl and beat with a fork until homogenous. Set a 12- or 14-inch frying pan, preferably nonstick, over medium-low heat. When the pan is hot, brush a thin coat of lard on the bottom of the pan. Imagine a rectangle 5 inches wide and 12 or 14 inches long on the bottom of the pan. Now, dip your fingers into the beaten egg and, with your fingers pointing straight down, move your hand back and forth so the egg drips off the tips of your fingers in ultrathin strands onto the imaginary rectangle. You can go freestyle or you can stick with the traditional crisscross pattern. Just make sure the weave is fairly tight (no more than ½ inch wide). Once the rectangle is adequately filled in, cover the pan and leave undisturbed just until the top of the egg net is no longer runny, no more than a few seconds. Don't overcook the net or it will be too brittle to roll. Position a banana pepper at the edge of one of the short sides of the rectangle. Using a rubber spatula and following the tapered contour of the pepper, roll the egg net around the pepper as snugly as possible, taking care not to break the net. Repeat until all the peppers are wrapped in an egg net, brushing the pan with more lard as needed and using the remaining egg if needed. Set the peppers aside; keep them warm.

To prepare the rice, put it in a fine-mesh sieve or colander and rinse it with the filtered water until the water runs clear and all of the grains are separate. Divide the rice evenly among four large soup bowls.

Other than the stuffed banana peppers that are best served slightly warmer than room temperature, the accompaniments are served at room temperature. Arrange the accompaniments and side vegetables and herbs on a large platter or divide them among four individual plates. Pour the flower-scented water over the rice and add the ice cubes, dividing them both evenly. Enjoy the rice while it is ice-cold, and never add the accompaniments to the rice bowls. The rice and scented water must be kept crystal clear throughout the meal. Transport a bite of one of the accompaniments right into your mouth with a spoon, then chase it down with three or four bites of the rice and water. The side vegetables and herbs are there to cleanse the palate between bites and to provide the sharp flavor and astringency to a dish whose primary flavors are sweet and salty.

On Rice Vermicelli (Khanom Jin)

Khanom jin is a type of rice noodle that resembles the Chinese-style rice noodles you see on the streets of Bangkok and in nearly every part of Thailand. And the Thai word *jin* in the name, which usually means "China" or "Chinese," has led many to believe that these noodles are of Chinese origin.

But the function and history of *khanom jin* tell a different story. In the Central Thai tradition, *khanom jin*, like rice, is always served on a plate—never in a bowl—and is eaten with a spoon and a fork. The noodles are also often served with the same curries that Bangkokians traditionally serve over rice. These two things, which do not apply to noodles of Chinese origin, show that the Thais regard this particular type of rice noodle as almost interchangeable with rice.

Most observers believe that *khanom jin* came to us through the Mon. According to this theory, *khanom* is a Mon word meaning "things made with flour" (dumplings, noodles, or cakes)—rice in this case—and *jin* is another Mon word, which some scholars suggest means "cooked."

Approaching *khanom jin* with this knowledge helps to make sense of its role in the cuisine of Bangkok and, though less important, to understand why it is eaten the way it is. Although Chinese-style noodles that come in a bowl are always eaten with a pair of chopsticks in one hand and a short spoon in the other, Bangkokians don't normally use chopsticks to eat *khanom jin*—just as they don't normally use chopsticks to eat rice on a plate.

Rice vermicelli with fish curry

ขนมจีนน้ำยา **KHANOM JIN NAM YA**

CURRY

12 ounces skinless snakehead fish (pla chon), trout, or tilapia fillets

1 cup coconut cream

1 cup coconut milk

3 tablespoons packed finely chopped fingerroot

1 tablespoon packed thinly sliced lemongrass (with purple rings only)

1 tablespoon packed finely chopped galangal (the more mature, the better)

1½ ounces shallots, cut into ½-inch cubes

3 large cloves garlic, halved crosswise

5 large dried Thai long or guajillo chiles, seeded, cut into 1-inch pieces, soaked until softened, and squeezed dry

2 tablespoons packed crumbled meat from Panfried Salted Fish Steak (page 327), or 8 anchovy fillets in oil, rinsed and finely chopped

1 tablespoon packed Thai shrimp paste

Fish sauce, for seasoning

1 (14-ounce) package dried rice vermicelli noodles (khanom jin), cooked according to package directions, drained, rinsed under running hot water, and drained again

6 medium- or hard-boiled eggs, halved

Side vegetables (see page 172)

Fish sauce, for serving

Dried red chile powder (page 323), for serving

Of the many one-plate meals that call for *khanom jin*, this one is among the most popular with Bangkokians and Central Thais. The coconut-based fish curry features the scent of fingerroot prominently, which is typical of most traditional dishes containing freshwater fish, especially snakehead fish, which is the traditional choice for this dish.

In all of my years of eating extensively in the city, I have never found any street stall that turns out a better version of this dish than what comes out of the kitchen of a good home cook. So don't be intimidated by the long ingredients list, as whipping up a plate of *khanom jin* covered with a thick, rich, deeply flavorful fish curry sauce is absolutely within your power. ♦ **Serves 6**

To make the curry, fill a 2-quart saucepan one-third full with water and bring to a boil over high heat. Add the fish fillets, turn the heat to a gentle simmer, and cook, undisturbed, until the fish flakes easily, 10 to 15 minutes, depending on the thickness of the fillets. Turn off the heat. With a slotted spoon, transfer the fish to a plate to cool. Discard all but 1 cup of the liquid from the pan, add the coconut cream and coconut milk to the cooking liquid, and set aside.

Put the fingerroot, lemongrass, galangal, shallots, and garlic in a small frying pan, place over medium heat, and toast, stirring constantly, until softened and slightly charred, about 3 minutes. Set aside to cool.

Put the chiles in a mortar. Add the toasted aromatics, salted fish, and shrimp paste and grind until smooth. Add the cooked fish and grind until smooth.

Bring the coconut milk mixture to a boil over high heat. The moment the liquid boils, spoon the fish paste into it and stir only once just to dissolve. Bring back to a boil, then lower the heat to medium, cover, and simmer for 2 minutes. Add the fish sauce to taste, taking into account the rice noodles and all of the side vegetables. Remove from the heat.

Divide the noodles among six dinner plates and ladle the sauce over the top. Place two boiled egg halves on the side of each plate. Arrange your choice of side vegetables around the noodles. Set fish sauce and dried red chile powder (for extra heat) on the table. Enjoy while still warm.

continued

Suggested Side Vegetables

- Fresh lemon basil leaves (best), Thai sweet basil leaves, or Mediterranean basil leaves (okay)

- Bean sprouts, refreshed in cold water for 5 minutes, then drained and patted dry

- Green cabbage, sliced into fine strips

- Cucumber slices

- Long beans, winged beans, or green beans, trimmed and thinly sliced crosswise or cut into 1-inch sticks

- Banana blossom, trimmed, thinly sliced against the grain into fine strips, soaked in acidulated water until serving, then drained and squeezed dry (optional but recommended)

- Pickled mustard greens, rinsed, squeezed dry, cored, and thinly sliced

- Bitter melon, halved lengthwise, seeds and fibrous core discarded, thinly sliced crosswise, blanched until tender-crisp, and drained

Rice vermicelli with coconut sauce and fish dumplings

ขนมจีนซาวน้ำ **KHANOM JIN SAO NAM**

4 ounces fresh young ginger

15 large cloves garlic

½ pineapple (from a 2-pound pineapple)

3 tablespoons finely chopped cilantro roots or stems

1 teaspoon ground white pepper

1 pound skinless firm white fish fillet, cut into 1-inch cubes and kept chilled

¼ cup crushed ice

1 egg white

1 tablespoon Thai tapioca starch or cornstarch

1¾ teaspoons salt

½ cup coconut cream

1½ cups coconut milk

1 tablespoon packed grated palm sugar or 2 teaspoons granulated sugar

1 (14-ounce) package dried rice vermicelli noodles, cooked according to package directions, drained, rinsed under running hot water, and drained again

3 tablespoons dried shrimp, soaked in hot water until softened, squeezed dry, and ground into fine, cottony flakes

Fish sauce, for seasoning

½ cup fresh lime juice

4 or 5 fresh bird's eye chiles, thinly sliced crosswise

4 medium- or hard-boiled eggs, halved

This old-school *khanom jin* dish is where freshness meets vibrant tang meets creaminess meets heat meets salty funkiness. In other words, it's everything in one bite. As is the case with most dishes that call for ingredients that are simply cooked or otherwise minimally handled, freshness is of utter importance. If there's a dish that can convince you to crack open a mature coconut and extract the milk from its meat from scratch, it's this one. It makes such a difference. ◆ **Serves 4**

Peel the ginger and cut it lengthwise and slightly on the diagonal into paper-thin slices. Stack the slices and slice again lengthwise into thin matchsticks 1½ to 2 inches long. Very thinly slice 12 of the garlic cloves crosswise. Peel the pineapple half, then cut the flesh into matchsticks about 1 inch long and ¼ inch thick and wide. Put the ginger, garlic, and pineapple in separate bowls, cover, and refrigerate.

Put the cilantro roots, pepper, fish, crushed ice, egg white, tapioca starch, ¾ teaspoon of the salt, and the remaining 3 garlic cloves in a food processor and process to an ultrasmooth, sticky paste, stopping to scrape down the sides of the bowl occasionally. Transfer the fish paste to a bowl, cover, and refrigerate.

Combine the coconut cream, coconut milk, the remaining 1 teaspoon salt, and the sugar in a 2-quart saucepan and bring to a boil over medium-high heat. When the coconut milk boils, immediately turn the heat to low so the liquid is barely bubbling. Fill a coffee mug with water and keep it near the stove.

Take the fish paste out of the refrigerator. Dip your fingers into the water, scoop up a little fish paste, shape it into a 1-inch ball, flatten the ball slightly, and then gently lower the ball into the coconut milk. Repeat, moistening your fingers from time to time, until the fish paste runs out. (It's okay if the gently bubbling coconut milk stops boiling altogether after a couple of fish dumplings have been added; as long as it produces steam, it is fine.) After the last dumpling goes in, cover the pan and leave it on low heat for 10 minutes before turning off the heat.

Divide the noodles evenly among four dinner plates. Ladle the coconut sauce and the dumplings over the noodles. Top with the ginger, garlic, pineapple, and dried shrimp flakes. Toss together before consuming. Invite diners to season their plates to taste with fish sauce, lime juice, and chiles, and serve the eggs on the side.

Rice vermicelli with chopped chicken curry and yellow chile–coconut sauce

ขนมจีนไก่คั่ว   **KHANOM JIN KAI KHUA**

YELLOW CHILE–COCONUT SAUCE

4 fresh orange Thai long chiles, cut into ½-inch pieces; or ½ large yellow bell pepper, seeded, deveined, and coarsely chopped, plus 4 or 5 fresh red bird's eye chiles or 1 large red jalapeño or serrano chile, cut into ½-inch pieces

¼ teaspoon salt

3 tablespoons vegetable oil

3 tablespoons coconut cream

SEASONING PASTE

¼ cup homemade red curry paste (page 317) or 2 tablespoons store-bought red curry paste

1 large fresh red Thai long, jalapeño, or serrano chile, seeded, deveined, and coarsely chopped

2 tablespoons finely chopped cilantro roots or stems

CHICKEN CURRY

1 pound skinless, boneless chicken breasts

4 ounces chicken livers (optional)

½ cup freshly extracted coconut cream, or ½ cup canned coconut cream plus 1 tablespoon extra-virgin coconut oil

1 cup coconut milk (or 1½ cups if adding the chicken livers)

¾ cup homemade chicken stock (page 323) or store-bought sodium-free chicken stock

1 tablespoon packed grated palm sugar

Fish sauce, for seasoning

1 (14-ounce) dried rice vermicelli noodles, cooked according to package directions, drained, rinsed under running hot water, and drained again

¼ cup thinly sliced green onions

¼ cup roughly chopped cilantro leaves and stems

This is a dish I recently discovered and fell for. Hard. You probably wouldn't know just by looking at it, but this is the one *khanom jin* dish that's different from all the others in this book—or anywhere else in Thailand. It's also unique to Bangkok.

When Bangkokians think of Portuguese Thai foods in the city, their minds usually go first to the little sponge cakes (page 290) that come out of the Kudi Chin community, the two-centuries-old Portuguese settlement on the west bank of the Chao Phraya. But many more dishes have long circulated within that community and in other Portuguese Thai communities in the city. This dish, which marries Thai rice vermicelli with a coconut-based sauce of red curry and chopped chicken, is one of the most delicious.

It was a way the homesick Portuguese, who married the locals and, in the mid-1700s, settled into the area that has now become the Thonburi side of Bangkok, re-created the taste of home, which, in this case, is most likely pasta with some sort of cream-based meat ragù. A new hybrid dish, *khanom jin kai khua*, was born, and it has been regularly served at Catholic holiday celebrations among Bangkokians of Portuguese descent since then.

This is my adaptation of the recipe given to me by Kanittha Sakunthong, chef and owner of Ban Sakunthong, a restaurant in the Portuguese Thai community of Kudi Chin. ◖ **Serves 4**

To make the chile-coconut sauce, in a mortar or small chopper, grind the chiles to a coarse puree. Stir in the salt, transfer the puree to a small frying pan, add the oil, and set over medium heat. Stir until the mixture sizzles and you start coughing a little, about 2 minutes. (If using the bell pepper, stir until most of the moisture evaporates.) Transfer to a small bowl, stir in the coconut cream, and set aside until serving.

To make the seasoning paste, in a mortar, grind together the red curry paste, chile, and cilantro roots to a smooth paste. Set aside.

To make the curry, cut the chicken into small pieces, then chop with a cleaver on a sturdy chopping block into a coarse grind. Transfer to a bowl, cover, and refrigerate until needed. Trim away any connective veins from the chicken livers, if using, and cut the livers into ½-inch dice.

In a 4-quart saucepan, combine the seasoning paste and coconut cream and set over medium-high heat. Stir until the paste is fragrant and the

continued

coconut fat separates, about 2 minutes. Add the coconut milk, stock, sugar, chicken, and chicken livers and stir to break up the chicken. Cook, stirring occasionally, until the chicken turns opaque, 6 to 8 minutes. Season to taste with fish sauce. Aim for sweet first and then salty, taking into account the bland noodles that will be served with the curry. Once it tastes good to you, remove the pan from the heat.

Divide the noodles evenly among four dinner plates. Top with the curry, followed by the green onion and cilantro. Serve immediately with the chile-coconut sauce on the side for diners to season their noodles as desired.

Rice vermicelli with lentil-peanut sauce

ขนมจีนน้ำพริก **KHANOM JIN NAM PHRIK**

8 to 10 dried bird's eye chiles, stemmed

2 tablespoons vegetable oil

2 ounces shallots

6 large cloves garlic

2½ cups water

⅓ cup pink (red) lentils

⅓ cup unsalted roasted peanuts

8 ounces shrimp, peeled and deveined

1 cup coconut cream

1 cup coconut milk

2 tablespoons chile jam, homemade (page 22) or store-bought

5 tablespoons tamarind paste, homemade (page 316) or store-bought

½ teaspoon salt

⅓ cup packed grated palm sugar

2 tablespoons coarsely chopped galangal

5 large dried Thai long or guajillo chiles, seeded, cut into 1-inch pieces, soaked until softened, and squeezed dry

1 teaspoon packed Thai shrimp paste

¼ cup homemade lard (page 28) or extra-virgin coconut oil

2 tablespoons fresh lime juice

¼ cup fresh juice and 1 tablespoon grated zest of bitter (Seville) oranges, or ⅓ cup fresh juice and 2 tablespoons grated zest of navel oranges

1 (14-ounce) package dried rice vermicelli noodles, cooked according to package directions, drained, rinsed under running hot water, and drained again

3 medium- or hard-boiled eggs, halved

This classic and resolutely Central Thai dish gets me to fall in love with Thai food over and over again. The interplay of salty, sweet, sour, creamy, nutty, and smoky is unrivaled. Add to that a vast array of textures and flavors from the traditional side vegetables (*mueat*) and you get something as close to perfection as food can ever get.

Although most recipes call for hulled mung beans (*thua thong*), my family's recipe—the one we've been making for decades—calls for pink lentils (often labeled "red lentils"), which in the past required a trip to Phahurat, Bangkok's Little India. I used to wonder why we insisted on using them when we could have used the hulled mung beans that were sold at every supermarket. Pink lentils (*masoor dal*) lend the sauce a delicate flavor, while hulled mung beans (*moong dal*) give it a nuttier flavor. It's just a matter of personal preference. ◗ **Makes 5 cups sauce; serves 6**

Combine the bird's eye chiles and oil in a small frying pan and set over medium heat. Stir until the chiles darken and are crisp, 3 to 4 minutes. Transfer to a plate and set aside.

Peel the shallots and garlic. Cut half of the shallots into ½-inch cubes. Cut the remaining shallots in half lengthwise, then place the halves cut side down and slice lengthwise paper-thin. Slice 3 garlic cloves crosswise as thinly as possible; keep the other 3 cloves whole. Set all of the shallots and garlic aside.

Pour 1 cup of the water into a 4-quart saucepan and prepare a heatproof plate; set both near the stove. Put the lentils in an 8-inch frying pan, set over medium heat, and toast, stirring constantly, until medium brown, about 10 minutes. Don't walk or look away, especially toward the end, or they may burn. You want the lentils to be toasted, smoky, and nutty, which is key to the success of this dish. The moment your eyes and nose tell you they are a mere second from going over to the dark side, immediately pour the lentils into the prepared water pan; this will instantly stop the cooking. Put the peanuts in the pan and toast in the same way until smoky and dark brown around the edges, about 10 minutes; transfer to the heatproof plate. Don't wash the frying pan just yet.

Put the lentil saucepan over high heat. Once it boils, cover, turn the heat to medium-low, and cook for 10 minutes. Uncover the pan, add the shrimp, re-cover, and cook until the shrimp are firm and opaque, 2 to 3 minutes.

continued

VEGETABLES

Trimmed banana blossoms, soaked in acidulated water until serving, then drained and patted dry

Crispy water spinach as detailed in Crispy Water Spinach Salad (see page 127)

Whole small edible flowers, prepared as for Crispy Water Spinach Salad (see page 127)

Leafless water spinach stems, thinly sliced on a sharp diagonal and sautéed briefly in a tiny amount of lard or vegetable oil

Transfer the contents of the pan, including all of the liquid, to a food processor. Put the coconut cream and coconut milk in the same saucepan. Meanwhile, process the lentils and shrimp to the consistency of coarse mustard and scrape every bit into the coconut cream mixture in the pan. Chop the peanuts into small pieces the size of a match head and add them to the pan along with the chile jam, tamarind, salt, and sugar; set aside.

Meanwhile, put the cubed shallots, whole garlic cloves, and galangal in the frying pan in which you toasted the lentils and toast them over medium heat, stirring constantly, until softened and slightly charred, 4 to 5 minutes. Transfer to a mortar or mini chopper. Add the toasted chiles and shrimp paste to the shallot mixture in the mortar or small chopper and grind to a smooth paste. Set aside.

Wipe the frying pan clean, then put the lard, sliced shallots, and sliced garlic in the pan and set over medium heat. Stir constantly until the shallot and garlic slices are golden brown and crisp, 5 to 7 minutes. Using a slotted spoon, transfer to a plate, leaving the lard in the pan. Put the pan back on the stove and crank the heat to medium-high. Add the chile paste and stir-fry until it thickens up somewhat and is fragrant, about 2 minutes, then remove from the heat.

Put the saucepan with the lentil-peanut mixture over medium-high heat. Add the remaining 1½ cups water and bring to a boil, stirring often. Stir in the fried chile paste along with the lard. Add the lime juice and the orange juice and zest. Since the dish is served without additional seasonings, taste the sauce and season further, if necessary, to achieve a flavor that's equally salty, sweet, and sour, then heat through, and remove from the heat.

Divide the noodles among four dinner plates, spoon a generous amount of the lentil-peanut sauce over the noodles, and place a boiled egg half on the side. Arrange the fried bird's eye chiles on the side for anyone who may want to crumble them up over their noodles for some heat (that said, these noodles aren't supposed to be very spicy hot). Arrange the vegetables around the noodles before serving.

A Mat and a Pillow

The contribution of Chinese immigrants to Thai cuisine in its present form is immense. Imagine Bangkok without noodles. Imagine Bangkok without anything cooked in a wok. Imagine Bangkok without "twin" crullers (page 281) and hot soy milk. Imagine Bangkok without egg noodles and barbecued pork (page 328). Imagine Bangkok without roasted duck or stewed pork leg (page 205). I think I'm going to faint. Countless dishes of Chinese origin are part of everyday life—dishes that have evolved into what everyone in Thailand sees as resolutely Thai.

But the Chinese have contributed to Thai society beyond the kitchen. The phrase *suea phuen mon bai*, literally "a floor mat [and] a pillow," has been used to describe the condition under which Chinese immigrants lived when they came to Thailand. Although Chinese had arrived and become part of the local culture long before the founding of Bangkok, it was the immigration at the beginning of the twentieth century, prompted by hardship in some southern Chinese provinces, that gave birth to the expression. The phrase is always used to demonstrate how with nothing more than a mat and a pillow to sleep on, and with hard work, perseverance, and entrepreneurial spirit, many of them became successful business owners.

In many Western countries, the presence and influence of Chinese immigrants are most visible in Chinatowns. But in Bangkok, the Chinese permeate nearly every square inch of the city, and the local Chinatown is a historic quarter in which the Chinese immigrants' way of life remains closer to what it once was.

The various groups of Chinese immigrants have brought with them different skill sets and cultures. In Bangkok, three groups dominated. The Teochew, the largest group, were known for rice and medicine trading as well as finance. The Hakka were known for being skilled tanners, miners, farmers, and financiers. And the Hainanese tended to gravitate toward cooking in restaurant or hotel kitchens. Over the last few decades, however, Chinese immigrants have fully assimilated into Thai society and such observations no longer apply. Culinary distinctions among these groups, on the other hand, can still be seen.

Plain rice porridge with assorted accompaniments

ข้าวต้มพุ้ยและกับ KHAO TOM PHUI LAE KAP

PICKLED HEARTS OF MUSTARD GREENS SALAD

6 ounces pickled mustard greens

Fresh lime juice, for seasoning

Fish sauce, for seasoning

2 fresh bird's eye chiles, thinly sliced crosswise

CHINESE SAUSAGE–CUCUMBER SALAD

6 ounces Chinese dried sweet sausage (lap cheong), cut crosswise on a 40-degree angle into ⅛-inch-thick slices

1 pickling or Persian cucumber, halved lengthwise, then cut on a 40-degree angle into ⅛-inch-thick slices

1 (1-ounce) shallot, halved lengthwise, placed cut side down, and cut lengthwise into paper-thin slices

Fish sauce, for seasoning

Fresh lime juice, for seasoning

3 or 4 fresh bird's eye chiles, thinly sliced crosswise

¼ cup coarsely chopped cilantro leaves and stems

4 hard-boiled duck eggs

1 recipe Preserved Radish Omelet with Crispy Basil (page 147)

1 recipe Panfried Salted Fish Steak (page 327)

1 recipe plain rice porridge (page 21)

The obsolete Thai name for plain rice porridge is *khao tom kui*, literally "rice porridge of the coolies (*kui*)," which some view as neutral in the old days. But the word, the Thai equivalent of the English *coolie*, has since become a derogatory term, so the word *phui*, or "to deposit food into the mouth rapidly with chopsticks" (which is how you eat rice porridge), has become more and more frequently used as a replacement. I'm following that new tradition here.

Plain rice porridge is a blank canvas that opens itself up to anything. And in Bangkok these days, the line between what is traditionally served with Chinese-style porridge and what is traditionally a Thai dish is so blurry that it may no longer exist. Here, I have put together a set meal of plain rice porridge and some accompaniments typically served with it. ◆ **Serves 4**

To make the mustard greens salad, rinse the mustard greens under running cold water and squeeze dry. Remove the leaves and the thin stems and reserve them for other uses (such as Rice Vermicelli with Fish Curry, page 171). Remove and discard the core and slice the heart and the thick stems close to the base crosswise into ¼-inch-thick slices and transfer to a serving bowl. Add just enough lime juice and fish sauce to achieve an equally salty and sour flavor. Stir in the chiles. (This accompaniment is served in a small portion and is considered more of a condiment than a vegetable dish.)

To make the sausage-cucumber salad, put the sausage slices in a 12-inch frying pan and set over medium-low heat. Stir and flip the slices around until they are browned on all sides, just a few minutes, and then transfer them to a bowl and let cool to room temperature. Stir in the cucumber and shallot slices and season to taste with fish sauce and lime juice. The dressing should be sour and salty enough to balance out the sweetness of the sausage. Stir in the chiles and cilantro and transfer to a plate.

Peel and halve the eggs, put them on a small plate, and set the plate on the table. Put the dishes of salads, the omelet, and the salted fish alongside the eggs. Heat the porridge until piping hot and then ladle into small soup bowls. Do not add the accompaniments directly to the porridge. Instead, invite diners to take a bite of one of the accompaniments and then to chase it with three or four bites of porridge. (The porridge should be piping hot throughout the meal, so keep it in its pan over the lowest heat setting and refill the bowls as needed.)

Rice soup with fish and soy-glazed pork

ข้าวต้มปลาบะเต็ง KHAO TOM PLA BA TENG

SALTED SOYBEAN SAUCE

¾ cup dark salted soybean paste

1 teaspoon grated fresh ginger

1 teaspoon minced fresh bird's eye chile (optional)

SOY-GLAZED PORK (OPTIONAL)

1 tablespoon homemade lard (page 28) or vegetable oil

6 ounces boneless fatty pork shoulder, cut into ⅓-inch cubes

2 teaspoons Thai dark soy sauce

1 tablespoon Thai thin soy sauce or Golden Mountain seasoning sauce

2 teaspoons crushed Chinese rock sugar or packed light or dark brown sugar

½ teaspoon ground white pepper

RICE SOUP

8 cups homemade chicken or pork stock (page 323) or store-bought sodium-free chicken stock

1 teaspoon salt

1½ pounds firm, white saltwater fish fillets, cut into 2-inch cubes

4 cups tightly packed cooked Thai jasmine rice (the drier and firmer, the better), kept warm

3 tablespoons preserved cabbage

½ cup cut-up Chinese celery or tender leaves and stalks of regular (Pascal) celery heart, in ½-inch pieces

3 tablespoons fried garlic and its oil (page 322)

Ground white pepper, for dusting

TABLE SEASONINGS

Fish sauce

Dried red chile powder (page 323)

Pickled chiles in vinegar (page 317), at room temperature (so they don't cool down the soup)

Certain things taste better against the backdrop of darkness—or that's how it seems. Among those brilliant dishes that emerge to illumine the nocturnal food venues in Bangkok is this rice soup with fish.

I like to use grouper in this soup, but nearly any fresh firm white saltwater fish will do. The rice soup with just fish is good enough to stand on its own, so the soy-braised pork included here is optional. I'm offering it as an option because that's how the soup is served at my favorite Bangkok purveyor of the dish. If you opt to make the pork, treat it as a condiment rather than another main protein, adding just a spoonful to each bowl. ⚜ **Serves 6**

To make the sauce, combine all of the ingredients in a small bowl and mix well. Set aside.

To make the glazed pork, put the lard in a wok or 8-inch frying pan and set over medium-high heat. When the lard is hot, add the pork, dark and thin soy sauces, sugar, and pepper and stir-fry until the pork is cooked through and the moisture in the pan has evaporated, about 10 minutes. The pork juices, the soy sauces, and the fat should create a dense, glossy glaze that coats the pork. Transfer the pork to a bowl and set aside.

To make the soup, fill a 2-quart saucepan halfway with water and bring to a boil over high heat. At the same time, put the stock in a 4-quart saucepan, cover, and bring to a boil over high heat. When the water boils, stir in the salt and then lower the heat so the water is bubbling gently. Add the fish pieces to the water and stir once very gently just to separate the pieces. Cook, without stirring, until the fish turns barely opaque, 1 to 2 minutes. Turn off the heat and, using a mesh skimmer, gently transfer the fish to a bowl and cover the bowl. When the stock boils, turn the heat to the lowest setting to keep it steaming hot.

Put the rice in a fine-mesh sieve or colander and hold it under running hot water to rinse off excess starch and to loosen up the grains. Shake off any excess water and add it to the stock. Turn the heat to high and bring the stock back to a boil for only 10 seconds. Then, before the rice has a chance to swell and expand too much, divide the soup among six large soup bowls. Top the bowls with the preserved cabbage, cooked fish, celery, fried garlic and oil, and a good dusting of pepper, in that order. Spoon some glazed pork to one side of each bowl and serve immediately. Because the stock is not salted, any saltiness comes from the pork and cabbage. Invite diners to season their own bowls at the table with soybean sauce, fish sauce, dried red chile powder, and pickled chiles.

Barbecued pork with sweet gravy on rice

ข้าวหมูแดง **KHAO MU DAENG**

1 recipe "Red" Barbecued Pork (page 328), with marinade reserved

3 tablespoons Thai dark soy sauce

2 teaspoons crushed Chinese rock sugar or packed light or dark brown sugar

½ cup distilled white vinegar

1 fresh green Thai long, jalapeño, or serrano chile, cut crosswise into ¼-inch-thick slices

2 ounces Chinese dried sweet sausage (lap cheong)

¼ cup plus 2 tablespoons hoisin sauce

1 tablespoon oyster sauce

3 tablespoons cornstarch

1¼ cups water, homemade chicken stock (see page 323), or store-bought sodium-free chicken stock

1 teaspoon white sesame seeds, toasted

¼ teaspoon toasted sesame oil

OTHER ACCOMPANIMENTS

4 cups cooked Thai jasmine rice, kept warm

2 large green onions, cut crosswise into 1-inch pieces

½ English cucumber or 2 Persian cucumbers, cut crosswise on the diagonal into ¼-inch-thick slices

2 medium- or hard-boiled eggs, halved

Even though *khao mu daeng* (literally "rice [and] red pork") is available everywhere in the city, the best versions are nearly always found at one of the decades-old shophouse eateries rather than at street carts. My maternal grandparents' house was only ten minutes away from Nai Sai, a shophouse eatery in the Prachachuen neighborhood that I consider one of the best makers of roasted and barbecued pork in Bangkok. This recipe is based on the flavors I remember from years of eating there.

Boneless pork butt is the best cut for the job. Pork loin, though acceptable, is not recommended. The barbecued pork is nearly always reddish (hence, the name "red pork"), the product of red food coloring. Although the most reputable vendors use the artificial red coloring conservatively, many others seem to live by the "more is more" philosophy. Beet juice, however, is my preferred coloring agent. That said, the red color isn't important, and some shops, including Nai Sai, don't use any coloring.

If you are feeling particularly indulgent, slice about 8 ounces Chinese-style roasted pork belly (homemade, page 318, or store-bought) and arrange it on the plate along with the barbecued pork.

Serves 4

Before you cook the barbecued pork, put every bit of the leftover marinade in a 1-quart saucepan, cover, and refrigerate. After the cooked pork has rested in a covered pan, collect the juices at the bottom of the pan and add them to the marinade in the saucepan, then re-cover and refrigerate.

Combine 2 tablespoons of the soy sauce, the rock sugar, the vinegar, and the chile in a bowl and stir to mix, then leave at room temperature until serving to allow the chile to mellow. (For an even better result, make this sauce 3 days ahead, refrigerate it in an airtight container, and let come to room temperature before using.)

Cut the barbecued pork on the diagonal against the grain into bite-size pieces about ⅛ inch thick. Cover and set aside at room temperature until serving.

Meanwhile, cut the Chinese sausage on the diagonal into slices about ¼ inch thick. Transfer the slices to an 8-inch frying pan and set over medium-high heat. Fry, stirring almost constantly, until the sausage is blistered and browned all over, just a few minutes (be careful, as this type of sausage tends to burn easily). Set aside.

continued

Remove the saucepan holding the marinade from the refrigerator. Whisk the hoisin sauce, oyster sauce, the remaining 1 tablespoon soy sauce, the cornstarch, and the water into the marinade, making sure there are no lumps. Place the pan over medium-high heat and bring to a boil, whisking constantly. About 1 minute after the mixture has reached a boil, it will begin to thicken quickly, so don't stop whisking. When the sauce is the consistency of runny yogurt (if too thick, add more water or stock) and glossy, remove from the heat and whisk in the sesame seeds and sesame oil.

Divide the rice evenly among four dinner plates. Arrange one-fourth of the barbecued pork on top of each rice portion and spoon one-fourth of the warm sauce over the pork. Arrange one-fourth each of the fried sausage, the green onions, the cucumber slices, and half a boiled egg on the side of each plate. Set the chile in soy sauce and vinegar on the table (to be used as needed only and sparingly) and serve right away.

Chicken and rice, Thai Muslim style

ข้าวหมกไก่ KHAO MOK KAI

2 tablespoons ghee

1 (2-inch) cube fresh ginger (1½ ounces), peeled and ground to a paste

4 large cloves garlic, ground to a paste

1 yellow or white onion, finely diced

2 teaspoons garam masala

1 cup water

½ teaspoon cayenne pepper

1 teaspoon ground turmeric

1 tablespoon mild curry powder

2 teaspoons salt

1 tablespoon granulated sugar

2 tablespoons plain whole-milk yogurt (not Greek yogurt)

4 bay leaves

4 skin-on, bone-in chicken thighs (1½ pounds total), trimmed of excess fat

4 chicken drumsticks (1 pound total)

RICE

2 cups raw Thai jasmine rice

2 (3-inch) cinnamon sticks

1½ teaspoons saffron threads steeped in 1 tablespoon hot water, or 1½ teaspoons ground turmeric

1 tablespoon ghee

½ teaspoon salt

5 Siamese cardamom or green cardamom pods, cracked

3 bay leaves

4 whole cloves

3 cups water, if using a rice cooker, or 3½ cups, if cooking on the stove top

Following my philatelist grandfather to the General Post Office to get first day of issue stamps was one of the highlights of my childhood. Not only did I learn about stamps and start collecting them but I also got to explore Bang Rak, the culturally rich, diverse neighborhood in which the post office is located. It was home to many dishes we didn't usually make in our kitchen. A chicken and rice stop at Jio, a halal eatery in the alleyway opposite the post office, was often on the agenda, and it was in that tiny, unassuming place that I had *khao mok kai* for the first time.

Muslims in Thailand have come from many places and have brought with them different traditions. The Thai rendition of what is known elsewhere in the world as chicken *biryani* is a staple of halal eateries throughout Bangkok and is popular inside and outside of the Thai Muslim population.

Jio's version looks a bit different from the norm, as the rice is cooked separately rather than in the same pot as the chicken and it tastes more curry-like. But because Jio is the place where I first fell in love with this fragrant, delicious, and satisfying dish, I follow its lead.

You can find the spices and the ghee at a South Asian store. If you can't find the round, light blond Siamese cardamom that imparts a slightly sweeter flavor and fragrance than green cardamom does, the latter will do. ◆ **Serves 4 generously**

Put the ghee in a 4-quart saucepan wide enough to accommodate the chicken in a single layer and heat over medium-high heat. When the ghee is hot but not smoking, add the ginger, garlic, onion, and garam masala and stir until the onion has softened, about 2 minutes. Add the water, cayenne, turmeric, curry powder, salt, sugar, yogurt, and bay leaves; stir to combine. Arrange the chicken thighs, flesh side down, in a single layer on the spice mixture and add water as needed to cover them barely. Bring to a boil, lower the heat so the liquid is simmering gently, cover, and cook for 20 minutes.

Uncover, add the chicken drumsticks, and then add more water to cover barely all of the chicken if needed. Bring the liquid back to a boil, then lower the heat to a gentle simmer, cover, and cook until the chicken drumsticks split around the ankles and the thighs are tender but still hold their shape, 40 to 45 minutes longer. Check the liquid from time to time and replenish with water if needed to maintain the original level. Remove and discard the bay leaves before serving.

continued

CUCUMBER RELISH

3 cloves garlic

1 cup packed fresh mint leaves

1 cup packed fresh cilantro leaves

2 fresh Thai long green chiles or jalapeño or serrano chiles, seeded and deveined

⅓ cup granulated sugar

⅓ cup distilled white vinegar

¾ teaspoon salt

1 pickling cucumber, ½ English cucumber, or 2 Persian cucumbers

To cook the rice, while the chicken is simmering, put the rice in a fine-mesh sieve and rinse under cold running water until the water runs clear. Transfer the rice to a rice cooker, add the cinnamon, saffron, ghee, salt, cardamom, bay leaves, cloves, and the 3 cups water and stir to combine. Cover the rice cooker and turn it on. When the rice cooker turns itself off, keep the cover on so the residual heat continues to steam the rice. After 10 minutes, fluff with a fork and discard the cinnamon sticks, cardamom pods, bay leaves, and cloves.

If cooking the rice on the stove top, put the rinsed rice in a 4-quart saucepan, add the remaining ingredients as directed for the rice cooker, using 3½ cups water, and stir to combine. Bring to a boil over medium-high heat, stirring often. Turn the heat to the lowest setting, cover, and cook until the rice is tender and all of the moisture has been absorbed, about 15 minutes. Remove from the heat and let stand, covered, for 15 minutes, then fluff with a fork and discard the spices as directed.

To make the cucumber relish, combine all of the ingredients, except the cucumber, in a blender and process until a somewhat fine puree forms (it will not be silky smooth). Transfer the mixture to a small saucepan and bring to a very gentle boil over medium heat, stirring often. Cook, stirring, for 1 minute, then transfer to a small heatproof serving bowl. Let cool to room temperature. Peel the cucumber and cut crosswise on a 40-degree angle into ¼-inch-thick slices. Arrange the slices in a shallow bowl and pour the cooled sauce over them.

Divide the rice evenly among four dinner plates and top with the chicken. Serve the cucumber relish on the side (to be enjoyed as a condiment and not a side vegetable).

Braised spareribs in salted soybean sauce on rice

ข้าวซี่โครงหมูอบเต้าเจี้ยว ❖ KHAO SI KHRONG MU OP TAO JIAO

3½ pounds pork spareribs, separated into individual ribs and halved crosswise

4 or 5 coins peeled fresh ginger, ⅛ inch thick

2 tablespoons oyster sauce

2 tablespoons dark salted soybean paste

2 tablespoons finely chopped cilantro roots or stems

4 large cloves garlic

½ teaspoon white peppercorns, cracked

1 to 2 tablespoons Thai thin soy sauce or Golden Mountain seasoning sauce

1 tablespoon Thai sweet dark soy sauce

2 tablespoons Chinese rice wine (shaoxing)

1 tablespoon crushed Chinese rock sugar or packed light or dark brown sugar

12 ounces Chinese broccoli, broccolini, or broccoli crowns

1 tablespoon cornstarch

¼ cup water

6 cups cooked Thai jasmine rice, kept warm

I can't think of a more exciting nighttime food activity in Bangkok than grazing along Yaowarat Road in Chinatown. I use the word *graze* because that's exactly what I do. I arrive on the scene with an empty stomach and amble along the main road and the adjoining alleyways, sampling as widely and as variedly as I can. (I don't live in the area, so I'm not going to drag my rear end all the way to Chinatown just to park it at a single shop or stall.)

As broadly as I eat, there is one stop that is always on my agenda: a little shop at the entrance of Yaowarat 9 alley, where I enjoy a plate of rice topped with tender soy-braised spareribs in an umami-rich salted soybean sauce.

Built around a whole slab of spareribs, this recipe yields a large amount. But even if you're cooking only for yourself, you'll still want to make the whole recipe, as it freezes and reheats well. The richness and oomph of the spareribs make the dish. No other cuts will do—not even baby back ribs. If you live near an Asian market, you can buy the ribs already separated and halved. If you don't, you'll need a sturdy cleaver, a solid chopping block, and good aim. ❖ **Serves 6**

Place the ribs in a 4-quart Dutch oven or braising pot. Scatter the ginger slices over the top. In a small chopper, combine the oyster sauce, soybean paste, cilantro roots, garlic, peppercorns, 1 tablespoon of the soy sauce, the sweet dark soy sauce, wine, and sugar and process until smooth. Pour the mixture over the ribs. Add water (use some to rinse the chopper bowl into the ribs so as not to lose any of the sauce) as needed to cover the ribs barely. Cover and bring to a boil over high heat. As soon as it comes to a boil, turn down the heat so the liquid is simmering gently and cook the ribs, stirring occasionally, until tender to your liking, 1 to 1¼ hours. (I like my ribs slightly chewy, so I usually pull them after only 45 minutes.) Check the liquid from time to time and replenish with water if needed to maintain the original level.

Meanwhile, trim off the tough stem ends from the Chinese broccoli. Cut the stalks crosswise on the diagonal into ¼-inch-thick slices. Cut the leaves crosswise into 2-inch pieces. If using broccolini, trim off the tough stem ends and leave the remainder whole; I think they're prettier that way. Alternatively, cut them crosswise into 2-inch sticks. If using broccoli crowns, cut them into 2-inch florets. Steam over boiling water until crisp-tender; keep warm.

continued

When the ribs are tender, turn off the heat, scoop out the ribs with a slotted spoon, and place them in a large bowl. Remove and discard the ginger. Then, using a large spoon, skim off some of the fat from the surface of the braising liquid. Take note of the level of the liquid left in the pot, then turn the heat to high, bring the liquid to a rolling boil, and boil, uncovered, until the liquid has reduced by half. Taste the liquid and adjust the seasoning with the remaining 1 tablespoon thin soy sauce if needed, taking into account the bland rice and steamed vegetables that will be served with the ribs and sauce. As the sauce continues to boil, in a small bowl, quickly whisk together the cornstarch and water and stir the mixture into the braising liquid, 1 tablespoon at a time, until a glossy, slightly viscous sauce forms with just enough body to coat the ribs. Lower the heat to medium, return the ribs to the pot, and stir to coat and heat through.

Divide the rice evenly among six dinner plates and top with the ribs and the sauce. Arrange the broccoli on the side of each plate and serve warm.

Coconut rice with green papaya salad, sweet shredded beef, and chicken red curry

ข้าวมัน-ส้มตำ-เนื้อฝอย-แกงไก่ ❖ KHAO MAN-SOM TAM-NUEA FOI-KAENG KAI

CHICKEN CURRY

2 tablespoons homemade red curry paste (page 317) or 1 tablespoon store-bought red curry paste

½ cup freshly extracted coconut cream, or ½ cup canned coconut cream with 1 tablespoon extra-virgin coconut oil

12 ounces skinless or skin-on, boneless chicken breasts or thighs, sliced against the grain on a 40-degree angle into bite-size pieces

½ cup coconut milk

2 teaspoons fish sauce, or as needed

2 teaspoons finely cut makrut lime leaves, in whisker-thin strips

8 fresh Thai basil leaves

COCONUT RICE

1½ cups raw Thai jasmine rice

½ cup coconut milk, preferably freshly extracted

1 cup water

1 tablespoon plus 2 teaspoons granulated sugar

½ teaspoon salt

½ cup coconut cream, preferably freshly extracted

1 recipe Sweet Shredded Beef (page 329)

According to written records, this traditional set meal has been a Central Thai and Bangkok specialty since the beginning of the twentieth century or even earlier. It was my grandparents' favorite family meal when they were young, and that love has been passed down to their children and grandchildren.

One of the stars of this set meal is a minimalist papaya salad that is quite different from the other versions—especially northeastern—with which most people are familiar. It doesn't involve pounding the papaya in the mortar. Instead, the fruit is shredded with a knife into uneven, crisp strands and then mixed with a simple dressing of fish sauce, palm sugar, tamarind paste, and lime juice in a bowl with none of the usual add-ins, such as peanuts, long beans, or tomatoes. The salad is served alongside coconut rice, which is the center of the meal; a small portion of sweet shredded beef, which is enjoyed sparingly as a savory-sweet condiment; and a small bowl of ultrasimple chicken red curry.

Traditionally, the ensemble is rather extensive. It includes all of the components just detailed, plus deep-fried fish and assorted fresh leaves and herbs, such as young star gooseberry leaves or wild betel leaves. The herbs, to be enjoyed in each bite, lend a mild astringency and acidity that balance out the sweetness of the beef and the richness of the rice and the curry. If you like, add these items to the combo. Otherwise, the four components included here are more than enough to make a satisfying meal. ❖ **Serves 4 to 6**

To make the curry, combine the curry paste and coconut cream in a 2-quart saucepan and set over medium-high heat. Stir until the paste is fragrant and the coconut fat separates, about 1 minute. Add the chicken, coconut milk, and fish sauce, plus water if needed so the liquid is flush with the chicken. Adjust the heat to a gentle simmer, cover, and cook until the chicken is cooked through, 3 to 4 minutes. Taste and adjust the seasoning with fish sauce if needed. (Aim for salty with no sweetness beyond the natural sweetness of the coconut, as the shredded beef with which the curry is served is quite sweet.) Stir in the lime leaves and basil and remove from the heat immediately.

To make the rice, which is best done in a rice cooker, put the rice in a fine-mesh sieve or colander and rinse under cold running water until the water runs clear. Transfer the rice to a rice cooker, add the coconut milk, water, sugar, and salt, and stir to combine. Cover the rice cooker and turn it on.

continued

PAPAYA SALAD

2 large cloves garlic

½ teaspoon white peppercorns

3 tablespoons dried shrimp, soaked in hot water until softened and squeezed dry

4 cups shredded green papaya (shred with a knife or a julienne shredder—never a box grater or coarse blade grater) about 2 inches long

Tamarind paste, homemade (page 316) or store-bought for seasoning

Fresh lime juice, for seasoning

Fish sauce, for seasoning

Grated palm sugar, for seasoning (optional)

Chopped fresh bird's eye chiles, for seasoning

As soon as the rice cooker turns itself off, uncover, pour the coconut cream evenly over the top of the rice (do not stir it in), and replace the lid. Keep the rice warm until serving.

Make the beef as directed.

To make the papaya salad, in a mortar, grind together the garlic and peppercorns to a fine paste. Add the dried shrimp and grind into fine flakes. In a bowl, combine the paste and papaya and mix with your hands, squeezing the papaya strands to soften them slightly. Season to taste with the tamarind paste and the lime juice in equal amounts, fish sauce, and palm sugar. Aim for a primarily sour flavor then salty with very little sweet. You can even leave out the sugar. Stir in the chopped chiles.

Fluff the rice with a fork to separate the grains and stir down some of the coconut cream on the surface. Divide the chicken curry among four to six small bowls. Divide the rice among four to six dinner plates (the rice is traditionally packed into a bowl and unmolded onto each plate, but you don't need to do that). Spoon the papaya salad onto one side of the rice and the beef onto the other. Serve immediately. Instruct diners to make sure each bite contains a little bit of each component.

Rice noodles with five-spice pork-tofu sauce

ก๋วยเตี๋ยวหลอด KUAI TIAO LOT

1 pound boneless pork shoulder or country-style pork ribs, cut into 1-inch cubes

2 teaspoons Chinese five-spice powder

⅓ cup Thai sweet dark soy sauce

2 tablespoons Thai thin soy sauce or Golden Mountain seasoning sauce

1½ tablespoons crushed Chinese rock sugar or packed light or dark brown sugar

8 ounces extra-firm tofu, cut into ½-inch cubes

½ teaspoon toasted sesame oil

2 ounces sweet preserved radishes (see page 344)

½ cup freshly made pork cracklings (page 28)

¼ cup homemade lard (page 28)

¼ cup fried garlic and ¼ cup fried garlic oil (page 322)

1½ pounds fresh rice noodle sheets, homemade (page 330) or store-bought, cut into 1-inch-wide strips; or 12 ounces ½-inch-wide dried rice stick noodles, cooked according to package directions, drained, rinsed under hot running water, and drained again

2 tablespoons tiny dried shrimp (see headnote)

3 cups bean sprouts

2 large green onions, thinly sliced crosswise

¾ cup packed cilantro leaves

TABLE SEASONINGS

About ¾ cup pickled chiles in vinegar (page 317), coarsely pureed

Fish sauce

Granulated sugar

Dried red chile powder (page 323)

This dish is often presented as noodle rolls (the *lot* in *kuai-tiao lot* means "tube"), the fillings tucked neatly inside soft rice noodle sheets, with a bowl of soy-based sauce—the dressing, if you will—on the side. But it arrives just as often fashionably disheveled, with the sauce already on the deconstructed noodle rolls. That's how it's served at one of my favorite food carts in Chinatown. Delicate yet chewy rice noodle strips dotted with tiny shrimp—dyed a curious shade of pink—are steamed in single-serving-size bamboo baskets and kept warm in the steamer. When an order comes in, the vendor puts the noodles on a plate and ladles over the pork and tofu braise that's been sleepily bubbling in a nearby brass pan. The dish is finished with a generous spoonful of pork cracklings and crispy garlic—ingredients that are vital elements rather than optional garnishes. At the table, the diner tosses the whole thing together as if it is a salad. The sauce is traditionally seasoned conservatively, so that diners can customize their noodle "salad" with fish sauce, vinegar, sugar, and dried red chile powder as they like.

The best type of tofu to use here is the extra-firm pressed variety that usually comes vacuum-packed instead of submerged in water in a plastic tub. Also, the best type of dried shrimp to use in this dish isn't the meaty kind but the tiny, crunchy dried shrimp—all shells with hardly any meat. In the United States, they tend to be found at Japanese or Korean supermarkets. ♦ **Serves 4**

Put the pork, five-spice powder, sweet dark soy sauce, thin soy sauce, and sugar in a 4-quart saucepan, add water to cover the pork barely, stir, and set over high heat. When the liquid begins to boil, cover, lower the heat so it simmers gently, and cook for 15 minutes. Add the tofu and if needed, more water to bring the liquid flush with the top of the pork and tofu. Re-cover, and bring the mixture back to a boil over high heat. Lower the heat to a simmer and continue to cook for 15 minutes longer. Stir in the sesame oil and remove the pan from the heat. Keep warm until serving.

Meanwhile, cut the preserved radishes into chunks, transfer to a food processor, and pulse until reduced to pieces the size of match head. Transfer the radishes to a fine-mesh sieve, rinse under cold running water for about 30 seconds, and squeeze bone-dry. Put the radishes in a small frying pan, set over medium heat, and toast, stirring constantly, until dry to the touch, 2 to 3 minutes. Transfer the radishes to a bowl, add the pork cracklings, lard, fried garlic, and fried garlic oil, and mix well. Set aside.

Combine the rice noodles and dried shrimp in a heatproof shallow bowl and toss to mix well. Place in a steamer tier and steam over boiling water until hot. Put the bean sprouts in a second shallow heatproof bowl and steam for just a few seconds until crisp-tender.

Divide the bean sprouts among four large dinner plates (the portions are pretty generous!). Layer the noodles on top, then ladle the pork and tofu braise over the noodles. Top with the pork crackling mixture, the green onions, and the cilantro leaves. Serve immediately. Invite diners to toss everything together like a salad, taste, and then season as they like with the table seasonings.

Beef yellow curry on rice, Chinatown style

ข้าวแกงกะหรี่เนื้อ **KHAO KAENG KARI NUEA**

CURRY PASTE

3 dried Thai long or guajillo chiles, cut into 1-inch pieces, soaked until softened, and squeezed dry

2 fresh red Thai long, jalapeño, or serrano chiles, seeded, deveined, and cut into 1-inch pieces

2 teaspoons finely chopped galangal

1 tablespoon finely sliced lemongrass (with purple rings only)

1 teaspoon finely chopped makrut lime rind or 3 makrut lime leaves, ribs removed and torn into small pieces

5 large cloves garlic

CURRY

1½ tablespoons homemade lard (page 28) or extra-virgin coconut oil

½ cup coconut cream

1½ tablespoons mild curry powder (Thai or any Southeast Asian brand)

1½ pounds boneless trimmed chuck roast (with as much sinew as you can find), cut against the grain on the diagonal into pieces about 3 inches long and 1½ inches wide

1 cup coconut milk

1 tablespoon packed grated palm sugar

1 teaspoon salt

1 to 1½ tablespoons fish sauce

½ cup water

1 tablespoon Thai tapioca starch or cornstarch

This rice-curry combo features the kind of *kari* curry, or "yellow curry," you see only in Bangkok Chinatown. Popularized by Chinese cooks, it has a slightly different flavor from the Thai Muslim version found elsewhere in the city and throughout the world. This yellow curry is made with a simple paste of fresh red chiles—uncommon in most Central Thai red curries, which use dried chiles—and fresh herbs and spices, rather than primarily dried spices. Also, true to its Chinese form, a thickener of tapioca starch or cornstarch always finds its way into the sauce—something that doesn't usually apply to traditional coconut-based Thai curries. Finally, it's a mild curry that even children can enjoy.

Jek Pui, with its much-photographed eating area along an old, tattered wall lined with stools, is one of the most popular vendors of this type of yellow curry. Nai Yong, anglicized as "Mr. Tall," also in Chinatown, is another famous vendor. This one-plate meal is the microcosm of Bangkok's Chinese-style rice-curry shop at its best.

 Serves 4 to 6

To make the paste, in a mortar or small chopper, combine all of the ingredients and grind to a very smooth paste.

To make the curry, transfer the paste to a 4-quart saucepan, add the lard, coconut cream, and curry powder, and set over medium-high heat. Stir-fry until the paste is fragrant and the coconut fat separates, 1 to 2 minutes. Add the beef, coconut milk, sugar, salt, 1 tablespoon of the fish sauce, and enough water so the liquid is flush with the beef and bring to a boil. Lower the heat to a gentle simmer, cover, and cook until the beef is tender but still holds its shape, about 1 hour. Check the liquid from time to time and replenish with water if needed to maintain the original level.

To prepare the sides, while the beef is cooking, put the sausage slices in a small frying pan and set over medium-low heat. Stir and flip the slices around until they are brown on all sides, about 2 minutes. (Be careful, as this type of sausage can burn easily.) Transfer to a small plate. Halve the cucumber lengthwise, then, with the cut side down, slice crosswise and straight down into ⅛-inch-thick slices. Cut the chiles crosswise and straight down into ⅛-inch-thick slices. If you prefer to lessen the heat, remove the seeds and veins. Set the sausage, cucumber, and chiles aside with the eggs until serving.

continued

SIDES

4 ounces Chinese dried sweet sausage (lap cheong), cut crosswise on a 40-degree angle into ⅛-inch-thick slices

1 small pickling cucumber or ½ English cucumber

2 fresh green Thai long or jalapeño chiles

4 to 6 medium- or hard-boiled eggs, halved

4 to 6 cups cooked Thai jasmine rice, kept warm

When the beef is ready, taste the sauce and adjust with the remaining ½ tablespoon fish sauce if needed. Make sure the level of the liquid is flush with the beef. If there is too much liquid, raise the heat and cook the curry, uncovered, to reduce the liquid. When that is done, adjust the heat so the curry is bubbling gently. In a small bowl, whisk together the water and tapioca starch, stir it into the curry, and then cook, stirring constantly, until the sauce is more viscous but still pourable, 1 to 2 minutes.

Divide the rice evenly among four to six dinner plates and spoon the curry over the rice. Arrange the egg halves and sausage, cucumber, and chile slices around the rice. Serve immediately.

Stewed pork hocks on rice

ข้าวขาหมู **KHAO KHA MU**

4 meaty pork hocks (about 3 pounds total)

4 hard-boiled eggs, peeled and with absolutely no spots of yolk exposed

4 star anise pods

1 teaspoon black peppercorns, coarsely cracked

5 whole cloves

2 (3-inch) cinnamon sticks

¼ cup Thai thin soy sauce or Golden Mountain seasoning sauce

¼ cup Chinese rice wine (shaoxing)

1½ tablespoons Thai sweet dark soy sauce

1 tablespoon oyster sauce

1 tablespoon crushed Chinese rock sugar or packed light or dark brown sugar

1 teaspoon salt

2 teaspoons fish sauce

3 large cloves garlic

6 fresh bird's eye chiles or 1 large jalapeño chile

½ teaspoon salt

½ teaspoon granulated sugar

¼ cup distilled white vinegar

8 ounces Chinese broccoli or 4 ounces pickled mustard greens

4 cups cooked Thai jasmine rice, kept warm

Few things make Bangkokians' hearts beat faster than the sight of a voluptuous pork leg stewed until the meat is tender and the skin—bronze and glistening—is tremulously silky. Of all the things for which we have the Chinese immigrants of old to thank, this Teochew specialty is among the top. And although these days you can find stewed pork legs on rice anywhere in the country, when it comes to abundance and quality, no place can surpass Bangkok.

Whole pork legs are used to make this dish commercially, with trotters offered in some places as well. Although not as meaty as the legs, trotters are sought after by anyone with a penchant for gnawing on bony, collagen-rich parts. This recipe calls for pork hocks because they're easy to find and practical for the home kitchen. They taste great prepared this way, too. Even Charoen Saeng, which is in the Bang Rak neighborhood and is one of the city's most popular *khao kha mu* shops, uses hocks. It's also where you're most likely to bump into me in Bangkok.

One thing is nonnegotiable, however—the pork must be cooked with the skin on. The rich, velvety skin is what makes this dish as glorious as it is. Bangkokians find the concept of stewing whole pork legs without skin incomprehensible. Even the skin-averse know that the only reason the meaty bits are so good is because they've been swimming in the same pot with the skin for hours. It's a case of deliciousness by association. ♦ **Serves 4 generously**

Put the pork hocks, cut side down, and the eggs in a 3- or 4-quart saucepan wide enough to accommodate everything in a single layer. Cut a 6-inch square of cheesecloth; put the star anise, peppercorns, cloves, and cinnamon in the center of the square; bring up the corners to form a purse; and tie securely with kitchen string. Drop the spice sachet into the pan. Add the thin soy sauce, wine, dark soy sauce, oyster sauce, sugar, salt, and fish sauce. Add enough water so the liquid is flush with the pork hocks and bring to a boil over high heat. Turn down the heat so the liquid is bubbling gently, cover, and cook until the meat is fork-tender and the skin is soft and silky yet the hocks hold their shape, about 3 hours. Check the liquid from time to time and replenish with water if needed to maintain the original level.

Remove from the heat and, using a large spoon, skim off the fat from the surface of the braising liquid. Re-cover and let the pork and eggs rest in the pan for 30 minutes.

continued

While the pork is cooking, in a blender, combine the garlic, chiles, salt, sugar, and vinegar and process until the garlic and chiles are reduced to the size of a match head. Transfer to a small saucepan, bring to a boil over medium heat, and boil, stirring often, for 1 minute. Let cool completely.

Leave the Chinese broccoli whole (some of us like to pick up a whole stalk, tender and crisp, with a fork and eat it like a large carrot stick) or cut it crosswise on a 40-degree angle into 2-inch pieces. If using pickled mustard greens, rinse well, squeeze dry, core, and slice crosswise into ¼-inch-wide ribbons. Set aside.

Once the pork has rested, remove it from the pan, remove the bones, and slice the meat against the grain into bite-size pieces. Remove the eggs from the pan and halve them lengthwise. Keep warm.

Remove and discard the spice sachet, place the pan over medium heat, and bring to a boil. Add the broccoli or mustard greens and blanch for 30 seconds. Using a slotted spoon, transfer the blanched vegetables to a plate and turn off the heat.

Divide the rice evenly among four dinner plates and top with the meat. Put 2 egg halves on one side of each plate and one-fourth of the blanched greens on the other. Spoon ½ to ¾ cup of the stewing liquid over each serving. Put the garlic-chile-vinegar sauce on the table for diners to add in tiny amounts. The role of the sauce is to balance the richness of the dish, rather than alter its flavor, which is primarily salty with a faint hint of sweet.

Fried rice with salted olives

ข้าวผัดหน้าเลี้ยบ **KHAO PHAT NAM LIAP**

10 salted Chinese olives, pitted or 1 (12-ounce) jar pitted Kalamata olives in brine, drained, rinsed, and well drained

4 large cloves garlic

8 ounces ground pork

1 tablespoon homemade lard (page 28) or vegetable oil

4 cups cooked Thai jasmine rice, kept cold

Dark or thin soy sauce, for seasoning

2 ounces ginger, preferably young, peeled and cut into fine matchsticks

2 ounces shallots, halved lengthwise, placed cut side down, and cut lengthwise into paper-thin slices

½ cup unsalted roasted cashews

4 to 6 fresh red bird's eye chiles, thinly sliced crosswise

2 limes, halved lengthwise around the core

8 to 10 cilantro sprigs

Salted Chinese olives (*nam liap*) are the star of this show. Their soft, pasty flesh lends not only a briny, earthy flavor to the rice but also a beautiful dark purple. That said, the salty fried rice by itself is something of a one-note ditty, and this is where the other components—none of them optional—come in.

Salted Chinese olives can be found in the canned or preserved foods aisle of any well-stocked Asian grocery store, and for the best result, you should seek them out. The cured green or black olives commonly found in U.S. markets—the ones you put in your martinis or salads—don't work as well. But a few years ago, I started experimenting with plump, almond-shaped, dark purple Kalamata olives in brine in this dish and was surprised to find that the result, though different, was quite good. So I have offered Kalamata olives as an option for anyone who cannot find salted Chinese olives. ♦ **Serves 4**

In a mortar or small chopper, grind together the olives and garlic to a smooth paste. Transfer the paste to a bowl, add the pork, and mix until the paste is evenly dispersed.

Put the lard in a wok and set over medium-high heat. When the lard is hot, add the pork mixture and cook, breaking up the pork as finely as possible with the blunt end of a wooden spatula, until cooked through, about 3 minutes. Add the rice and stir-fry until everything is well mixed and heated through. Add the soy sauce to taste.

Divide the fried rice evenly among four dinner plates. Arrange the ginger, shallots, cashews, chiles, and lime halves around the rice. Garnish with the cilantro sprigs and serve immediately. Invite diners to squeeze the lime halves over their portion, then mix everything together as if a salad.

Kindness on the Death Railway

In the early twentieth century, Hua Hin, a town in Prachuap Khiri Khan Province, was the most popular beach vacation spot among the elite of Bangkok. They traveled there on the newly constructed two-hundred-mile railway that connected the west bank of the Chao Phraya in Bangkok to the southern seaside town.

Rail travel was novel and glamorous back then, and rail dining was all about luxurious imported items that weren't available to everyday people. And no item on the menu of the Bangkok–Hua Hin train was more luxurious and popular than fried rice made with butter, sausage, peas, and European seasoning sauces. It was expensive and a marker of status, much as foie gras, *burrata*, or lobster is today. Of course, try to charge modern-day Bangkokians a lot of money for the same fried rice now and they would laugh at you.

But it's not the once-glamorous route south out of Bangkok that has affected me since I was a child. It is the route going west, laced not with luxury but with grimness and suffering.

On the weekends, the State Railway of Thailand arranged a special guided train trip to Kanchanaburi, home of the famous bridge over the Khwae Yai river, and my grandparents; mother; many uncles, aunts, and cousins; and I often took advantage of the program. We would reserve a whole car for our family on the historic route, and we would eat the famous "train" fried rice together while our grandparents recounted the tumultuous events of their youth.

We learned about how this Death Railway had claimed the lives of tens of thousands of local laborers and prisoners of war from various countries, primarily Britain, Australia, the Netherlands, and the United States. We'd make a stop at the war cemetery and look at the names of the people who never got to go back to their respective homes. As a kid, I wondered about them. Did they have any hope the war would end and they'd be able to go home? Were they bitten by mosquitoes? Were they fed?

Nearly the only bright spot amid all those grim ruminations was the story my grandparents told us about Boonpong Sirivejjabandhu, a Thai pharmaceutical merchant who used the canteen management contract he had with the Japanese troops to deliver food, medicine, money, radio batteries, and letters to the POWs by hiding those items in bamboo baskets filled with vegetables. The story of how Boonpong and his family risked their lives to save those of the POWs was also told in various memoirs. Because of this man, my grandfather said, many lives were saved. You look at the world at its worst and you feel despair. But if you look more closely, he continued, you will find that kindness always prevails.

"Train" fried rice

ข้าวผัดรถไฟ **KHAO PHAT ROT FAI**

2 teaspoons Thai thin soy sauce or Golden Mountain seasoning sauce

½ teaspoon ground white pepper, plus more for dusting

¼ cup liquid from red fermented tofu

¼ cup ketchup

2 tablespoons homemade lard (page 28) or vegetable oil

1 tablespoon pork cracklings (page 28; optional)

4 large cloves garlic, minced

3 eggs, lightly beaten

8 ounces yellow or white onions, cut lengthwise into ½-inch-wide wedges

1 Roma tomato, cut lengthwise into ½-inch-wide wedges

1 pound pork shoulder, sliced thinly against the grain into bite-size pieces

3 cups tightly packed cooked Thai jasmine rice, cold

SAUCE

2 or 3 fresh bird's eye chiles, thinly sliced crosswise

¼ cup fish sauce

SIDES

1 small pickling cucumber or 2 Persian cucumbers, peeled and sliced crosswise ¼ inch thick

4 green onions, trimmed

2 limes, halved lengthwise around the core

I don't travel by train that much nowadays, but when I want to relive the trips our family took to Kanchanaburi and the memory of the "train" fried rice (see page 210), I visit Mit Ko Yuan, an old restaurant in the Giant Swing area of Rattanakosin Island, where a version of the fried rice is still served. Their minimalist rendition is decidedly more Chinese than European, much less indulgent, and is made with the liquid from *tao hu yi* (tofu cubes fermented with red rice yeast) that both tints the rice pink and gives it a heady flavor. This recipe is my adaptation of Mit Ko Yuan's version. ⚜ **Serves 4**

In a small bowl, stir together the soy sauce, pepper, tofu liquid, and ketchup. Set it near the stove.

Put the lard, cracklings, and garlic in a wok or 14-inch frying pan and set over high heat. Stir until the garlic is fragrant, 30 to 40 seconds. Add the eggs and scramble until partially set. Add the onions and cook without stirring too much, 2 to 3 minutes. You want them to brown a little and the moisture in the wok to evaporate. Add the tomato wedges and pork and cook them the same way you cooked the onion until the pork has firmed up with some pink still remaining, about 3 minutes. Use a rubber spatula to scrape every bit of the prepared sauce into the wok, then add the rice and stir-fry until well blended and heated through. Turn off the heat.

To make the sauce, in a small serving bowl, stir together the chiles and fish sauce and set it on the table for anyone who may want this Thai equivalent of salt and pepper shakers.

Divide the warm fried rice evenly among four dinner plates. Arrange some cucumber slices, a green onion, and a lime half on each plate. Invite diners to squeeze the lime over their rice and to eat bites of the cucumber and green onion alternating with bites of the rice.

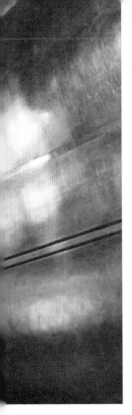

In Remembrance of Queens Khao Man Kai

"This place is full of history," said Boonyong Panpanichgul, as we sat down for a talk. "I get sad thinking about how it will all disappear in just a few weeks."

Queens, a longtime eatery in Old Town Bangkok specializing in Hainanese Thai specialties, was closing. When I walked into the shop earlier that fine afternoon in October 2012 to interview the maker of my favorite chicken and rice, it was the last thing I expected to hear. When I started eating the plate of *khao man kai* before me, I was happy as a lark. Little did I know that when the news hit me during the fifth bite, I would be plunged into the first stage of grief: denial.

"No," I said, stunned. It's the sort of thing people in denial usually say.

But it was true. After sixty years, this *khao man kai* shop would be no more. None of his children or grandchildren wanted to take over the business, he explained, and the place was going to be converted by the new owner into a gold shop. A gold shop. I watched myself move seamlessly into the anger stage.

Much of the Wang Burapha neighborhood, the place to see and be seen back in the early post–World War II era, had changed over the years, but Queens had stayed the same since the beginning. The built-in clay stove from the late 1940s near the stairs, the dumbwaiter covered in cobwebs in the back, the wood ceiling fans, the glass cabinet in the front where poached chickens hung, the tables, the chairs, the booths.

The booths. That thought shot me past the stage of grief right into depression.

One of those booths was where my father and I, two *khao man kai* fanatics, used to sit on our dates until he got sick and passed away. Dad would have his *khao man kai* with the soy-ginger-chile sauce, and I, not being able to handle ginger and chile yet, would drizzle the syrupy sweet dark soy sauce over mine.

The place was brimming with the memories of Boonyong's father, too. In 1939, he had escaped the poverty of Hainan Island in southern China along with many other young compatriots and sailed along the coast of Vietnam all the way to the island of Samui, in southern Thailand. Not speaking a word of Thai, he earned a living by laboring day and night in a coconut grove until he had put together enough money to travel to Bangkok. His plan was to find a better job and make more money so that his wife, whom he'd left behind in Hainan, could join him in the new country. Then the war broke out and life continued to be hard for him for a few more years. Finally, after lots of tears and sweat, he bought this shophouse and started cooking.

Queens began as a cook shop (see page 138), just as most restaurants run by Hainanese chefs did in the old days, and its clientele was made up of the crowds that went in and out of its namesake, the once hip but now long-defunct Queens Theater. A few years later, the shop was converted into a low-key eatery featuring *khao man kai* and a handful of other Hainanese Thai specialties. This prompted the then twenty-five-year-old Boonyong to quit his job as a hotel receptionist and take over the cooking, and he has been the main person behind the glass chicken cabinet ever since.

"I'll miss many of my customers who have become our friends," Boonyong looked around, nodding to himself. "But it's been a good run—I'm ready to quit." His wife, who walked over to the table with a plate of Chinese-style fresh spring rolls (page 35) for me, nodded in agreement. Both in their seventies, Boonyong and his wife could definitely do without standing all day, putting together plate after plate after plate of *khao man kai*. Boonyong had made a promise to continue this business after his father's passing, and he'd kept it faithfully for almost five decades. I guess knowing that you have given your all to something makes it easier to accept the end of it.

Our conversation turned to the cooking technique at that point, and Boonyong's face lit up instantly. When people are passionate about what they do, it shows in their voice, their face, their demeanor. He wanted me to make it at home, and he wanted you to make it at home.

As I took one last look at the booth where Dad and I used to sit, I reflected on the hardworking, dedicated people who had made it possible for us to enjoy such good food for so many years. Then I swallowed that knot in my throat, said my good-bye to Queens, and walked away.

Poached chicken on rice with soy-ginger sauce

ข้าวมันไก่ **KHAO MAN KAI**

Spotting a *khao man kai* shop in Bangkok is not difficult. First, there are many of them. Second, it's hard to miss the row of poached whole chickens hanging in a glass cabinet right at the front of the shop. Of the many contributions of Chinese immigrants to the city's culinary scene, the Thai adaptation of Hainanese poached chicken on rice is one of the most popular. It is the ultimate comfort food for many Bangkokians, and whenever I'm asked what I want my last meal to be, it's always a toss-up between *khao man kai* and grilled chicken with sticky rice. I like it that much.

I don't know what this one-plate meal looked like when it was first made commercially in Bangkok. But long before I was born, *khao man kai* had already taken on a canonical, immutable form: boneless (always!) chicken sliced against the grain into long strips and arranged on a mound of fragrant rice, cooked in chicken fat and broth, with cool crisp cucumber slices on the side and a sprig or two of cilantro as a garnish. The dish comes with a piquant sauce of salted soybeans, garlic, ginger, and chiles. A bottle of sweet dark soy sauce is always set on the table for the chile-averse and for young children. Finally, a small bowl of piping-hot broth for sipping accompanies every plate. Most of the time, bite-size chunks of Chinese winter melon—the most traditional option—are floating in the broth. But these days, it's not uncommon to see chunks of daikon or small pieces of pickled mustard greens instead.

The poaching method described here may seem strange, but this is my home adaptation of what many renowned shops, including Queens (see page 214), do. The goal is to heat the chicken as minimally as possible to get it to the point where it's thoroughly cooked but not a smidge beyond that. Once cooled to room temperature, the perfect serving temperature for the chicken, the meat is tender and lushly juicy yet still firm. For this poaching method to work, it's important that the chicken be whole and within the specified weight range. One modification I have made to the traditional method is the use of chicken stock as the poaching liquid. Most vendors start the process with plain water. However, they have a huge advantage over home cooks in that they poach a large number of chickens in the same pot of water each day, thereby turning plain water into deeply flavorful broth. At home, where you'll likely poach just one chicken at a time—though water remains an option—the use of chicken stock is an extra step worth taking to achieve maximum flavor. ◆ **Serves 6 generously**

continued

POACHED CHICKEN AND SIPPING BROTH

2 quarts homemade chicken stock (page 323), store-bought sodium-free chicken stock, or water

1 teaspoon salt

1 whole chicken, no less than 3¼ pounds and no more than 3¾ pounds

2 tablespoons Thai thin soy sauce or Golden Mountain seasoning sauce

1 pound Chinese winter melon, peeled, seeded, and cut into 1-inch cubes

Fish sauce, for seasoning

Ground white pepper, for seasoning

SAUCE

2 ounces ginger (about 5 inches long and 1½ inches in diameter), peeled

8 large cloves garlic

3 or 4 fresh bird's eye chiles

¼ cup dark salted soybean paste

¼ cup distilled white vinegar

3 tablespoons granulated sugar

2 tablespoons Thai thin soy sauce or Golden Mountain seasoning sauce

1 tablespoon Thai sweet dark soy sauce

2 tablespoons water

To poach the chicken, put the stock in a 4-quart saucepan, stir in the salt, and bring to a boil over high heat. If possible, select a relatively wide, shallow pan—just deep enough for the water to keep the chicken barely submerged—rather than a narrow, deep one, as it will make getting the chicken in and out of the pan easier. Insert a sturdy wooden spoon inside the cavity of the chicken all the way to the neck end. Consider this your chicken "handle," which you'll be using throughout the process. Gripping firmly on the handle, gently lower the chicken into the pot and try to fill its cavity with as much boiling stock as possible. Lift the chicken straight up from the stock and then tilt it at a 45-degree angle so the stock in the cavity pours back into the pot. Repeat this another four times within the next minute. This helps to equalize the temperature of the stock inside and outside the chicken cavity to ensure even cooking.

Once this is done, lower the chicken, breast side down, back into the pan. Remove the handle and turn down the heat to the lowest setting so the liquid steams but doesn't bubble at all, cover tightly, and poach undisturbed for 30 minutes (use a timer).

To make the sauce, meanwhile, using a cutting board and a sharp knife, chop the ginger, garlic, and chiles into pieces about the size of a match head. Transfer them to a small saucepan; add the soybean paste, vinegar, sugar, thin and dark soy sauces, and water; and set over medium heat. Bring the mixture to a boil, lower the heat to a gentle simmer, and cook for 30 seconds. Remove from the heat and let cool.

After 30 minutes have passed, uncover the chicken and, using your "handle," transfer it to a plate. Raise the heat to high and bring the liquid to a boil. Using the spoon again, dunk and drain the chicken five times as before. Then lower the chicken, breast side up, back into the pan. This time turn off the heat completely, cover tightly, and poach undisturbed for another 30 minutes.

When the chicken is ready, lift it from the pot, draining off any water in the cavity, and transfer it to a large bowl, cover the bowl with plastic wrap, and leave it to cool to room temperature. Reserve the poaching liquid.

To make the rice, meanwhile, put the rice in a fine-mesh sieve or colander and rinse under cold running water until the water runs clear. Shake off the excess water and set aside.

Using a large spoon, spoon the fat that has risen to the surface of the poaching liquid into a glass measuring cup. Add just enough of the poaching liquid to make a total of 1½ cups of liquid and reserve.

RICE

2 cups raw Thai jasmine rice

¼ cup rendered chicken fat (preferably) or vegetable oil

4 large cloves garlic, minced

1½ cups water

¼ teaspoon salt

4 thin slices ginger, peeled (optional)

4 pandan leaves, tied together into a knot (optional)

SIDES

1 pickling cucumber, peeled and cut crosswise on the diagonal ¼ inch thick

¼ cup packed cilantro leaves

Put the ¼ cup chicken fat in a heavy 3- or 4-quart saucepan and set over medium-high heat. When the fat is hot, add the garlic and stir until fragrant, about 1 minute. Add the rice and stir gently to separate the grains. Add the water, salt, ginger, pandan leaves, and reserved 1½ cups mixture of chicken fat and broth and stir to mix. Cover and bring the mixture to a boil, stirring once. Immediately turn the heat to low, cover, and cook undisturbed until the rice has absorbed all of the liquid and is cooked through, 10 to 12 minutes.

To make the sipping broth, while the rice is cooking, bring the liquid remaining in the chicken pan to a boil over high heat. Add the winter melon cubes and more water (or chicken stock, if you have extra on hand) as needed to cover the melon by 1 inch. Turn the heat to medium, cover, and simmer until the melon is tender but not mushy, 7 to 8 minutes. Season the broth to taste with fish sauce and pepper. Keep the broth hot while you work on the other components.

The chicken will now have cooled to slightly warmer than room temperature. Drain off any liquid that may be inside the cavity and pat it dry. Separate the chicken into quarters, bone the quarters, and cut the meat against the grain into ½-inch-thick slices. (The chicken juice should be clear. The meat will be firm, yet slightly pinkish, however, which is a sign that it has been properly poached.) Keep the chicken covered until serving.

Everything should now be ready to assemble the plates. Fluff the rice and discard the ginger and pandan leaves. For each serving, put a mound of warm rice on a dinner plate and top it with the now room-temperature chicken pieces. Divide the sauce among individual dipping sauce bowls. Arrange the cucumber slices on one side of the plate and the cilantro leaves on top of the chicken. Ladle the hot broth into small individual soup bowls, sprinkle with pepper, and place a bowl alongside each plate of rice and chicken. Invite diners to sip the broth between bites of the chicken and rice to, as the Thais put it, help things glide down the esophagus more smoothly.

Stir-fried glass noodles with chicken and vegetables in fermented tofu sauce

สุกี้แห้งไก่ SUKI HAENG KAI

SAUCE

1 tablespoon mashed
red fermented tofu

2 tablespoons liquid from
red fermented tofu

1 tablespoon distilled
white vinegar

1 tablespoon oyster sauce

1 tablespoon granulated sugar

2 tablespoons homemade lard
(page 28) or vegetable oil

4 large cloves garlic, minced

6 ounces skinless, boneless
chicken breasts or thighs,
cut against the grain
on a 40-degree angle into
bite-size pieces

2 cups napa cabbage slices
(2-inch squares)

3 ounces glass noodles,
soaked in room-temperature
water for 15 minutes, drained,
cut into 6-inch lengths, and
blotted dry

3 eggs, lightly beaten

¾ cup Chinese celery sticks or
the heart of regular (Pascal)
celery, in 1-inch lengths

1 cup water spinach sticks,
in 2-inch lengths

TABLE SEASONINGS

Fish sauce

Granulated sugar

Distilled white vinegar

Dried red chile powder

This is a flavorful noodle stir-fry that makes you feel like someone has just reduced an entire hot pot spread (see page 261), including the sauce, into this one plate. The flavor and scent of fermented tofu comes through loud and clear in this strongly seasoned dish, so to love this stir-fry, you first have to love that red tofu. ◆ **Serves 2**

To make the sauce, in a small bowl, stir together the mashed tofu, tofu liquid, vinegar, oyster sauce, and sugar. Dissolve the sugar as best you can. Set aside.

Heat the lard in a large wok or 14-inch frying pan set over high heat. When the lard is hot, add the garlic and stir-fry until fragrant, about 30 seconds. Add the chicken and stir-fry until opaque, 2 to 3 minutes. Add the cabbage and glass noodles and, using a rubber spatula, scrape every bit of the prepared sauce into the wok. Stir-fry until the noodles have absorbed all of the liquid in the pan, 7 to 8 minutes. Make a well in the middle of the noodles and pour the eggs into it. When the eggs are barely set, after about 10 seconds, add the celery and water spinach and stir everything together. When the celery and water spinach have wilted, take the wok off the heat.

Divide the stir-fry evenly between two dinner plates and serve immediately with the table seasonings.

"Mama Dearest"

For more than a decade, I've been watching how everyone and their sainted grandmother are in competition to see who can serve the most "authentic" Thai food in both Thailand and the United States. In Thailand, especially in Bangkok, restaurants have been hot on the retro trend, which some view as a yearning by the middle class for the idyllic old days. At the same time, many Thai restaurants in the United States have been striving to make their dishes and concepts more region specific, employing, to an often humorous degree, the Christmas light–oilcloth-covered table–retro country music formula as a template for the "real" Thailand. In the current climate, the mere mention of the word *fusion* typically elicits a derisive response.

Yet, there in a quiet, dark corner sits the gaudily clad Mama, a cigarette in a foot-long holder in one hand and an ostrich feather fan in the other. With a large mole at one corner of her mouth paired with a self-satisfied smirk, she watches the comings and goings of crazes and trends with the kind of poise and nonchalance that can only come from knowing what a hot commodity she is. And she's not mistaken.

By "Mama," of course, I mean the popular Thai instant ramen brand that has become the generic word for all instant noodles. The gatekeepers of "authenticity" never want to talk about the Thais'—particularly the Bangkokians'—obsession with instant noodles. Mama noodles are a guilty pleasure. Everyone loves them, but few formally recognize them as part of the Thai eating culture. Yet anyone who has spent more than a short vacation in Thailand knows how ubiquitous Mama is. These packaged noodles come in a dizzying array of flavors that occupies an entire supermarket aisle, much like breakfast cereals in America. Thais consume them not because they don't know or can't afford better things to eat. They consume them because they love them.

What about Thais living in the United States? They love Mama, too. How much? We were all reduced to a bunch of sad orphans when Mama mysteriously disappeared from the shelves of many Thai grocery stores during the 2011 floods in Thailand. Those were dark days we'll be telling our children and grandchildren about for years to come.

Creamy tom yam noodle soup with shrimp

บะหมี่ต้มยำกุ้งน้ำข้น ❖ BAMI TOM YAM KUNG NAM KHON

14 ounces plain dried ramen noodles (dried squiggly noodles in square cakes)

8 cups homemade chicken stock (page 323) or store-bought sodium-free chicken stock

3 makrut lime leaves, lightly bruised and torn into small pieces

5 slices galangal, about ⅛ inch thick

1 large lemongrass stalk, cut into 1-inch pieces and bruised

1 (12-ounce) can evaporated milk or 1½ cups coconut milk

½ cup chile jam, homemade (page 22) or store-bought

½ cup fresh shrimp tomalley or faux river prawn tomalley (page 29; optional but recommended)

1 pound jumbo or colossal shrimp (U8 size), peeled and deveined

About ½ cup fish sauce

¾ to 1 cup fresh lime juice

Dried red chile powder (page 323), for seasoning

¼ cup coarsely chopped cilantro leaves and stems

¼ cup fresh sawtooth coriander leaves, cut crosswise into ½-inch-wide pieces (optional)

Lime slices

This recipe is a from-scratch version of a Mama soup (see page 221) variation Bangkokians love, a spin-off of the classic *tom yam* soup with shrimp with the addition of ramen. But just when you think it can't be any more inauthentic, there's more: the soup gets its creaminess from milk.

Over the past few decades, dairy products, which were once unimaginable in Thai cooking, have been slowly making their way onto local dinner tables. In an ideal—and idealistic—world, the creamy version of the classic *tom yam* is made with coconut milk, the only kind of milk Thai cooks used in the past and should be allowed to use in the present and future, as the gatekeepers of "authenticity" would tell you. Bangkokians know, however, that restaurants and street carts hardly share that sentiment.

This recipe is my minimalist adaptation of the creamy *tom yam* noodles with river prawns served at a famous Bangkok shop, where people regularly line up in the middle of the night for a table. It contains evaporated milk, which is what noodle-shop vendors all over the city—not just that specific shop—use. If you can't or won't have it, coconut milk is the option. ❖ **Serves 4**

Fill a 4-quart saucepan halfway with water and bring to a boil over high heat. Add the noodles and cook until al dente, 5 to 7 minutes. Drain into a colander and rinse under running cold water to remove the excess starch. Shake off the excess water and set aside.

Rinse out the saucepan, pour the stock into it, and bring to a boil over high heat. Add the lime leaves, galangal, and lemongrass, then immediately turn the heat to medium-low so the stock barely bubbles. Cover and steep for 2 minutes. Remove the herbs with a mesh skimmer and discard.

Stir the milk, chile jam, tomalley, and shrimp into the gently bubbling stock and cook until the shrimp turn opaque, about 2 minutes. Return the noodles to the pan and check the level of the liquid. If needed, add water (or stock) so the solids are covered by 2 inches; bring to a hard boil, then immediately turn off the heat. While the broth is steaming hot and before the noodles swell, quickly season the broth with the fish sauce, lime juice, and chile powder to taste. The broth should be primarily sour and then salty, with the sweetness coming from the chile jam, and it should be as spicy as your palate allows (this soup must be boldly seasoned to be good, so don't hold back on the seasonings).

Ladle the noodles and the broth into four large soup bowls. Divide the shrimp evenly among the bowls and top with the chopped cilantro, sawtooth coriander, and lime. Enjoy the soup while it is steaming hot.

Egg-wrapped glass noodle pad thai with shrimp

ผัดไทยวุ้นเส้นกุ้งห่อไข่ PHAT THAI WUN SEN KUNG HO KHAI

3 tablespoons packed grated palm sugar

2 tablespoons tamarind paste, homemade (page 316) or store-bought

2 tablespoons fish sauce

2 tablespoons homemade lard (page 28) or vegetable oil

2 tablespoons fresh shrimp tomalley or faux river prawn tomalley (page 29)

2 tablespoons pork cracklings (page 28)

3 large cloves garlic, minced

¼ cup finely chopped sweet preserved radish (see page 344)

2 tablespoons dried shrimp

4 ounces extra-firm tofu, cut into matchsticks

10 large shrimp, peeled and deveined

3 ounces glass noodles, soaked in room-temperature water for 15 minutes, drained, cut into 6-inch lengths, and blotted dry

½ cup cut-up Chinese garlic chives, in 1-inch lengths

¾ cup bean sprouts

4 eggs

2 tablespoons homemade lard (page 28) or vegetable oil

SIDES AND SEASONINGS

1 lime, halved lengthwise around the core

2 wedges trimmed banana blossom, 1 inch thick, soaked in acidulated water until serving, then drained and patted dry (optional)

1 cup bean sprouts, refreshed in cold water for 5 minutes, then drained and patted dry

4 Chinese garlic chives, each trimmed to 5 inches

Coarsely ground unsalted roasted peanuts

Fish sauce

Granulated sugar

Dried red chile powder (page 323)

Pad thai, a dish whose worldwide popularity began in Bangkok, is traditionally made with thin rice noodles. But this chewier glass-noodle version is also popular in the city. My recipe mimics the more rustic version of the classic, employing lard and cracklings and prawn tomalley, just as pad thai vendors did in the old days.

The egg crepes and the noodles are cooked in two different pans and the dish needs to be assembled as quickly as possible, so you'll need to have two pans, one preferably nonstick, on two burners at the same time. For the best result, look for the firmest tofu you can find, preferably one sold vacuum-packed rather than immersed in water in a plastic tub. ◆ **Serves 2**

To make the sauce, in a small bowl, stir together the palm sugar, tamarind, and fish sauce, dissolving the sugar as best you can. Set aside.

To make the noodles, put the lard, tomalley, and cracklings in a large wok or 14-inch frying pan and set over high heat. When the lard is hot, add the garlic, preserved radish, dried shrimp, and tofu and stir until the garlic is fragrant, about 1 minute. Add the large shrimp and stir until partially cooked, about 1 minute. Turn the heat to medium-high; add the noodles and the reserved sauce and stir until the noodles have absorbed all of the moisture and the large shrimp are thoroughly pink and opaque, 7 to 8 minutes. (The noodles should be soft but chewy; if they are too rubbery, add a little water as needed.) Stir in the chives and bean sprouts and immediately remove the wok from the heat.

To make the egg crepes, crack the eggs into a bowl and beat with a fork until homogenous. Heat 1 tablespoon of the lard in a second large wok or 14-inch frying pan, preferably nonstick, and set over medium heat. When the lard is hot, pour in half of the beaten egg and tilt the pan back and forth so the egg forms a thin, hole-free round about 12 inches in diameter. When the top of the egg sheet appears firm but still glossy, after about 1 minute, spoon half of the glass-noodle mixture onto an imaginary 4-inch square in the center. Using a heatproof rubber spatula, fold the two sides of the egg sheet over the noodle mound and then the top and bottom to form a square pocket. Press lightly on the seam to secure it. Using a large metal spatula, transfer the pocket, seam side down, to a dinner plate. If desired, cut a large X across the surface of the pocket and peel back the petals to reveal the noodles. Repeat with the remaining 1 tablespoon lard, beaten egg, and noodle mixture.

Serve the egg-wrapped noodles with the lime halves, banana blossom wedges, bean sprouts, and chives on the side of each plate. Advise diners to squeeze the lime over their noodles and help themselves to the seasonings on the table as desired.

Stir-fried angel hair rice noodles with water mimosa and shrimp

เส้นหมี่ผัดผักกระเฉดใส่กุ้ง SEN MI PHAT PHAK KRACHET SAI KUNG

2 cups cut-up trimmed water mimosa, in 2-inch pieces, or 8 ounces asparagus spears (about ⅓ inch in diameter), tough stem ends removed and cut on a 40-degree angle into 2-inch lengths, or 6 ounces samphire (whole)

1 tablespoon salt

6 ounces large shrimp, peeled and deveined

2 heaping tablespoons fresh shrimp tomalley or faux river prawn tomalley (page 29)

1 tablespoon fish sauce

1 tablespoon oyster sauce

¼ cup homemade chicken stock (page 323) or store-bought sodium-free chicken stock

4 teaspoons granulated sugar

3 tablespoons fresh lime juice

1 large fresh red Thai long, jalapeño, or serrano chile, seeded, deveined, and minced

2 fresh red bird's eye chiles, minced

2 tablespoons homemade lard (page 28) or vegetable oil

4 large cloves garlic, minced

4 ounces Wai Wai brand dried angel hair rice noodles, soaked in lukewarm water for 15 minutes, drained, patted dry, and cut into 6-inch lengths

Ground white pepper, for dusting

Water mimosa (*phak krachet*), a freshwater aquatic plant found throughout Southeast Asia and in South America, typically floats on the water's surface, supported by the white spongy tissue that gives buoyancy to its stems. Trimmed of the white sponge and pinkish roots, its shoots and tender stems are consumed both raw, as a relish crudité, and cooked, in sour curry and stir-fries. When prepared correctly—flash fried over high heat or ever-so-briefly cooked—*phak krachet* has a crunchy texture and uniquely irony flavor that are delicious, qualities that this noodle stir-fry shows off beautifully.

Fresh water mimosa grown in Florida sometimes shows up at Thai stores in large U.S. cities, but in areas where it cannot be found, asparagus is a good substitute. Samphire, also known as sea beans or sea asparagus, works well, too, though its naturally briny flavor tends to make salting the sauce tricky. When it comes to the noodle choice, however, there's no flexibility. Although many noodle dishes allow you to use any type of noodle, this dish stands with its arms akimbo and tells you only angel hair rice noodles (*sen mi*) will do. But even if tradition weren't a factor, I would tell you the same thing. These superthin noodles are the easiest to work with and the most eager to drink up the sauce without getting soggy or falling apart.

This recipe represents the flavoring and cooking method employed at two restaurants in the city, Je Ngor and So Nah Wang, whose noodle-mimosa stir-fries are unrivaled. Shrimp tomalley is so important to the success of this dish that I don't consider it optional. If you can't find it, my faux tomalley is an excellent stand-in. And if you want to serve more than two people, make the recipe in batches, rather than doubling it. ◆ **Serves 2**

Fill a 2-quart saucepan halfway with water and bring to a boil over high heat. Meanwhile, fill a large bowl with ice-cold water and set it near the stove. When the water boils, add the water mimosa (or asparagus or samphire) and blanch for 30 seconds, then transfer with a mesh skimmer to the ice water. Turn down the heat so the water is only steaming. Stir in the salt and shrimp, and when the shrimp appear half-translucent and half-opaque, transfer them to the same ice water. Drain both ingredients, shake off the excess water, and keep them on a plate near the stove.

In a bowl, stir together the shrimp tomalley, fish sauce, oyster sauce, stock, sugar, lime juice, and chiles. Set the sauce near the stove.

Heat the lard in a large wok or 14-inch frying pan over high heat. When the lard is hot, add the garlic and stir-fry until fragrant, 15 to 20 seconds. Using a rubber spatula, scrape every bit of the reserved sauce into the wok and boil very briefly just until the sugar melts. Immediately add the noodles and stir constantly until they have absorbed all of the sauce, with no moisture visibly sizzling anywhere. Stir in the blanched water mimosa and the shrimp and stir-fry just until the shrimp turn fully opaque and everything is heated through, about 1 to 2 minutes.

Divide the stir-fry evenly between two dinner plates, dust with pepper, and serve immediately.

Angel hair rice noodles with coconut sauce

หมี่กะทิ MI KA-THI

EGG RIBBONS

4 eggs

½ teaspoon salt

1 tablespoon homemade lard (page 28) or vegetable oil

COCONUT SAUCE

2 tablespoons fresh shrimp tomalley or faux river prawn tomalley (page 29)

4 ounces shallots, cut into ¼-inch dice

1 cup coconut cream

2 cups coconut milk

½ cup light salted soybeans (rinse and drain the beans, then mash to a semismooth paste)

4 ounces shrimp meat, coarsely chopped

4 ounces ground pork

¼ cup packed grated palm sugar

¼ cup tamarind paste, homemade (page 316) or store-bought

NOODLES

¼ cup fresh shrimp tomalley or faux river prawn tomalley (page 29)

1½ cups coconut milk

1 tablespoon liquid from red fermented tofu

½ cup canned tomato sauce (not ketchup)

8 ounces Wai Wai brand dried angel hair rice noodles, soaked in lukewarm water for 15 minutes, drained, patted dry, and cut into 6-inch lengths

4 ounces bean sprouts, refreshed in cold water for 5 minutes, then drained and patted dry

¾ cup cut-up Chinese garlic chives, in 1½-inch pieces

This is an old-school noodle dish that's becoming harder and harder to find in Bangkok. But what stings even more is that the most common rendition of it—the one often sold from street carts—is so poorly done. And that comes from someone with a relatively high tolerance for bad food.

Some cooks, whom I respect, season (and tint) their noodles with red fermented tofu, and some use tomato sauce. Some insist shrimp tomalley appear in the dish—in the noodles, in the sauce, or in both. To be safe, I've listed all three ingredients here according to the way this dish has always been made in my family. One thing everyone agrees on, however, is that the bright pink noodles (tinted with red food coloring) of the street version should not be tolerated.

Mi ka-thi means "coconut (rice angel hair) noodles," hinting at the importance of the coconut in this recipe. The scent of freshly extracted coconut milk is what takes this dish to a great height, so use it if you can. Otherwise, good-quality canned or boxed coconut milk without thickeners will do. ◆ **Serves 4 generously**

To make the egg ribbons, crack the eggs into a bowl, add the salt, and beat together with a fork until homogeneous. Warm the lard in a 12-inch frying pan (preferably nonstick) over medium heat, swirling the pan so the fat evenly coats the surface. Pour the beaten egg into the pan and tilt the pan back and forth so the egg forms a thin sheet that covers the bottom. When the top of the egg sheet looks fairly firm but is still glossy and the bottom of the sheet moves when you shake the pan, flip the egg sheet and immediately take the pan off the heat, allowing the residual heat to cook the egg further. Let cool, then slide onto a cutting board and cut in half. Roll up each half into a tight scroll and cut each scroll crosswise into ¼-inch-wide slices to form ribbons. Set the ribbons aside.

To make the sauce, combine the shrimp tomalley, shallots, and ½ cup of the coconut cream in a 2-quart saucepan and set over medium heat. Stir until the shallots are softened, about 2 minutes. Add the remaining ½ cup coconut cream along with the coconut milk, soybean paste, shrimp meat, pork, sugar, and tamarind and raise the heat to medium-high. Cook, stirring constantly to break up the shrimp and pork into ¼-inch chunks, until cooked through, 6 to 7 minutes. Remove from the heat and cover to keep warm.

continued

Angel hair rice noodles with coconut sauce, continued

GARNISH AND SIDES

1 large fresh hot red chile or ¼ red bell pepper, seeded, deveined, and cut lengthwise into ⅛-inch-wide strips (optional)

2 limes, halved lengthwise around the core

4 wedges trimmed banana blossom, 1 inch thick, soaked in acidulated water until serving, then drained and patted dry (optional)

4 ounces bean sprouts, refreshed in cold water for 5 minutes, then drained and patted dry

8 Chinese garlic chives, trimmed to 5 inches

To make the noodles, combine the tomalley, coconut milk, fermented tofu liquid, and tomato sauce in a 12-inch frying pan over medium heat. When the mixture boils, add the noodles and stir until all of the liquid has been absorbed, 2 to 3 minutes. Taste the noodles to see if they are too chewy. If they are, add water as needed and keep stirring until the noodles are soft but not soggy. Stir in the bean sprouts and chives, then immediately remove the pan from the heat. Let the noodles rest for 5 minutes to allow the residual heat to wilt the bean sprouts and chives.

To serve, divide the noodles evenly among four dinner plates. Top with the egg ribbons and then garnish with the chile strips. Arrange the lime halves, banana blossom wedges, bean sprouts, and chives around the noodles. Divide the coconut sauce evenly among four bowls and set a bowl next to each plate. Invite diners to spoon the sauce over the noodles and to add a squeeze of lime. Bites of banana blossom, bean sprouts, and chives are alternated with bites of the dressed noodles. The astringency of the sides helps balance the creaminess of the sauce.

Hand-rolled rice noodle soup with pork dumplings

เกี๊ยมอี๋น้ำหมูสับ KIAM I NAM MU SAP

HAND-ROLLED NOODLES

2 cups water

1½ cups Thai tapioca starch

½ cup Thai rice flour, plus more for dusting

½ cup Thai glutinous rice flour

½ teaspoon salt

2 tablespoons homemade lard (page 28) or vegetable oil

NOODLE SOUP

12 cups homemade chicken or pork stock (page 323) or store-bought sodium-free chicken stock

1 pound ground pork

1 tablespoon Thai thin soy sauce or Golden Mountain seasoning sauce

½ teaspoon ground white pepper, plus more for dusting

Fish sauce, for seasoning

2 tablespoons preserved cabbage

2 cups bean sprouts

1 large green onion, trimmed and thinly sliced crosswise

¼ cup packed cilantro leaves

2 tablespoons fried garlic (page 322)

2 tablespoons fried garlic oil (page 322)

TABLE SEASONINGS

Fish sauce

Granulated sugar

Pickled chiles in vinegar (page 317)

Dried red chile powder (page 323)

Jiam bi i or *jiam bi*, localized into the Thai language and most popularly known as *kiam i*, are Teochew-style noodles made by hand rolling dough into thin, round dumplings with pointy ends. In Thailand, the noodles are made with varying ratios of rice flour and tapioca starch that produce light and tender noodles that hold their shape in hot broth. These same noodles are often made with wheat starch (not to be confused with wheat flour) elsewhere in Southeast Asia, which yields a chewier noodle.

Hand rolling the noodles one at a time may sound like hard work, but you'll find that the dough is simple to make and easy to handle.

Serves 4

To make the noodles, put the water in a small saucepan, preferably one with a pouring spout, cover, and bring to a boil over high heat. You will not need all of the water, but it is better to have more than you need. While the water is heating, combine the tapioca starch, rice flour, glutinous rice flour, salt, and lard in a large bowl and stir until the lard is evenly dispersed. Get a sturdy wooden spoon ready. The moment the water comes to a full boil, remove the pan from the heat. With one hand, slowly pour the boiling water in a thin stream into the center of the flour bowl. At the same time, with the spoon in the other hand, stir the flour and water together briskly. Immediately stop adding water the moment you have a stiff, shaggy ball of dough that cleans the bottom and sides of the bowl. (If in doubt, err on the side of too little water, as you can always add more if the dough proves too dry.) Knead the dough lightly just to bring it together, then form it into a smooth ball and wrap it tightly with plastic wrap. Place it on the work surface, invert the bowl over it, and let rest for 20 to 30 minutes.

Divide the dough into four equal portions. Place one portion on the work surface and keep the remaining portions covered. Roll the dough into a rope ½ inch in diameter. If the dough becomes too sticky to shape, dust your hands and the work surface with rice flour (don't use tapioca starch or glutinous rice flour for dusting). Cut the rope crosswise into 1-inch pieces. Using your palm, gently roll each piece back and forth against the work surface to form an elongated dumpling-like noodle. It should be about 4 inches long and ¼ inch thick in the middle, with both ends gradually tapering into a sharp point. As the noodles are shaped, leave them uncovered on the work surface to allow their exteriors to dry out a bit. Repeat with the remaining dough portions.

continued

To make the soup, pour the stock into a 4-quart saucepan, cover, and bring to a boil over high heat. Meanwhile, in a bowl, combine the pork, soy sauce, and pepper and mix well. When the stock boils, turn the heat to medium. Using a pair of teaspoons, shape the seasoned pork into ½-inch dumplings and drop them into the simmering stock. When all of the dumplings float to the surface, season the stock with the fish sauce to taste (work quickly to prevent the stock from evaporating too much or you will end up with too little broth). Cover and turn the heat to the lowest setting to keep the soup broth steaming hot.

Fill a second 4-quart saucepan halfway with water and bring to a rolling boil over high heat. Line each of four large soup bowls with 1½ teaspoons of the preserved cabbage and set the bowls near the stove. When the water boils, add the bean sprouts and blanch for 20 seconds. Using a mesh skimmer, scoop out the bean sprouts, shaking off any excess water, and divide them evenly among the bowls. Lower the heat to medium-high, gently drop the rolled noodles into the water, and stir them once to keep them from sticking together. The moment the noodles float to the surface, scoop them out with the skimmer and drop them into the broth. Turn up the heat to high to bring the soup to a boil. The moment the liquid starts to bubble, turn off the heat. Ladle the soup into serving bowls.

Top with the green onion, cilantro, fried garlic, garlic oil, and a light dusting of the pepper. Serve with the table seasonings for diners to season their noodles to taste.

Wide rice noodles in fermented soybean broth with seafood

เส้นใหญ่เย็นตาโฟ **SEN YAI YEN TA FO**

CRUNCHY SQUID

8 cups water

2 cups food-grade lye water or ½ cup baking soda

1 whole dried squid (1 to 1½ ounces)

YEN TA FO SAUCE

3 large cloves garlic

3 tablespoons liquid from red fermented tofu

1 tablespoon red fermented tofu, mashed to a smooth paste

½ cup canned tomato sauce

2 teaspoons fresh juice from raw beets

2 tablespoons granulated sugar

1 tablespoon distilled white vinegar

1 teaspoon salt

NOODLE SOUP

3 quarts homemade pork or chicken stock (page 323) or store-bought sodium-free chicken stock

1 pound 1-inch-wide fresh flat rice noodles, homemade (page 330, formula 2) or store-bought

½ ounce dried white fungus, soaked in warm water for 30 minutes, drained, and cut into 4 pieces

4 (2-inch) cubes pork blood cake (optional)

8 fish balls, homemade (page 325) or store-bought

4 ounces fried fish sausage, homemade (page 326) or store-bought, thinly sliced

8 large shrimp, peeled and deveined

8 fried tofu puffs, halved

Pink isn't usually a color associated with food, especially a savory dish. But this noodle soup, as found on the streets of Bangkok, is as pink as they come, thanks to either red fermented tofu or, among less virtuous vendors, red food dye.

I make my own sweet-and-sour *yen ta fo* sauce at home, even though it is available in glass jars at most Thai grocery stores (an option you can choose, if you don't mind red food dye). The combination of red fermented tofu, tomato sauce, and beet juice that I use gives me everything I love about this pink noodle dish but with all natural ingredients. The beet juice makes the broth a darker shade of pink than what you'd normally see, but it doesn't affect the taste.

In Thailand, this soup traditionally calls for so-called crunchy squid, which is dried squid soaked in alkaline water to achieve a chewy yet crunchy texture. The squid is easy to find in Thailand but not in the United States, so I have instructions for making it here (look for the dried squid and the lye water in Asian markets). You will need to begin preparing it 5 days in advance of making the soup, or you can replace it with 8 ounces of fresh squid.

You will need to visit an Asian grocery store for the dried white fungus (also known as snow ear fungus or silver ear fungus), the tofu puffs, and the pork blood cakes. Look for the white fungus in cellophane packages in the dried foods aisle and for the deep-fried tofu puffs in the refrigerated section. Check the refrigerated section for the pork blood cakes, which usually come submerged in water in a plastic tub. ⬥ **Serves 4**

To make the crunchy squid, mix 4 cups of the water with 1 cup of the lye water or ¼ cup of the baking soda in a large nonreactive bowl. Add the squid, making sure it is fully submerged, and leave uncovered at room temperature for 2 days. Dried squid normally comes already cleaned and butterflied, so there's no need to gut it. If the skin is still intact, however, you want to peel it off with your hands; it should come off easily at this stage. Rinse the squid and discard the soaking liquid. Refill the bowl with the remaining 4 cups water and remaining 1 cup lye water or ¼ cup baking soda, add the squid, and leave to soak for another 3 days.

Remove the squid from the soaking liquid and discard the liquid. Rinse the squid thoroughly, scraping off any slimy mucus on the surface, and pat dry. Cut the squid into bite-size pieces. If you are using fresh squid, clean them,

continued

3 cups packed water spinach sticks, in 1-inch lengths

2 tablespoons fried garlic (page 322)

2 tablespoons fried garlic oil (page 322)

4 wonton skins, each folded in half to form a triangle and shallow-fried until crisp and golden brown

TABLE SEASONINGS

Pickled chiles in vinegar (page 317)

Dried red chile powder (page 323)

Granulated sugar

Fish sauce

slit the body of each one so it lies flat, score it on the "wrong" side in ¼-inch crosshatches, and then cut into 2-inch squares.

To make the sauce, combine all of the ingredients in a 1-quart saucepan and bring to a boil over medium heat, stirring constantly. Remove from the heat and set aside to cool.

To make the noodle soup, fill a 4-quart saucepan three-fourths full with water and bring to a boil over high heat. Put the stock in a second 4-quart saucepan and bring to a boil over high heat on another burner. Meanwhile, divide the cooled sauce evenly among four large soup bowls.

When the water boils, add the noodles and blanch just until heated through and softened, about 20 seconds. Using a mesh skimmer, scoop out the noodles, shaking off any excess water, and divide them among the four bowls. One at a time, blanch the fungus, squid, pork blood cubes, fish balls, fish sausage, shrimp, tofu puffs, and water spinach in the same way and divide them evenly among the bowls. When the broth comes to a boil, ladle it over the contents of the bowls. Top each bowl with the crispy garlic and garlic oil. Stick a fried wonton skin to one side of each bowl. Serve immediately with the table seasonings—everyone is going to need them.

On "Dry" Noodles

Noodle genres are clearly defined in Bangkok and in all of Thailand in general. And the demarcation lines that separate their territories are clear to the locals. It's understood that each shop specializes in a specific type of noodle or a family of noodles with common characteristics, and expectations are set accordingly. For example, you wouldn't walk into a boat noodle shop looking for stir-fried noodles with gravy, and you wouldn't walk into a *khanom jin* shop looking for egg noodles with barbecued pork.

Noodle soups in some form are common in nearly every corner of the world, and people innately know how to approach them. Dealing with stir-fried noodles or noodles topped with a sauce is also straightforward. But I have found that a subtype of noodle made according to Chinese Thai tradition—the noodles offered on nearly every street corner in Bangkok— seems to confuse many first-time visitors. "Dry" noodles are served with almost no seasoning, no broth, and, not counting some uncommon exceptions, no sauce except for the occasional light drizzle of sweet dark soy. What to do?

A bowl of these ubiquitous street noodles, which are generally referred to as *kuai tiao* (or *bami*, in the case of egg noodles) *nam/haeng* (noodles [that come] with/without broth), always starts the same way. The vegetable— usually bean sprouts—and the noodles of your choice are put into a small wire basket or mesh skimmer and blanched by dipping them into simmering water. The excess water is then shaken off and both ingredients are transferred to a bowl. A spoonful of garlic oil and a couple of glugs of fish sauce are mixed in immediately so the noodles won't clump up. Some preserved cabbage is usually added next, followed by the protein—meats or meatballs. A ladle of hot broth will go over everything at this point, if that's what you've specified earlier. If not—and let's pretend that's the case—those things are all you get. Then, with a light dusting of ground white (never black) pepper and a pinch of chopped green onion and cilantro on top, that bowl is complete and on its way to your table.

With a bowl of noodles before you, brothless and almost unseasoned, you know you must do something, so you reach out to the caddy of seasonings on the table. You add some more fish sauce to the bowl, and then, because you like it tart, you add a big spoonful of vinegar. You also want some sweetness, so you reach for the granulated sugar, and some crunch and creaminess, which a spoonful of ground peanuts will deliver. Finally, you want a little heat, and that's what the dried red chile powder is for.

With a short spoon in one hand and a pair of chopsticks in the other, you toss it all together—with ease because that spoonful of garlic oil does such a good job of lubricating everything. You taste your creation and then you keep adding a little bit of this and that until it doesn't need anything else. Your perfect bowl of dry noodles is ready.

Dry noodles are a noodle salad. Had the garlic oil and all the seasonings been mixed together separately and then drizzled onto the naked noodles, meat, and vegetables before everything was mixed together, the salad label would be more obvious. The Thais don't ever call a bowl of dry noodles a salad, reserving the term *yam* (salad) for traditional Thai salads. But the way dry noodles are handled and consumed is exactly that: a composed main-course salad that you, not the noodle chef, create the dressing for.

Jade noodles with barbecued pork

บะหมี่หยกแห้งหมูแดง BAMI YOK HAENG MU DAENG

12 ounces Chinese flowering mustard greens (yu choi sum)

2 pounds fresh jade noodles, homemade (page 332) or store-bought

¼ cup fried garlic oil (page 322)

2 tablespoons fried garlic (page 322)

1 tablespoon fish sauce

1 recipe "Red" barbecued pork (page 328) or 1 pound store-bought Chinese-style barbecued pork, thinly sliced against the grain into bite-size pieces

Ground white pepper, for dusting

2 tablespoons thinly sliced green onions

2 tablespoons coarsely chopped cilantro leaves and stems

TABLE SEASONINGS

Fish sauce

Granulated sugar

Pickled chiles in vinegar (page 317)

Dried red chile powder (page 323)

Ground unsalted roasted peanuts

I'll never forget the day my aunt, who had just completed her graduate studies in the United States, sat down to read me *Green Eggs and Ham*. But even better than the book itself was the special lunch she made after: green noodles and green "ham," with egg noodles tinted the color of dark jade with the juice of Chinese broccoli and barbecued pork dyed bright Kelly green.

For an adult, all-natural version of this, look for jade egg noodles (or just sub the regular yellow egg ones).

"Dry" egg noodles with barbecued pork and Chinese flowering mustard greens is among the most popular noodle dishes in Bangkok. The pok-pok of two bamboo sticks banged together outside the house gate—a Pavlovian bell of sorts—is a sound Bangkokians know well. It heralds the arrival of an itinerant tricycle vendor of egg noodles with barbecued pork who provides daily sustenance for anyone living deep inside the city's many labyrinthine alleyways.

This is a bowl of noodles I'd eat in a boat, with a goat, in a house, with a mouse, here and there—I'd eat it anywhere. ♦ **Serves 4**

Fill a 4-quart saucepan halfway with water and bring to a rolling boil over high heat. Grab a medium bowl and a large bowl and set them near the stove. Trim the tough stems off the mustard greens and cut the tender stems and leaves crosswise into 2-inch pieces. Loosen up the noodle strands.

When the water boils, drop in the greens and stir to submerge them. Blanch for 20 seconds, then fish them out with a mesh skimmer, shaking off any excess water, and transfer to the prepared medium bowl. While the water is still boiling, drop in the noodles and stir. If using store-bought noodles, cook for 40 to 50 seconds; for homemade noodles, allow 1 minute and a few seconds. Use a large mesh skimmer to fish out the noodles and then hold them under hot running water to rinse off the excess starch. Shake off all excess water and transfer to the large bowl.

Immediately add the fried garlic oil, fried garlic, and fish sauce to the noodles and mix well with a pair of chopsticks, shaking and loosening the noodle strands as you go, until the strands are thoroughly coated with the oil (work quickly so the noodles stay warm). Divide the noodles evenly among four large bowls. Arrange the blanched greens on one side of the noodles and the sliced pork on top and in the center of the noodle mound. Dust each bowl with the pepper. Sprinkle the green onions and cilantro on top. Serve with the table seasonings, inviting diners to season their noodles to taste—treating their bowl as a noodle salad that they can "dress" as they like. Toss well before enjoying.

Egg noodles with Hakka meatballs

บะหมี่แห้งลูกชิ้นแคะ BAMI HAENG LUK CHIN KHAE

MEATBALLS

4 ounces fatty ground pork, kept very cold

6 ounces shrimp, peeled and deveined, kept very cold

¼ cup Thai tapioca starch

1 egg white

¼ teaspoon salt

2 teaspoons Thai thin soy sauce or Golden Mountain seasoning sauce

¼ teaspoon ground white pepper

¼ cup thinly sliced green onions

6 tofu puffs (1-inch cubes)

6 extra-firm tofu cubes (1-inch cubes)

NOODLES

6 ounces bean sprouts, refreshed in cold water for 5 minutes, then drained and patted dry

2 pounds fresh egg noodles, homemade (page 332) or store-bought

¼ cup fried garlic (page 322)

¼ cup fried garlic oil (page 322)

¼ cup pork cracklings (page 28)

1 tablespoon fish sauce

3 tablespoons preserved cabbage

¼ cup thinly sliced green onions

¼ cup coarsely chopped cilantro leaves and stems

Ground white pepper, for dusting

TABLE SEASONINGS

Fish sauce

Pickled chiles in vinegar (page 317)

Granulated sugar

Dried red chile powder (page 323)

You won't find meat-stuffed tofu cubes in the style of the Hakka Chinese on every Bangkok street corner. Although the Hakkas are among the most prominent groups of Chinese in Bangkok, stuffed tofu is primarily served at home. And if you do see it for sale, it is usually in the form of dumplings—or "meatballs," as they are known in the city—in noodle dishes offered at Hakka-style noodle shops.

The meat can be fish, pork, or a combination of fish and shrimp and/or pork. The extra-firm tofu is the type that comes submerged in water in a plastic tub, not the dense type sold vacuum-packed. The deep-fried tofu puffs can be found in the refrigerated section at most Asian stores. Do not confuse them with Japanese tofu pouches, *aburaage*, which are great for sushi but won't work here.

Although worth the effort, this recipe is quite involved. That's unavoidable, however, as we're replicating the work of a professional noodle vendor who opens his shop each morning with hundreds of meatballs of various types already prepared and ready for swift assembly. Save this dish for a weekend when you have more time and you're having friends over for dinner. ◆ Serves 4

To make the meatballs, in a food processor, combine the pork, shrimp, tapioca starch, egg white, salt, soy sauce, and pepper and process until the mixture turns pale and is ultrasmooth and sticky. Use a rubber spatula to scrape every bit of the meat paste out into a bowl, then stir in the green onions, cover with plastic wrap, and refrigerate for 30 minutes.

Cut each tofu puff and extra-firm tofu cube in half. You should have a total of 24 tofu pieces each 1 by 1 by ½ inch. Using a teaspoon moistened with water, smear just enough of the meatball paste onto the cut side of each tofu piece to create a dome that rises about ½ inch above the tofu piece and reaches about halfway down its sides. The meat paste should cover the top part of the tofu cube snugly, like a bicycle helmet on your head. When you look at what is in your hand right now, it should have the size of the original tofu cube, except half of it is made up of meat paste. Continue until you have helmeted all 24 tofu pieces.

Bring water to a rolling boil in a steamer pot. Working in batches if necessary, steam the meatballs until the meat paste is opaque and firm, about 5 minutes. Cover and set aside. (Alternatively—and this helps add more textural contrast to the dish—you can deep-fry half of each type of meatball until golden brown and crisp. This way, you get both steamed and deep-fried dumplings in one bowl, which I love.)

To make the noodles, fill a 4-quart saucepan three-fourths full with water and bring to a boil over high heat. Drop the bean sprouts into the boiling water and blanch for 15 seconds. Using a mesh skimmer, fish them out, shaking off any excess water, and transfer them to a bowl. Blanch the steamed tofu meatballs and naked meatballs (not the fried ones, if you made any) in the boiling water for 30 seconds, just to reheat and refresh them, then transfer them to another bowl and keep warm.

Loosen up the noodle strands, then immediately drop the noodles into the boiling water, stir well, and cook until they are soft but still retain some chew, a little over 1 minute for homemade noodles and 40 to 50 seconds for store-bought noodles. Using a large mesh skimmer, fish out the noodles and then hold them under hot running water to rinse off the excess starch. Shake off excess water and transfer to a large bowl. Add the fried garlic, garlic oil, cracklings, and fish sauce and mix well with a pair of chopsticks, shaking and loosening the noodle strands as you go, until the strands are thoroughly coated with the oil (work quickly so the noodles stay warm).

Divide the bean sprouts evenly among six large bowls and top them with the preserved cabbage. Layer the noodles over them. Divide the meatballs evenly among the bowls, arranging them on top of the noodles. Top with the green onions and cilantro. Dust each bowl with the pepper and serve immediately with the table seasonings, inviting diners to season their noodles to taste.

Spicy thin rice noodle soup with pork and assorted fish balls

เส้นเล็กต้มยำ SEN LEK TOM YAM

SEASONINGS

¼ cup dried red chile powder (page 323)

¼ cup vegetable oil

¼ cup fish sauce

¼ cup fresh lime juice

4½ teaspoons granulated sugar

½ cup pickled chiles from pickled chiles in vinegar (page 317)

¾ cup ground unsalted roasted peanuts

NOODLE SOUP

3 quarts homemade chicken or pork stock (page 323) or store-bought sodium-free chicken stock

2 cups bean sprouts, refreshed in cold water for 5 minutes, then drained and patted dry

¼ cup preserved cabbage

1 pound dried thin rice noodles, soaked in warm water for 20 minutes and drained

¼ cup fried garlic oil (page 322)

4 tablespoons fried garlic (page 322)

4 tablespoons pork cracklings (page 28)

1 (6-ounce) piece boneless pork loin, boiled in water just until tender, drained, and thinly sliced against the grain into bite-size pieces

8 ounces fatty ground pork, scattered in simmering water, stirred to create separate grains, and drained

6 fresh sawtooth coriander leaves (better), finely cut crosswise, or ¼ cup packed cilantro leaves (good), coarsely chopped

Most noodle dishes arrive barely seasoned, leaving that step up to the diner. But *tom yam* pork noodle soup lands on the table brimming with salty, vinegary sour, citrusy sour, nutty, spicy, smoky flavors—in other words, ready to eat. Despite the appearance of *tom yam* on its name tag, this soup does not contain the lemongrass, galangal, and *makrut* lime leaves associated with the traditional Thai *tom yam*. Newer versions of this dish often come embellished with a coddled egg. If you'd like to offer them, put the eggs in a heatproof bowl and pour in boiling water to cover. After exactly 6 minutes, replace the hot water with ice-cold water to stop the cooking. ◆ **Serves 6**

To make the seasonings, combine the chile powder and oil in an 8-inch frying pan and set over medium-low heat. Fry, stirring constantly, until the chile turns dark brown (open the windows, as it will be smoky), 5 to 7 minutes. Transfer to a small heatproof bowl and let cool. Scoop out only the chile (reserve the oil for another use) and transfer it to a second small bowl. Add the fish sauce, lime juice, vinegar, sugar, chiles in vinegar, and peanuts and stir well. Taste the mixture to see if our tastes align. If not, adjust it to your liking. That said, this noodle soup is typically sour, followed by salty and sweet. Make sure the seasoning is strongly flavored, as you will be diluting it with the soup. Divide the seasoning evenly among six large soup bowls.

To make the soup, put the stock in a 4-quart saucepan and bring to a boil, covered, over high heat. Turn the heat to the lowest setting so the stock is steaming. Fill a second 4-quart saucepan three-fourths full with water and bring to a rolling boil. Add the bean sprouts to the boiling water and cook until tender-crisp. Using a mesh skimmer, scoop them out of the water, shaking off any excess water, and divide among the bowls with the seasonings. Keep the water boiling. Divide the preserved cabbage evenly among the bowls. Drop the noodles into the boiling water and cook, stirring constantly, until soft but still chewy, less than 1 minute. Drain the noodles into a colander, rinse under running hot water to remove the excess starch, and shake off any excess water. Working very quickly to keep the noodles from getting cold, transfer the noodles to a large bowl, add the garlic oil, and mix well with a pair of chopsticks, shaking and loosening the noodle strands as you go, until the strands are thoroughly coated with the oil (work quickly so the noodles stay warm). Divide the noodles evenly among the bowls. Top each bowl with 1 tablespoon each of the fried garlic and pork cracklings. Divide the pork slices and ground pork evenly among the bowls, arranging them on top. Top each bowl with equal amounts of the sawtooth coriander and green onions.

¼ cup thinly sliced
green onions

12 fish balls, homemade
(page 325) or store-bought

12 poached fish sausage slices
(page 326)

12 fried fish sausage slices
(page 326)

EMBELLISHMENTS

4 coddled eggs (see headnote;
optional)

4 wonton skins, each folded
in half to form a triangle and
shallow-fried until crisp
and golden brown (optional)

Raise the heat under the stock to high and bring to a rolling boil. Add the fish balls and simmer just long enough to heat through. Remove with the skimmer, shaking off any excess water, and divide them evenly among the bowls. Top each bowl with equal amounts of steamed fish sausage slices and fried fish sausage slices. Ladle the hot stock into each bowl. Crack a coddled egg into one side of each bowl, stick a fried wonton next to it, and then serve immediately. Invite diners to stir well before eating to disperse the seasonings at the bottom of their bowls.

Nautical Eats

Bangkok wasn't once dubbed the Venice of the East for nothing. Almost everywhere you now find roads, there used to be canals of all widths and lengths. And one of the most beautiful things the canals ever brought to Bangkokians is boat noodles.

The answer as to where the tradition of selling noodles out of a small paddle boat started is still debated. Some say it originated in the nearby province—once a powerful kingdom—of Ayutthaya. Others say it began in Rangsit, a town in Pathum Thani Province, north of Bangkok and south of Ayutthaya. Still others insist noodles had been sold from boats in Bangkok before anyone ever heard of boat noodles in either of those provinces. Thus far, no one has been able to provide anything other than anecdotal evidence.

What I do know is that boat noodles were in Bangkok long before I was born. When one of my paternal aunts built her house by San Saep canal in eastern Bangkok, as much as we were excited about her new house and the prospect of visiting her in that part of town, we were also excited about the prospect of sitting by the canal and eating noodles.

Around noon each day, a vendor would come by on a boat—a vehicle and a kitchen all in one. People in houses near the canal would flag him down, and he'd assemble noodles for them right from the boat. The diners would sit on the pier, eat noodles until they'd had their fill, and then leave behind stacks of empty bowls. One of my uncles could eat as many as thirty bowls in one sitting. Although I could never go beyond six bowls as a kid, thirty for an adult with a healthy appetite was not out of the ordinary.

This was because each bowl was tiny, barely big enough to contain food larger than a young kid's fist. Transported on a small boat and handed back and forth between the vendor (and table runner) on the boat and the customers on the pier, the bowls had to be that small. This also means that a bowl of boat noodles was devoured in no more than three polite bites.

That canal is no more, which is also true of many others in the city. And when the canals left, boat noodles went with them. These days, except in some old communities by the river in the suburbs or nearby provinces, the only boat noodles you get in Bangkok are made in a shophouse on land. The size of the bowls is the same as in the past, however, and the restaurant often has a decorative boat somewhere inside that serves as a symbol of life in the old days.

Boat noodles

ก๋วยเตี๋ยวเรือ **KUAI TIAO RUEA**

SPICE SACHET

1 teaspoon white peppercorns, coarsely cracked

1 teaspoon Sichuan peppercorns, coarsely cracked

1 teaspoon coriander seeds, coarsely cracked

2 star anise pods

3 (3-inch) cinnamon sticks, smashed into small shards

1 lemongrass stalk, smashed and then sliced thinly

4 or 5 slices galangal, ¼ inch thick, smashed

4 large cloves garlic, smashed

5 cilantro roots, smashed, or ½ cup coarsely chopped cilantro stems

BROTH

3 quarts sodium-free beef stock

2 pandan leaves, tied together into a knot

1 head Thai pickled garlic

1 tablespoon liquid from red fermented tofu

2 teaspoons dark salted soybean paste, mashed to a smooth paste

¼ cup coconut cream

1 tablespoon Chinese rice wine (shaoxing)

1 tablespoon Thai dark soy sauce

2 tablespoons distilled white vinegar

2 tablespoons crushed Chinese rock sugar or packed dark brown sugar

Thai thin soy sauce or Golden Mountain seasoning sauce, for seasoning

¾ cup beef blood (thawed if frozen)

This recipe comes from my uncle-in-law, a native of Ayutthaya Province, who has combined the typical Bangkok-style boat noodles (see page 248) with the seasoning practice of Ayutthaya-style boat noodles. It includes the addition of coconut cream, which helps keep the blood-thickened broth from curdling too much. He has also discovered that he likes to make humble boat noodles with well-marbled, tender, awfully expensive Wagyu beef, a version he has thought of calling "yacht noodles." And although we all sighed and shook our heads when we heard about his beef choice, we decided he was right after we tasted his boat noodles. A cut of good-quality tender beef works well here because it is blanched only briefly and, therefore, retains its natural sweetness.

One niche ingredient you'll need to seek out for this typical version of boat noodles is beef blood or pork blood. Both are sometimes available fresh or frozen in an Asian grocery store. Failing that, try a butcher shop specializing in European blood sausages, which should be able to direct you to a source.

This makes four supersize bowls. But if you'd like to split it up into several three-bite portions to experience Bangkok back when canals and waterways ruled, go ahead and do so. ⬥ **Serves 6**

To make the sachet, cut an 8-inch square of cheesecloth. Put all of the ingredients in the center of the square, bring up the corners to form a purse, and tie securely with kitchen string. Put the sachet in a 4-quart saucepan.

To make the broth, add the stock, pandan leaves, and pickled garlic to the saucepan, making sure the sachet is submerged. Bring to a boil over high heat, lower the heat to a simmer, cover, and cook for 15 minutes.

Meanwhile, to cook the solids, fill a second 4-quart saucepan three-fourths full with water and bring to a boil over high heat.

While waiting for the water to boil, remove the sachet, pandan leaves, and pickled garlic from the stock and discard. Add the tofu liquid, soybean paste, coconut cream, wine, dark soy sauce, vinegar, and sugar to the broth and stir well. Taste the broth, then add thin soy sauce to taste. Turn the heat to low to keep the broth steaming.

When the water boils, add the bean sprouts and water spinach and blanch for 10 seconds. Using a mesh skimmer, scoop out the vegetables, shaking off any excess water, and divide among four large soup bowls. While the water is still boiling, drop in the noodles and cook, stirring constantly, until

continued

SOLIDS

2 cups packed bean sprouts

2 cups cut-up water spinach tender stems and leaves, in 2-inch lengths

1 pound dried thin rice noodles, soaked in room-temperature water for 20 minutes and drained

3 tablespoons fried garlic (page 322)

2 tablespoons fried garlic oil (page 322)

3 tablespoons homemade lard (page 28)

½ cup pork cracklings (see page 28)

18 beef meatballs, homemade (page 324) or store-bought

1 pound well-marbled boneless beef (such as chuck steak or rib-eye steak) or tenderloin, very thinly sliced against the grain on a 40-degree angle into bite-size pieces

2 tablespoons thinly sliced green onions

2 fresh sawtooth coriander leaves, finely cut crosswise

1 tablespoon coarsely chopped cilantro leaves and stems

OPTIONAL SIDES

Store-bought fried pork rinds (seasoned with salt only)

Bean sprouts, refreshed in cold water for 5 minutes, then drained and patted dry

Fresh Thai sweet basil

TABLE SEASONINGS

½ cup dried red chile powder (page 323), fried over medium-low heat in ½ cup vegetable oil until the color of mahogany then cooled

Fish sauce

Granulated sugar

Pickled chiles in vinegar (page 317)

soft but still chewy, less than 1 minute. Drain the noodles into a colander, rinse under running hot water to remove the excess starch, and shake off any excess water. Transfer to a large bowl, add the fried garlic, garlic oil, lard, and cracklings, and mix well with a pair of chopsticks, shaking and loosening the noodle strands as you go, until the strands are thoroughly coated with the oil (work quickly so the noodles stay warm). Divide evenly among six large soup bowls.

Turn your attention back to the broth. Turn the heat to medium-high. Drop the meatballs into the broth and then add the beef, stirring to separate the pieces. When the beef is partially cooked with just a bit of pink remaining, less than 1 minute, using the skimmer, fish it out along with the meatballs and divide among the bowls. Turn the heat to medium-low. With one hand, slowly drizzle the blood into the broth while stirring with the other hand. Heat through only briefly without turning up the heat. Ladle the broth over the noodles in the bowls. Top with the green onions, sawtooth coriander, and cilantro and serve immediately with the sides and the table seasonings for the diners to add as they like.

Rice noodle rolls with pork in peppery broth

กวยจั๊บน้ำใส **KUAI JAP NAM SAI**

8 ounces dried kuai jap noodles (rice flakes)

1 (12-ounce) piece boneless pork loin

1 teaspoon salt

2 quarts homemade pork or chicken stock (page 323) or store-bought sodium-free chicken stock

2 tablespoons white peppercorns (no substitute)

2 teaspoons Thai thin soy sauce or Golden Mountain seasoning sauce

8 ounces store-bought Chinese-style roasted pork belly, homemade (page 318) or store-bought, cut into bite-size pieces

2 tablespoons cilantro leaves, coarsely chopped

2 tablespoons finely chopped green onions

1½ tablespoons fried garlic and its oil (page 322)

TABLE SEASONINGS

Fish sauce

Granulated sugar

Dried red chile powder

Pickled chiles in vinegar (page 318)

Anyone wandering at night on Yaowarat, the main street of Bangkok's Chinatown, is unlikely to miss Uan Pochana, a little shop directly in front of an old, sketchy theater. You can see throngs of people gathering around it from yards away, and whenever I have the chance, I stop by too.

I go there mainly to watch the man who runs this shop at work. He is the epitome of concentration. With the tasks of taking orders and running tables left to others, he never has to look up from his work counter, and he rarely does. In all of these years, I've never heard him say anything to anyone. There's something Jedi-like about the way he directs his mental energy and his focus to assembling bowl after bowl of noodles that I find inspiring. Maybe he's a Skywalker we haven't met, or maybe he just really likes making noodles.

But I also go there to eat his *kuai jap nam sai*, a clear soup of rice noodle rolls with pork and miscellaneous porcine parts popular with many Bangkokians. The version at Uan Pochana is deservedly famous, but it's also so peppery that my tongue goes numb, my throat gives out, and my whole body is reduced to a puddle of sweat after a few bites. At home, I make my own, less peppery *kuai jap*. But if you want to bring Uan Pochana into your kitchen, I suggest adding at least 1 tablespoon freshly ground white pepper, which is nowhere near the amount used there. If you take a few sips of the broth and you haven't thought about its extreme pepperiness, you haven't wondered if there might be a mistake in the recipe, and beads of sweat haven't formed on your forehead, you haven't added enough pepper.

Kuai jap noodles (often misleadingly referred to as "rice flakes") are about 2 inches square and are sold dried. As they cook, they elongate slightly and curl up into tight cigar-like rolls. These are not noodles you want to cook al dente or serve without broth. You want them swollen and soft and swimming in liquid. ♦ **Serves 4**

Fill a 4-quart saucepan halfway with water and bring to a boil over high heat. Add the noodles while stirring briskly, then stir nonstop for the first couple of minutes to keep the noodles separate as they curl into tight rolls. Boil for a total of 5 minutes, then turn off the heat. Cover the pan and leave the noodles to "bloom" in the hot water (don't worry; they won't overcook).

Meanwhile, place the pork loin and salt in a 2-quart saucepan and add water to cover by 1 inch. Bring to a boil, uncovered, over high heat. Lower the heat so the water is boiling gently and simmer the pork until it is cooked through, 8 to 10 minutes depending on the size and the thickness. Remove from the heat and, using a slotted spoon, transfer the pork to a plate. Cover and leave to cool. Don't throw out the cooking liquid just yet.

Put the stock in a 4-quart saucepan. Measure out 2 cups of the liquid in which you cooked the pork loin and strain it through a fine-mesh sieve into the stock. Cut a 4-inch square of cheesecloth. Coarsely crack 1 tablespoon of the peppercorns in a mortar and transfer them to the center of the cheesecloth. Bring up the corners to form a purse and tie securely with kitchen string. Drop the sachet into the stock and add the thin soy sauce. Cover the saucepan to minimize evaporation and bring to a boil over high heat. Turn the heat to the lowest setting and let the peppercorns steep for 15 minutes. Meanwhile, thinly slice the pork loin against the grain into bite-size pieces and grind the remaining 1 tablespoon peppercorns finely; set both aside.

Using a slotted spoon, scoop the warm noodles out of the saucepan, shaking off any excess water, and divide them evenly among four large soup bowls. Divide the pork belly and the pork loin into four equal portions and arrange them on top of the noodles. Discard the peppercorn sachet and ladle the hot broth over the noodles and pork in each bowl. Top each bowl with equal amounts of the cilantro, green onions, and fried garlic and its oil. Serve piping hot with the ground white pepper and the table seasonings for diners to season their noodles to taste, encouraging them to add as much ground white pepper as they can handle in order to experience the true taste of Bangkok Chinatown.

Crispy angel hair rice noodles with beef and Chinese broccoli stalks

เส้นหมี่กรอบราดหน้าเนื้อ SEN MI KROP RAT NA NUEA

MEAT

12 ounces boneless chuck or sirloin steak, very thinly sliced against the grain on a 40-degree angle into pieces about 3 inches long and 1 inch wide

1 tablespoon vegetable oil

1 egg white, lightly beaten

1 tablespoon Thai tapioca starch or cornstarch

1 tablespoon Chinese rice wine (shaoxing)

1 tablespoon Thai thin soy sauce or Golden Mountain seasoning sauce

½ teaspoon ground white pepper

¾ teaspoon baking soda

SAUCE

12 ounces Chinese broccoli with voluptuous stalks, or 16 stalks broccolini

4 cups homemade chicken stock (page 323) or store-bought sodium-free chicken stock

⅓ cup Thai tapioca starch (best) or cornstarch (okay)

2 tablespoons Thai thin soy sauce or Golden Mountain seasoning sauce

1 tablespoon Thai dark soy sauce

2 tablespoons oyster sauce

2 teaspoons granulated sugar

½ teaspoon ground white pepper

4 large cloves garlic, minced

Most of the rice noodles with gravy (*rat na*) in Bangkok follow the Teochew tradition, which translates to a light gravy with a sharp, briny, funky note of salted soybean paste. This recipe, however, is a clone of a popular dish served at Jak Kee, a noodle shop near the Victory Monument, in the Ratchathewi neighborhood, where the rice noodles lean toward the Cantonese tradition, with a more viscous gravy and the mellow, salty undertone of oyster sauce.

This signature dish comes with angel hair rice noodles (*sen mi*) deep-fried until crisp and then broken up and gathered into a mound in the center of a plate. They arrive topped with a thick, glossy sauce that includes velvety beef, tenderized with baking soda, and crunchy whole Chinese broccoli stalks, which you pick up with a fork and munch on in the manner of Bugs Bunny consuming a carrot.

Eating this plate of noodles requires a strategy: start from the outer layer of the mound and work your way toward the center. The outside has been cloaked with the gravy, so it's the first part to go soft. As you work your way in, the gravy gradually closes in on the interior. That's the beauty of Jak Kee crispy noodles with gravy; with each bite you get noodles in a different stage of crispiness. I can never get enough of this dish. ◈ **Serves 4**

To prepare the meat, in a bowl, combine the beef, oil, egg white, tapioca starch, wine, soy sauce, and pepper and mix well. Cover and refrigerate for at least 3 hours or up to overnight. About 30 minutes before you are ready to start cooking the recipe, knead the baking soda into the beef and let the beef come to room temperature.

To ready the ingredients for the sauce, trim the leaves off of the Chinese broccoli and keep them for other uses (you can leave some tender leaves at the top on, if desired, but the broccoli stalks at Jak Kee are typically served leafless). Slice about ½ inch off the tough end of each stalk and then trim the stalks to about 5 inches long. Each stalk should be about ⅓ inch thick. If they are thicker, split them in half lengthwise. If using broccolini, trim the tough stem ends if needed. In a bowl, whisk together the stock, tapioca starch, thin and dark soy sauces, oyster sauce, sugar, and pepper. Set aside.

To fry the noodles, pour the oil to a depth of 2 inches into a wok and heat to 350°F to 370°F. Line a sheet pan with paper towels and set it near the stove. While waiting for the oil to heat up, separate the noodles into eight small

continued

NOODLES

Vegetable oil, for deep-frying

6 ounces Wai Wai brand dried angel hair rice noodles

Ground white pepper, for dusting

TABLE SEASONINGS

Fish sauce

Pickled chiles in vinegar (page 317)

Dried red chile powder (page 323)

bunches. Turn on the faucet and give the noodles, a bunch at a time, a quick cold "shower" by running them through the water just long enough to moisten them. The shower should last no more than 4 seconds. Shake off any excess water and spread the noodles out on the counter. When the oil is hot, drop the noodles, a bunch at a time, into the oil and step back immediately to avoid the splattering, which will last no longer than 3 seconds. In just seconds, the noodles will puff up into a disk that covers the surface of the oil, crisp up, and turn a pale gold. Flip the disk once to ensure even cooking, then, when the bubbling quiets down, use a mesh skimmer to transfer the noodles to the prepared sheet pan. Repeat with the remaining noodle bunches. Each bunch should take less than 1 minute to cook.

When the last bunch of noodles has been fried, pour off all but about 2 tablespoons of the oil from the wok and set the wok over high heat. Now, return to the sauce and meat. Add the garlic to the hot oil and stir-fry until fragrant, 30 to 40 seconds. Add the beef and stir-fry until most of the pink is gone, about 3 minutes. Give the stock mixture a quick whisking (the starch will have settled on the bottom) and pour it into the pan, then add the broccoli and cook, stirring often, until the sauce thickens and turns glossy, 2 to 3 minutes. Check the consistency of the sauce; it should be viscous but pourable. If it's too thick, stir in a bit of water as needed. Remove the wok from the heat.

Divide the fried noodles evenly among four dinner plates. The noodles will be eight large, clunky disks. Use your hands to squeeze them, breaking them into ½- to ¾-inch pieces, and then form the broken noodles into a mound about 6 inches across and 1 inch high in the center of the plate. Ladle the sauce, beef, and broccoli stalks over the noodle mounds. Dust the top with pepper and serve immediately with the table seasonings.

Round rice noodles with beef stew and shrimp paste sauce

ขนมจีนไหหลำแห้งเนื้อ KHANOM JIN HAI LAM HAENG NUEA

2 pounds boneless beef shank, cut into 2-inch cubes

3 tablespoons Thai sweet dark soy sauce

2 tablespoons oyster sauce

2 (3-inch) cinnamon sticks

2 star anise pods

3 whole cloves

¼ cup Chinese rice wine (shaoxing)

1 tablespoon packed Thai shrimp paste

2 large cloves garlic

5 or 6 fresh bird's eye chiles

⅓ cup distilled white vinegar

1 teaspoon granulated sugar

1 (20-ounce) can whole bamboo shoots, rinsed, drained, and cut into bite-size pieces

1 pound dried Jiangxi rice sticks or 3 pounds fresh or frozen udon noodles

3 tablespoons cornstarch

¼ cup water

1½ teaspoons toasted sesame oil

6 ounces pickled mustard greens, rinsed, squeezed dry, cored, and thinly sliced

2 large green onions, thinly sliced crosswise

½ cup packed cilantro leaves

⅓ cup unsalted roasted peanuts, coarsely chopped

1 tablespoon white sesame seeds, toasted

Overshadowed by its exponentially more famous cousin, Poached Chicken on Rice with Soy-Ginger Sauce (page 217), this culinary gift from southern China has never enjoyed the limelight it richly deserves. Not many shops in Bangkok make it, and I can count on the fingers of a single hand the ones that make it well. I guess that's why many people—even some of the city's longtime residents—don't know it exists.

That's a shame. Of the many noodle dishes introduced to Bangkok by southern Chinese immigrants, this is my favorite. A dish of fat, chewy rice noodles under a blanket of succulent beef in a spiced soy-based sauce is already sublime, and a scattering of fragrant, crunchy toasted sesame seeds and crushed peanuts on top makes it even more memorable. But the pièce de résistance is the shrimp paste sauce on the side. It's the only table seasoning traditionally used with this noodle dish, and it's the only one you need.

This dish calls for fresh round rice noodles that measure just shy of ¼ inch thick when cooked. They are hard to find even in Bangkok, where all of the shop owners I spoke with told me they order them directly from a factory. Your best bet in the United States is to use fresh or frozen Japanese udon noodles (even though they are wheat noodles), which should be easy to find. But if you live near a large, well-stocked Asian store, look for Jiangxi rice sticks (*lai fan*) or *bún bò huế* rice sticks in the dried noodles aisle and cook them in boiling water as you would dried pasta. They are the best stand-in. ⚜ **Serves 4 generously**

Put the beef, soy sauce, oyster sauce, cinnamon, star anise, cloves, and wine in a 4-quart saucepan and add water so the liquid is flush with the beef. Cover the pan and bring to a boil over high heat. As soon as the liquid boils, stir the contents of the pan to mix well and then immediately lower the heat so the liquid is simmering gently. Cover and cook the beef for 3 hours. Check the liquid from time to time and replenish with water if needed to maintain the original level.

Meanwhile, to make a serving sauce, combine the shrimp paste, garlic, chiles, vinegar, and sugar in a small chopper or blender and process until smooth. Transfer the sauce to a small serving bowl and set aside. If you prefer a mellower flavor, transfer the sauce to a small saucepan and simmer it over medium-low heat for 1 minute before transferring it to the serving bowl to cool.

continued

After the beef has been cooked for 3 hours, stir in the bamboo shoots and enough water so the liquid is flush with the solids. Re-cover and cook at a gentle simmer for another 30 minutes, then check to see if the beef is ready. It should be tender but still hold its shape. If it is still a bit tough, cook for another 15 to 30 minutes.

Just before the beef is ready, cook the noodles according to the package directions, drain well, rinse under hot running water, and reserve.

Uncover the beef and check the amount of liquid. You now want to reduce the liquid to half of its original amount, so crank the heat to medium-high and bring the liquid to a boil. Working quickly, whisk together the cornstarch and water in a small bowl and stir the mixture into the stew. Cook, stirring constantly, until the liquid has reduced and is thick and glossy, about 1 minute. Remove the pan from the heat and stir in the sesame oil.

Quickly divide the pickled mustard greens evenly among four large bowls. Arrange the noodles on top, then ladle the beef stew over the noodles. Top with the green onions, cilantro, peanuts, and sesame seeds. Serve immediately with the shrimp paste sauce for diners to add to their noodles to taste.

Hot pot, Bangkok style

สุกี้หม้อไฟ ❖ SUKI MO FAI

MEATS

2 pounds tender, quick-cooking meats and/or seafood of choice (weighed after peeling)

12 to 16 fish balls, homemade (page 325) or store-bought

SAUCE

3½ cups Thai Sriracha sauce

2 tablespoons finely mashed red fermented tofu

1 tablespoon Thai thin soy sauce or Golden Mountain seasoning sauce

½ cup Thai oyster sauce or ⅓ cup Chinese oyster sauce

⅓ cup granulated sugar

¼ cup white sesame seeds, toasted and crushed just until broken up

1 tablespoon toasted sesame oil

½ cup packed finely chopped fresh sawtooth coriander

½ cup packed finely chopped cilantro (1 cup if sawtooth coriander is unavailable)

½ cup finely chopped garlic

Plump fresh bird's eye chiles, as many as you like, finely chopped

VEGETABLES

Napa cabbage, separated into individual leaves

Water spinach, trimmed of tough bottom ends

Chinese celery, trimmed of the roots and halved crosswise

Enoki mushrooms, trimmed of the roots and separated into tiny bunches

Fresh baby corn ears

Green onions, cut crosswise into 1-inch sticks

This recipe mimics the Cantonese-style hot pot served at MK, Bangkok's best-known hot pot restaurant. It's the place where I grew up eating hot pot and still do, even though many of the city's younger cool kids have moved on to newer, shinier spots.

Hot pot is fun, because it is a communal meal by nature. Diners sit around a table at the center of which is a shallow pot of broth simmering on a one-burner portable stove, electric or butane-fueled. All of the ingredients—still raw and fresh—are arranged on large platters by the cook who at this point can simply sit back and let his or her guests take over the cooking. Diners put what they want in a personal-size wire basket and dunk it in the broth, cooking it in just a few seconds, and transfer it to their personal soup bowl along with some hot broth. Using a pair of chopsticks, they dip the cooked morsels of food in the sauce in their personal sauce bowl, and enjoy them along with a few sips of the broth. This repeats until the food is gone, the broth is no more, and the conversation is dying down—a leisurely process that takes as long as they want it to.

To make the sauce, you need Thai Sriracha. Shark and Sriraja Panich are the two brands available in the United States that will work in this recipe, or you can make your own (see page 319). You can play around with the meats, vegetables, and other items, however. Quick-cooking cuts of beef such as tenderloin, sirloin, or rib-eye steak are good choices here, as are boneless chicken meat, pork loin or tenderloin, shellfish, and fish fillets. Quick-cooking and mild-tasting vegetables such as napa cabbage, Chinese water spinach, flowering mustard greens, and white mushrooms work well. What I've listed in this recipe are the foods most associated with hot pot in Bangkok. ❖ **Serves 4**

To prepare the meats, slice the meats as thinly as possible against the grain on a 40-degree angle into bite-size pieces. If using seafood, remove any inedible parts and cut as needed into bite-size pieces. Arrange the meats, seafood, and fish balls on a large platter, keeping them separate and leaving room for the eggs, which you will add later. Cover and refrigerate until serving.

To make the sauce, whisk together the Sriracha sauce, fermented tofu, Thai thin soy sauce, oyster sauce, and sugar in a 2-quart saucepan. Set over medium-high heat and bring to a gentle boil, whisking constantly. Remove from the heat, whisk in the sesame seeds and sesame oil, and

continued

MISCELLANEOUS

4 eggs

3 ounces glass noodles, soaked in room-temperature water for 15 minutes, drained, cut into 6-inch lengths, and blotted dry

1 pound jade noodles, homemade (page 332) or store-bought, cooked, drained, and lightly greased with some fried garlic oil (page 322)

8 ounces soft tofu, cut into 1-inch cubes

BROTH

4 quarts homemade chicken stock (page 323) or store-bought sodium-free chicken stock (you may not use all of it, but it's better to have more than you need on hand)

Thai thin soy sauce or Golden Mountain seasoning sauce, for seasoning

leave to cool. Once the sauce has cooled, stir in the sawtooth coriander and cilantro. Put the garlic and chiles in separate bowls for diners to add to their sauce to taste.

Assemble a nice selection of vegetables and arrange them on a large platter, keeping them separate, and set the platter on the table. Remove the platter of meat and seafood from the refrigerator. Set the eggs in the spot you have left for them and place the platter on the table. Arrange the noodles and tofu on a platter. Set each place at the table with a soup bowl, a small sauce bowl, a pair of wooden chopsticks, a soup spoon, a wire basket, and a small ladle.

To make the broth, pour the stock into a saucepan that's about 12 inches wide and 4 to 5 inches deep and bring to a simmer on a portable one-burner stove set in the middle of the dining table. Add just enough soy sauce to give it some flavor. Don't add too much, as the sauce packs a lot of flavor. Set the pot in the center of the table.

Divide the sauce evenly among the sauce bowls. Invite diners to tear the vegetables into bite-size pieces and, using a wire basket, dunk them into the simmering broth to blanch them, stirring with the tips of their chopsticks for even cooking. Do the same for the meats, seafood, and tofu. The noodles have already been cooked, so a quick dip into the broth is enough to revive them. The eggs can be cracked into a small bowl, beaten lightly with a chopstick, and drizzled into the simmering broth to create egg drops. Diners can also dip a piece of meat into the beaten eggs before blanching it in the broth to get a tender piece of blanched meat with a silky coating of eggs. The sauce is there to dip the cooked meats and vegetables in or to flavor the broth (with all the solids in it, of course), to taste, in each diner's individual bowl. There are no hard and fast rules when it comes to hot pot, however. Have fun.

Mussel fritters

หอยทอด HOI THOT

SAUCE

1 large fresh red Thai long or jalapeño chile or 2 serrano chiles, seeded and deveined

2 large cloves garlic

¼ cup distilled white vinegar

¼ cup water

3 tablespoons granulated sugar

1 teaspoon cornstarch

FRITTERS

¼ cup plus 2 tablespoons Thai rice flour

2 tablespoons Thai glutinous rice flour

3 tablespoons Thai tapioca starch

1 teaspoon baking soda

½ cup raw mussel or oyster juice or bottled clam juice

½ cup very cold water

½ teaspoon salt

¼ teaspoon ground white pepper, plus more for dusting

8 ounces shucked raw mussels, shucked raw oysters, or thawed, frozen shucked mussels

½ cup plus 1 tablespoon homemade lard (page 28) or vegetable oil

8 ounces beans sprouts, refreshed in cold water for 5 minutes, then drained and patted dry

3 eggs, lightly beaten

1 green onion, thinly sliced crosswise

2 tablespoons coarsely chopped cilantro leaves and stems

Hoi thot is often referred to as "mussel omelet," but I find that term misleading. When is the word *omelet* ever used to describe something that has more batter than eggs? This dish is more accurately dubbed panfried mussel fritters or pancakes.

When it comes to mussel fritters, you want to go old-school. Nowadays, many newer places turn out thin, crêpe-like, crisp, brittle mussel pancakes that readily break into shards (often because wheat flour–based tempura mix is used in the batter). But traditional—and in my opinion, the best—*hoi thot* is sticky and chewy on the inside and crisp on the outside—something you absolutely cannot achieve if you skimp on the frying fat.

Most specialized shops cook the fritters on a flat griddle or a large, round steel pan with a flat bottom. The parents of one of my best friends used to own a *hoi thot* shop, and in high school, I helped them out enough times one summer break to know how to work this large pan. So pull out your heaviest pancake griddle or large cast-iron frying pan seasoned so well that nothing sticks to it and use it. Lacking those options, your best bet is a frying pan at least 14 inches in diameter and as shallow as they come.

In Bangkok, *hoi thot* shops typically use shucked raw mussels. Their juice, when mixed with the batter, produces fritters with a sweet scent and a savory flavor. And since the mussels are cooked only briefly—in a light protective shroud of batter and eggs—they retain their natural sweetness, which adds to the overall flavor of the dish. These desirable attributes are greatly diminished if you start with cooked or frozen mussels. If you live where fresh mussels are unavailable, however, you can substitute bottled clam juice for half of the water in the batter, or you can replace the mussels with shucked raw oysters, which always come with their juice. Be sure to cut the oysters into pieces the size of a shucked mussel. ◆ **Serves 2**

To make the sauce, in a blender, combine the chile, garlic, vinegar, and water and puree until smooth. Strain through a fine-mesh sieve into a small saucepan, pressing hard against the solids with a rubber spatula to extract as much liquid as possible. Discard the pulp. Whisk the sugar and cornstarch into the strained liquid, making sure there are no lumps. Put the pan over medium heat and warm, whisking constantly, until the sauce has thickened and is glossy, 1 to 2 minutes. Thin it out with more water as needed to achieve the consistency of kefir. Transfer the sauce to a small serving bowl and let cool.

To make the fritters, in a bowl, whisk together both rice flours, the tapioca starch, baking soda, mussel juice, water, salt, and pepper until smooth. Stir in the mussels.

Grab two spatulas and two dinner plates and set them near the stove. Set a large griddle or frying pan over high heat and add 1 tablespoon of the lard. When the lard is hot, add the bean sprouts and stir-fry just until slightly wilted but still very crisp, about 20 seconds. Divide them evenly between the two plates. Wipe the griddle or pan clean and put it back on the burner over medium-high heat.

Add ¼ cup of the lard to the griddle or pan. When the lard is hot, give the batter one big stir and then pour it onto the hot surface into a circle about 10 inches in diameter. Use the spatulas to distribute the mussels evenly across the surface. When the fritter is crisp and brown on the bottom, 2 to 3 minutes, spread the eggs evenly over the surface and flip the fritter. It will probably break when you flip it, but that's to be expected. Distribute the remaining ¼ cup lard around the periphery of the fritter. Fry the fritter, flipping it as needed to cook the eggs, until it is crisp on the outside, 2 to 3 minutes.

Divide the fritter evenly between the plates, placing it on top of the bean sprouts. Dust each plate with pepper, then sprinkle with the green onion and cilantro. Serve immediately with the prepared sauce.

Sweets

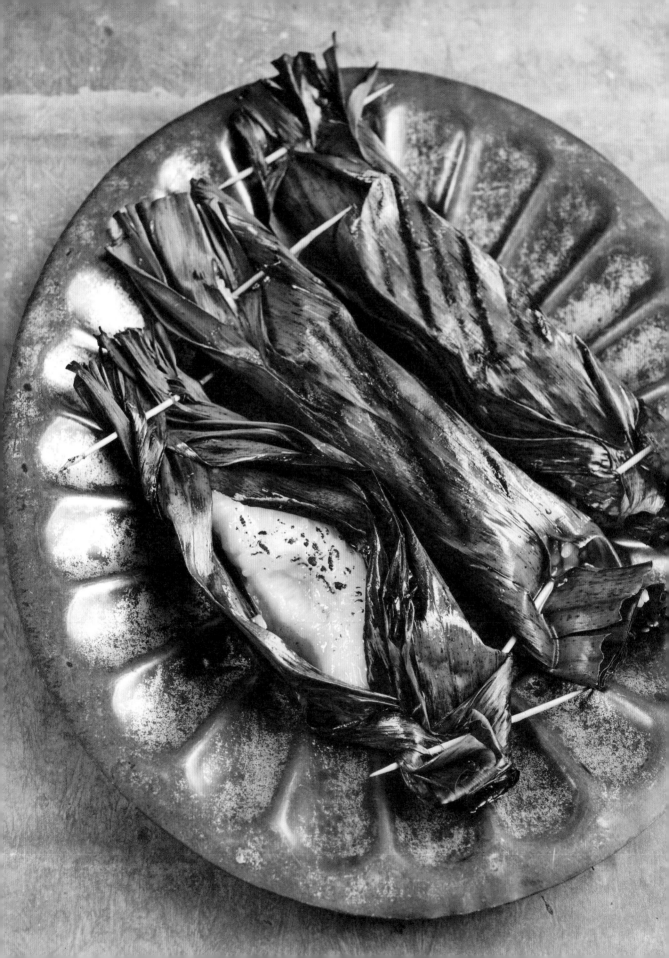

Grilled sweet sticky rice with banana filling

ข้าวเหนียวปิ้งไส้กล้วย KHAO NIAO PING SAI KLUAI

1¾ cups Thai white glutinous rice, rinsed until the water runs clear and soaked for 2 hours

¼ cup coconut cream

1 cup coconut milk

¼ cup extra-virgin coconut oil

⅓ cup granulated sugar

½ teaspoon salt

1 pound (about 12) banana leaves

6 fully ripe nam wa or Burro bananas (about 2½ ounces each), peeled and halved lengthwise

If while roaming the streets of Bangkok, you chance upon these banana-leaf packets on a grill, their contents hidden and their exteriors randomly singed and burned, do not turn away from them. Despite their rustic appearance, these delicious packets conceal warm, slightly sweet sticky rice richly perfumed with the smokiness of the charred wrapper and with a piece of soft, gooey *nam wa* banana at the center. In recent years, this common Thai banana cultivar has become easier to find in Asian grocery stores in the United States. It tastes sweet with a little tang and has a flavor redolent of—and this may sound odd but is true—pineapple and summer berries. Thai *nam wa* bananas have come to be synonymous with Burro bananas, and both can be used interchangeably, though in the United States the two are slightly different.

Banana leaves are usually sold frozen in large, flat packages at Asian or Latino stores. They need to be completely thawed and wiped down before being used. ❧ **Makes 12 packets**

Drain the sticky rice and steam it according to the instructions on page 18, stopping when it has barely turned glossy and is still dry (it will be cooked again), about 20 minutes. Remove from the heat.

While the rice is still hot, combine the coconut cream, coconut milk, coconut oil, sugar, and salt in a 2-quart saucepan and bring to a boil, stirring to dissolve the sugar. Remove the pan from the heat and stir in the hot sticky rice, making sure every grain is separate and coated with the coconut syrup. The mixture will appear soupy at this point, but don't panic. Cover the pan tightly and leave the rice undisturbed at room temperature for 1 hour.

Meanwhile, wipe the banana leaves clean with a damp cloth, then cut into 12 pieces each 12 by 10 inches, with the 10-inch side parallel to the leaf grain. Have ready 24 toothpicks.

After an hour, the rice will have absorbed the hot coconut syrup, cooled, and become firmer. At this point, it should be fully cooked but not soft, and tender enough to eat. Use a butter knife to divide it, directly in the saucepan, into quarters. Then divide each quarter into three equal wedges. Lay a piece of banana leaf, dull side up and with a long side facing you, on a work surface. Place a portion of the sticky rice in the center of the leaf. Use your fingers to form the rice into a flat, oblong bed parallel with the grain of the leaf. The bed should be about the length of a banana half and twice its

continued

width. Press a banana half firmly into the center of the rice bed. Using your fingers, gently fold the overhangs of the sticky rice over the banana half and manipulate it so it covers the banana entirely. With the banana leaf positioned in such a way that its grain is perpendicular to your body, lift up the left edge of the leaf and fold it along the grain over the filled sticky rice, tucking it in tightly. Continue to roll from left to right, forming a compact packet. Secure each end with a toothpick, positioned as close to the rice as possible. Trim off the overhangs, leaving only about 1 inch on each end. Repeat with the remaining banana leaves, sticky rice, and banana halves.

To grill the packets, light natural wood charcoal and allow it to burn until you have low coals under a heavy layer of ash. Grill the packets directly over the coals, flipping them every 5 minutes, until the leaves are thoroughly charred and the packets are heated through. This should take 35 to 45 minutes. Alternatively, place an oven rack in the lowest position in the oven and preheat the broiler (if your broiler is adjustable, set it at low). Arrange the banana packets on a large sheet pan, place the pan on the oven rack, and broil the packets, flipping them every 5 minutes, until the leaves are charred and the packets are heated through, about 40 minutes (fewer, if your broiler automatically sets at high).

Leave the packets to cool for about 15 minutes before serving. Leftover packets can be frozen, then thawed overnight in the refrigerator and baked in a preheated 350°F oven until softened and heated through, 30 minutes.

Tapioca and Thai muskmelon in iced coconut–palm sugar syrup

สาคูแตงไทยน้ำกะทิ SA-KHU TAENG THAI NAM KA-THI

2 cups water

½ cup uncooked tapioca pearls (the smallest type)

Grated palm sugar, for sweetening

1 cup coconut milk

½ teaspoon salt

2 cups packed cubed fully ripe Thai muskmelon or semiripe but very sweet cantaloupe or honeydew melon, in ½-inch cubes

1 cup crushed ice

The second quarter of each year marks the arrival of the hot season in Bangkok. Although it happens annually, even people who have lived in the city their entire lives shudder at the thought of it. The month of April is especially—to play it down—infernal. All anyone wants to do is take an ice-water bath and sit in front of an air-conditioner. Going outside? You won't want to wear anything more than just enough to avoid arrest. It is no wonder that when 60°F weather rolls around in December, the whole city bundles up in a winter coat and rejoices.

But the hot season is also when nature hands us durians, mangoes, mangosteens, marian plums, and many other fruits as a way of apologizing for turning on the heat full blast. Thai fruits are already excellent any time of year, but in the summer, they're incomparable.

One local fruit that peaks in the hot season but doesn't get much attention is the Thai muskmelon (*taeng thai*). The oblong melon has light green skin marked with yellow streaks and yellowish orange flesh similar in color to that of cantaloupe but with a more acidic than sweet flavor. *Taeng thai* may not suit everyone's palate, but when it is fully ripe and so soft and fragile that a hard stare could make it sob, it releases a unique, staggeringly fragrant scent. The Thais love it.

The more traditional sidekick of Thai muskmelon in an iced dessert like this one would be lemon basil seeds that have been soaked in water until they develop a translucent, mucilaginous covering, much like chia seeds. But in this recipe, I have paired this fragrant melon with cooked tapioca pearls. Either way, this is a cold, refreshing dessert that helps cool you down even if your summer is nowhere near as hot as a Bangkok summer. ◆ **Serves 4**

Put the water in a 1-quart saucepan, cover, and bring to a boil over high heat. Add the tapioca pearls and 1 tablespoon palm sugar and stir a couple of times to prevent clumping. Cover and lower the heat so the water is gently simmering. After 5 minutes, give the tapioca another stir, then re-cover and continue to cook until the tapioca pearls are translucent and the liquid becomes mucilaginous, about 5 minutes longer. Some of the white specks may remain inside the tapioca pearls even when the pearls are fully cooked. To be sure the tapioca is ready, taste a small spoonful. The pearls should be completely soft and chewy with nothing hard and gritty at the center. (If not, stir in more water, 2 to 3 tablespoons at a time, and simmer gently until the pearls are soft.)

continued

Add the coconut milk and salt to the tapioca and stir to combine. While the mixture is still warm, add more palm sugar to the pan, 1 tablespoon at a time and tasting as you go, until the mixture tastes like syrup. Keep in mind that you will be adding ice to the mixture, so you need to add more sugar than you think prudent, as the ice will melt into the soup and dilute it.

Once the taste suits you and the sugar has fully dissolved, let the tapioca cool to room temperature. Divide the tapioca mixture evenly among four dessert bowls (large enough to hold twice the volume of each portion), then divide the melon and crushed ice among the bowls. Stir everything together and serve. Let the ice melt a little before taking the first bite.

Sour mango and salty palm sugar caramel dip

มะม่วง-น้ำปลาหวาน   MAMUANG-NAM PLA WAN

3 or 4 dried bird's eye chiles, stemmed

1½ cups packed soft, sticky, dark pure palm sugar from Thailand, or ¾ cup each packed grated light, hard palm sugar and packed dark brown sugar

¼ cup water

¼ cup fish sauce

1 teaspoon packed Thai shrimp paste

3 tablespoons dried shrimp, soaked in hot water until softened, squeezed dry, and ground into fine, cottony flakes

2 ounces shallots, halved lengthwise, placed cut side down, and cut lengthwise into paper-thin slices

1 pound sour green mangoes, peeled, cut lengthwise into slices ¼ inch thick and kept covered and chilled

You can't wander more than a couple of blocks in any busy pedestrian area in Bangkok without seeing at least one fruit cart filled with all kinds of peeled and trimmed seasonal fruits resting on large blocks of ice. You just point at what you want and the vendor will chop it up, put it in a plastic bag along with a couple of bamboo skewers and a small packet or two of chile-salt-sugar dip, and hand it to you.

But the pairing of green mango and salty palm sugar caramel dip is in a class of its own. This snack has sour, salty, sweet, and spicy all in one perfect ensemble. The fish sauce and dried shrimp up the ante, contributing a funky umamic element to that classic foursome.

The best mangoes to use here are the sour green mangoes that are rock hard, so hard you can squeeze them with all your might and they won't give. These mangoes can be found at Southeast and South Asian grocery stores (do not use the green-red type). Any tart, crisp fruits, such as Granny Smith apples, work well, too. I've even come to prefer them over mangoes these days. ⚜ **Makes 1½ cups caramel dip; serves 4**

Toast the chiles in a small frying pan over medium heat, stirring often, until brittle, about 2 minutes. Set aside.

Combine the sugar, water, fish sauce, and shrimp paste in a 1-quart saucepan and set over medium heat. Stir until the sugar has melted and the shrimp paste has dissolved, about 2 minutes. Continue to boil for 1 minute longer, then remove from the heat. Stir in the dried shrimp and shallots and let cool to room temperature. The dip will thicken slightly as it cools. If it is stickier and thicker than maple syrup, which means it is not good for dipping, thin it with warm water as needed.

Scrape the dip into a small serving bowl and crumble the toasted chiles on top. Serve with the mango slices.

Lychees in iced syrup with young ginger and green mango

ส้มฉุน SOM CHUN

2 ounces very young ginger (best) or mature ginger (okay)

½ small sour green mango (from an 8-ounce mango)

1 (1-ounce) shallot, halved lengthwise, placed cut side down, and cut lengthwise into paper-thin slices

3 tablespoons vegetable oil

1 cup granulated sugar

1 cup flower-scented water (page 23) or plain water

¼ teaspoon salt

36 fresh lychees, peeled and pitted

3 cups crushed ice

Although this iced dessert has been around for longer than a century, you will likely find it only in homes where traditional Thai food has been made for generations or in one of the few restaurants that offers time-honored dishes. The flavor combination here seems unusual. The idea of pairing sweet lychees and tart green mango in iced syrup with slivers of young ginger already sounds strange. But when crispy fried shallots are added to the mix, beads of nervous perspiration usually form on folks' foreheads. But of the many Thai iced desserts I have tried, none is more elegant, refreshing, or delicious than this one.

The sweet-and-sour marian plum that appears in markets during Bangkok's hottest months is my first choice for this dessert. But other sweet and slightly tart tropical fruits, such as pineapple and rambutan, also work well. In the United States, I've used fresh strawberries and navel or blood orange segments, and I've been pleased with the results. Lychees seem to be the most popular choice, however, so I've decided to use them here. ◆ **Serves 6**

Peel the ginger and cut lengthwise on a slight diagonal into paper-thin slices about 2 inches long. Stack the slices and then cut lengthwise into whisker-thin strips. (If you use mature ginger, follow the same procedure, then rinse the strips in cold water until the water runs clear, and squeeze them dry.) Put the strips in a small bowl, cover, and refrigerate until serving. Peel and cut the mango the same way, then place in a separate bowl, cover, and refrigerate until serving.

Line a small plate with a paper towel and set near the stove. Put the shallot slices and the oil in an 8-inch frying pan and set over medium heat. When the shallot slices are sizzling, turn the heat to medium-low and cook, stirring almost constantly, until the slices are light brown and crispy, about 10 minutes. Using a slotted spoon, transfer the shallots to the prepared plate. Discard the oil or reserve it for another use.

Combine the sugar, water, salt, and lychees in a 2-quart saucepan and set over high heat. Stir just until the sugar and salt have dissolved, then remove from the heat and let cool.

Spoon the cooled lychees and syrup into six dessert bowls. Divide the ice evenly among the bowls and stir just to combine. Top with the ginger slivers, green mango slivers, and crispy shallots. Serve immediately. Advise diners to stir together all of the components before enjoying.

Steamed bread with dipping custard

ขนมปัง-สังขยา KHANOM PANG-SANGKHAYA

COCONUT DIPPING CUSTARD

3 egg yolks

1 tablespoon plus 2 teaspoons cornstarch

¼ cup granulated sugar

½ cup coconut milk

½ cup evaporated milk or half-and-half, plus 2 tablespoons for topping (optional)

2 tablespoons pandan juice concentrate (page 337)

6 cups cubed soft white sandwich bread, in 1½-inch-thick slices, steamed until warm, and cut into 1½-inch cubes just before serving

I was first introduced to this Bangkokian classic at On Lok Yun, a near century-old coffee shop in Phra Nakhon District. It's at old Chinese-style coffee shops like this where Bangkokians, especially those from my grandparents' and parents' generations, went for an all-day breakfast of hot coffee with condensed milk, fried or coddled eggs with Maggi seasoning sauce and a dash of ground white pepper, ham, panfried cocktail franks, and, yes, this combo of impossibly soft white bread and creamy, fragrant custard.

But *khanom pang-sangkhaya* isn't a breakfast-only item. You can enjoy it throughout the day at mall food courts or old-school coffee shops across the city. Night markets, including Chinatown, also offer it well into the late night hours. In other words, you can enjoy it any time.

Makes 1½ cups custard; serves 4

To make the custard, combine the egg yolks, cornstarch, sugar, coconut milk, ½ cup of the evaporated milk, and pandan juice concentrate in a 1-quart saucepan and whisk until smooth. Set the pan over medium heat and cook, whisking constantly, until the custard thickens to the consistency of sour cream, 5 to 6 minutes. Transfer to a bowl, cover, and let cool to slightly warmer than room temperature.

Drizzle the remaining 2 tablespoons of evaporated milk on top of each bowl and serve with the bread cubes, hot off the steamer.

Thai Tea Variation

Mix 2 tablespoons of unsweetened Thai tea powder with 6 tablespoons boiling water and leave to cool. Strain, pressing out every bit of liquid, and measure out 2 tablespoons to use in place of the pandan juice concentrate.

Twin crullers

ปาท่องโก๋ PA THONG KO

500 grams (4 cups)
all-purpose flour, plus more
for dusting

15 grams (1 tablespoon)
vegetable oil

¼ teaspoon active dry yeast

30 grams (2 tablespoons plus
1 teaspoon) granulated sugar

4 grams (¾ teaspoon) double
acting baking powder

8 grams (1¾ teaspoons)
baking ammonia powder

2 grams (½ teaspoon)
alum powder

20 grams (3½ teaspoons) salt

2 grams (½ teaspoon)
baking soda

350 grams (1½ cups) water,
at room temperature

Vegetable oil, for deep-frying

Sweetened condensed milk
or warm coconut dipping
custard (see page 279),
for serving

In the early 1800s, Siam exported a variety of goods to China by sea: teakwood, rice, ivory, tin, and spices. On the way back, the junks carried goods from China, such as silk, pearls, gold, silver, and satin fabric—all products high in value but low in weight. Beautiful stone statues from China were used as ballasts to stabilize the ships in heavy seas. These old stone statues (*ap chao*) are now used to decorate various historic places in Bangkok, including the Grand Palace and the Temple of Dawn (Wat Arun).

A stone lioness that now overlooks the Chao Phraya from an obscure corner of the prestigious Thammasat University came to Siam in exactly that way. But she didn't come alone. She came with a male companion, a lion. But when her ship was sailing along the Chao Phraya, approaching its destination, a storm broke out and the ship sank. Once the storm died down, the people who lived by the river dove into the water to retrieve the sunken ship and the goods it carried. While the lion vanished into the far reaches of the river, the lioness was found in the wreckage and placed in its current spot. Legend says that the sounds of a lioness wailing for her mate can be heard on some nights.

Not everything that has come from China gets separated, however. These crullers always come in pairs, and the pairs pair well with others. You can dip them in sweetened condensed milk or dipping custard (page 279), you can tear them into pieces and eat them with rice soup (page 186), or you can enjoy them with a mug of hot soy milk for breakfast. And if you should hear wailing at any time while eating them, that's me crying out for another plate of *pa thong ko*. Since the goal here is to create light and crisp crullers with airy pockets inside—never bready or dense—you absolutely need a reliable scale. There is no room for error, so measuring by volume will not do. You will also need alum powder (potassium aluminum sulfate), which is found in the spice aisle of most groceries, as well as baking ammonia—don't worry, the smell fades as the dough sits—which is often found at stores specializing in Middle Eastern and/or Greek ingredients. **Makes 24 pairs**

In a large bowl, combine the flour, the oil, yeast, sugar, baking powder, ammonia, alum, salt, baking soda, and water and mix with a wooden spoon just until combined. The dough will appear dimply and disturbingly wet, but don't panic. Cover the bowl tightly with plastic wrap and leave at room temperature for 10 to 12 hours.

continued

Dust a work surface lightly with all-purpose flour (keep about 1 cup around, though you're probably not going to use all of it). Using a rubber spatula, scrape every bit of the dough out of the bowl onto the floured surface. Divide the dough in half (a kitchen scale comes in handy here). Form each half into a ball. The dough will be sticky, and you will need to dust your hands with flour and maybe add more flour to the work surface. The key to creating the desired open texture of the finished crullers is to keep the dough as wet as possible, however, which means you don't want to disturb the hydration level by using more flour than is absolutely necessary to shape it. Cover the dough with an overturned bowl and let rest for 20 to 30 minutes.

Using your hands and a dough scraper, flatten and shape each dough portion into a rectangle of even thickness that is exactly 4 inches wide and 12 inches long. Use the dough scraper to cut each rectangle crosswise into 12 strips, each 1 inch wide. Then cut the 12 strips in half crosswise. You should have a total of 48 dough strips. Fill a small bowl with cold water and keep the bowl and a chopstick or a spoon with a long, thin handle handy.

Pour the oil to a depth of 2 inches into a wok or Dutch oven and heat to 350°F. Set a cooling rack on a sheet pan (or line the sheet pan with paper towels) and place it near the stove.

Using the water and the chopstick (or spoon handle), lightly moisten the center of a dough strip, covering about ½ inch. Put a second strip of dough on top of the first strip, aligning them. Press them together at the moistened area. Pick the formed cruller off of the work surface by its ends, stretch it out gently so it is 2 inches longer, and then carefully lower it into the hot oil. Assemble an additional three or four crullers the same way and fry them in one batch, flipping them around almost constantly. The oil temperature will drop to 325°F to 340°F; keep it in that range. You need to fry the crullers for a full 3 minutes for them to cook all the way through and develop honeycomb-like holes inside. If you let the oil get too hot, the crullers will burn before they are ready, so monitor the temperature closely. After 3 minutes, the crullers will be golden brown and crusty. Using a mesh skimmer, transfer them to the cooling rack. Repeat the forming, stretching, and frying with the remaining dough strips.

Serve the crullers warm with sweetened condensed milk. Leftover fried crullers can be refrigerated in an airtight container for a couple of days and warmed in a preheated 350°F oven until heated through. Reheated crullers won't be restored to their just-made glory, of course, but they will still be good.

Coconut rice pudding cakes

ขนมครก KHANOM KHROK

BATTER

½ cup raw long-grain white rice, preferably Thai jasmine, soaked in water for 5 to 6 hours and drained

1 cup Thai rice flour

1 cup limestone solution (page 336)

1 cup full-fat coconut milk

¼ cup granulated sugar

¼ teaspoon salt

TOPPING

¼ cup Thai rice flour

1 cup coconut cream

1 cup full-fat coconut milk

3 tablespoons granulated sugar

½ teaspoon salt

About ¼ cup extra-virgin coconut oil, for greasing the pan

OPTIONAL ADD-INS

¾ cup finely sliced green onions (green parts only), cooked corn kernels, or steamed but firm finely diced kabocha pumpkin, or ¼ cup of each

If you make a Venn diagram of traditional Thai desserts and things made from coconut milk, sugar, and rice, you may get something close to a perfect circle. This speaks not of repetitiveness—far from it. It's actually a testament to the creativity of Thai cooks in concocting myriad distinct snacks and desserts from these three locally available ingredients. Most resplendent among such creations are *khanom khrok*. They're what I eat nearly every day when I'm in Bangkok, what I look forward to when I'm about to return to Bangkok, and what I think about when I lie awake in the middle of the night missing Bangkok.

But the thought of this street snack also makes me sad for the good old days. I miss how the coconut rice pudding cakes of my childhood were made in a clay pan over charcoal. I miss how the cakes picked up a hint of smoke from the burning coals. I miss how they were transferred from the hot clay pan to the to-go container of fresh banana leaves and how the heat from the cakes lightly steamed the leaves, causing them to release a sweet, tea-like fragrance. These days, nearly every vendor makes these pudding cakes in a cast-iron pan over a gas burner and serves them in a Styrofoam box. The cakes are still quite good, but the nostalgia factor is largely gone.

This snack isn't difficult to make at home, but you do need a special pan. A cast-iron or nonstick Danish pancake (*æbleskiver*) pan works well, as does a Japanese pancake (*takoyaki*) pan. Both pans are widely available in the United States at specialty cookware stores or online. They have half-spherical hollows that are a tad deeper than those of a *khanom khrok* pan, so the cakes take slightly longer to cook. No matter what type of pan you use, make sure its diameter is the same as the diameter of your stove burner to ensure every hollow receives equal heat. ♦ **Makes 48 small cakes, each about 1¼ inches in diameter and ¾ inch deep**

To make the batter, combine all of the ingredients in a blender (preferably high speed) and process until perfectly smooth. Check carefully to make sure there are no lumps or grit. Transfer the batter to a bowl and set aside.

To make the topping, in a second bowl, combine all of the ingredients and whisk until smooth. Set aside.

Keep a 1-tablespoon measuring spoon and a 1-teaspoon measuring spoon handy. You'll be using them to ladle the batter and the topping into the cake pan. I don't recommend eyeballing amounts or using spoons that aren't

continued

measuring spoons. The amount of batter and of topping that goes into each cake must be exact to achieve the intended ratios of crisp, soft, and gooey and sweet and salty. The batter yields 3 cups (48 tablespoons), and the topping yields 2 cups (96 teaspoons). Each cake should consist of 1 tablespoon batter and 2 teaspoons topping. Keep this ratio as a guide if you need to make adjustments to accommodate the type of pan you are using.

Set the pan (see headnote) over medium-high heat and heat until hot. To test if it is hot enough, splash a tiny drop of water into a hollow. If the water drop jumps around and quickly evaporates, the pan is ready. Brush some oil over the entire surface of each hollow. Use the 1-tablespoon measuring spoon to give the batter a stir, then ladle 1 tablespoon of batter into each hollow, filling it about three-fourths full. Slowly tilt the pan back and forth a few times so the batter coats the entire interior of each hollow all the way to the rim. You want some of the batter to attach itself to the sides long enough to form a lacy, delicate edge as the remainder trickles back down to the bottom. Cover the pan and cook until the surface of each cake turns opaque around the edges but still looks undercooked, 3 to 5 minutes depending on the depth of the hollows. Use the 1-teaspoon measuring spoon to give the topping a stir, then ladle 2 teaspoons of topping into each hollow, filling them. Cover and cook until the topping is no longer runny but still jiggles slightly when the pan is shaken, about 2 minutes. You can leave the cakes plain or you can add about ½ teaspoon of one of the optional add-ins on top of each cake. Using a spoon with a thin, pointed bowl or a butter knife, gently pry the cakes out of the hollows and transfer them to a platter to cool slightly and set into soft, quivering pudding inside. Repeat until you run out of both the batter and the topping. Before cooking each batch of cakes, remember to grease the hollows with the coconut oil and to stir the batter and the topping (the flour will sink to the bottom of the bowls). Enjoy the cakes while they are still warm and the shells are still crisp.

The Kudi Chin Community

It's amazing how a quick ride on the Chao Phraya Express boat can take you from the bustling, congested business districts of Silom and Sathon to a quaint pier on the west bank of the river where you find yourself in a tranquil world—a world that you can hardly believe still exists in the city.

Following the fall of the former capital of Ayutthaya in 1767, descendants of the Siamese who married the Portuguese workers living among them moved into this part of Thonburi and established a village now known as the Kudi Chin community. Located not too far from the famous Temple of Dawn, this quiet slice of Bangkok is older than the city itself by roughly two decades. Fortunately, it has somehow managed to escape the talons of gentrification since its founding.

Many things make the Kudi Chin community a charming place to visit, such as the Victorian "gingerbread" architecture. But what Bangkokians love most about this old Portuguese Thai village are its little sponge cakes, which are known as *khanom farang kudi chin*, literally "foreigners' treat(s) from the Kudi Chin community."

Santa Cruz Church is at the heart of the community, both spiritually and physically, and the small wooden pavilion that stands near the front of the church is a favorite spot of mine. I often go to sit there by myself just to clear my head, as I watch the boats pass by. On a breezy day, the unmistakable scent of freshly baked cakes from Lan Mae Pao, one of the community's oldest bakeries, permeates the air.

What makes the Kudi Chin cakes interesting is that the local bakers bake them the same way their ancestors did, in an "oven" powered by hot coals. The batter is baked in small, hand-forged, fluted tart pans that sit on a bed of hot gravel set above the coals that act as the heat regulator. A thin sheet of aluminum is set on top of the pans, and then hot coals are placed on the aluminum. Because of this inspired setup, the little cakes come out evenly browned and crisped on all sides.

Why the small tart pans? Why not just pour the batter into one large cake pan? The anatomy of these small, round, spongy cakes is important. Each one measures 1 inch thick and about 3½ inches in diameter. Smaller ones are about 2 inches in diameter. I finish a larger one in exactly four bites and a smaller one in two bites. With each bite, I get the perfect ratio of crunchy sugar-strewn top, crisp and crackly exterior—enhanced by the fluted edges—and light, fluffy, moist interior. That's the beauty of the Kudi Chin cakes.

Kudi Chin sponge cakes

ขนมฝรั่งกุฎีจีน **KHANOM FARANG KUDI CHIN**

3 tablespoons unsalted butter, melted

¾ cup all-purpose flour

½ teaspoon baking powder

¼ teaspoon salt

½ cup granulated sugar

3 duck eggs (preferably), or 3 whole chicken eggs plus 1 egg yolk (to mimic the fattiness of duck eggs), at room temperature

2 teaspoons fresh lime or lemon juice

1 teaspoon vanilla extract

⅓ cup raisins or a mixture of raisins and thinly sliced dried persimmons (traditional) or dried mangoes (good)

The fact that these sponge cakes are best enjoyed fresh out of the oven cannot be overstated. If you need to store them for later, however, wrap the cooled cakes individually with parchment paper or plastic wrap, and place them in an airtight container. Stored this way, the cakes will keep at room temperature for 24 hours, in the refrigerator for 7 days, or in the freezer for 3 months. Just before eating them, reheat them briefly in the oven or toaster oven at 350°F, just until the exteriors have regained their signature crispiness.

This recipe calls for baking the cakes in fluted aluminum tartlet pans with bottoms measuring 2 inches across and flared sides, the type used for baking Hong Kong–style egg tarts. I have chosen them because they're the easiest to find and they yield cakes that are similar in appearance to true Kudi Chin cakes. **Makes eighteen 2-inch cakes**

Position an oven rack at the very bottom of the oven and a second rack in the upper third of the oven. Preheat the oven to 350°F. Arrange 18 fluted tartlet molds with flared sides, each 2 inches in diameter at the bottom, on a sheet pan and brush the bottoms and sides generously with the butter.

In a bowl, stir together the flour, baking powder, and salt. Set aside. Set 1 tablespoon of the sugar aside. Put the remaining sugar, the eggs, and the lime juice in the bowl of a stand mixer fitted with the balloon attachment. Beat on high speed until the mixture turns pale yellow and doubles in volume. When you lift the beater, the mixture should fall slowly from it and form a ribbon-like pattern on the surface that stays for at least 3 seconds before dissolving. Gently stir in the vanilla.

Sift the flour mixture, one-third at a time, into the egg mixture, folding in each addition with a large rubber spatula before adding the next. Do not overmix. Divide the batter evenly among the prepared tartlet molds.

Place the sheet pan on the bottom rack and bake the cakes for exactly 2 minutes. Open the oven door and, without removing the pan from the oven, gently (so as not to deflate the batter) decorate the tops of the cakes with the raisins and then sprinkle the reserved sugar evenly over the tops. Close the oven door and continue to bake for another 5 minutes. Move the pan from the bottom rack to the top rack and continue to bake until the tops of the cakes are golden brown and the centers spring back when lightly pressed with a fingertip, about 10 minutes longer.

Remove the cakes from the oven and leave to cool in the molds for 5 minutes before unmolding. Using the tip of a knife, gently pry the cakes out of the molds and transfer them to a cooling rack. Let cool completely before serving.

Golden threads

ฝอยทอง FOI THONG

1 cup egg yolks (from about 10 duck eggs or 12 chicken eggs)

1½ cups granulated sugar

1½ cups flower-scented water (page 23) or plain water

2 fresh or frozen pandan leaves, folded and tied together into a knot (optional)

You can't talk about Thai desserts without mentioning Maria Guyomar de Pinha, known as Thao Thong Kip Ma among the Siamese in the Ayutthaya period. Although details are scarce, it's generally believed that this Portuguese Japanese woman, who lived from the mid-1600s to the early 1700s, was responsible for creating and popularizing hybridized Portuguese Thai desserts, most of them egg based, in the royal palace. Many of these desserts are still made and enjoyed widely today.

One of the most notable among those egg-based desserts is golden threads, in which thread-thin strands of egg yolk are cooked in sugar syrup. It has become part of the family of gold-colored desserts that Thais serve at auspicious events as a symbol of prosperity and good fortune.

The *foi thong* made by cooks in modern-day Thailand is very sweet. I've had its Spanish and Portuguese counterparts and neither is anywhere near as sweet as the Thai version. This is something to be enjoyed in small bites and sparingly—perhaps with a cup of hot jasmine tea.

To make these egg threads, you'll need a *foi thong* dispenser, a cone-shaped tool with two tiny openings at the point, or a homemade substitute: using scissors, snip a tiny corner, no more than 1 millimeter wide, off of a 1-quart resealable plastic bag. ◆ **Makes 12 ounces; serves 4 to 6**

Ready a large, double-layered square of cheesecloth or muslin. Run the egg yolks through the finest-mesh sieve you have into a bowl. Use a rubber spatula to push the yolks through the mesh and to scrape away what oozes out on the other side. Pour the sieved yolks onto the center of the cloth, gather up the corners to form a bag, then squeeze hard to force the yolks out through the cloth back into the bowl. (Do your best not to lose too much volume during the double straining.)

Place a large plate, a wooden chopstick, and a *foi thong* dispenser (see headnote) near the stove. Put the sugar, water, and pandan leaves in a wide braising pan or saucepan and bring to a rapid boil over high heat, stirring to dissolve the sugar. Lower the heat to medium so the liquid still bubbles but not as vigorously. Transfer the yolks to the *foi thong* dispenser, stopping the flow with a finger. Remove and discard the pandan leaves. Remember the current level of syrup in the pan, as you will need to maintain this level throughout the process.

continued

Holding the dispenser over the pan, let the yolks flow into the boiling syrup in a thin, continuous circular stream twenty times around the edge of the pan, then stop the flow with your finger. Using the chopstick, scoop up the egg threads from the pan, shaking off the excess syrup, and fold them into a neat skein on the plate. Repeat until you have used all of the egg yolks. Along the way, the level of the syrup in the pan will reduce and the syrup will become too thick. This is because some of it has been lost through evaporation and some has left the pan along with the finished egg threads. You will need to add more water to maintain the original level.

You should have about 24 (½-ounce) skeins. Once cooled, the golden threads can be enjoyed right away or stored in an airtight container in the refrigerator for up to 2 weeks. Strain the cooled syrup and use it for other purposes. Enjoy these supersweet delicate threads in small amounts.

Baked custard with fried shallots

ขนมหม้อแกงไข่ **KHANOM MO KAENG KHAI**

¼ cup fried shallot oil
(page 322)

1 cup packed grated
palm sugar, or ¾ cup packed
dark brown sugar

2 tablespoons Thai rice flour

6 eggs plus 3 egg yolks
(preferably duck eggs)

1½ cups freshly extracted
coconut cream (if using
canned coconut milk,
use ¾ cup coconut milk
with ¾ cup water)

½ teaspoon salt

2 fresh or frozen pandan
leaves

¼ cup fried shallots
(page 322)

Even though the custard has become synonymous with Petchaburi Province, a center of palm sugar production south of Bangkok, this dessert originated in the Chao Phraya basin, most likely in the 1600s Portuguese kitchens of Ayutthaya. It is a classic example of a Western dessert, an egg-based custard, and a Western technique, baking, meeting local Thai ingredients, coconut and palm sugar. We don't know if fried shallots were used in the early versions of this dish, but a traditional rendition made today always includes this savory element.

Khanom mo kaeng literally means "dessert [or pudding] [made in] curry pot," which suggests that it was made in a clay pot in the old days. Based on remnants of the primitive ovens still used in Bangkok's Kudi Chin community of Portuguese Thais and in some rural areas in Thailand, it's likely the dessert was "baked" with hot coals both underneath the pot and on its lid to cook and brown the top and the bottom.

In modern-day Thailand, this custard is baked in a small, shallow square pan. In a home oven, I've found the custard turns out best if it is baked in a water bath, which ensures a better texture, and then broiled to brown the top. This is especially true with this version, which is eggy rather than starchy. This recipe is best made with freshly extracted coconut cream. But if that is not an option, the best substitute, counterintuitively, is the milk underneath the cream layer in a can or a box that is thinned out further with water. ⬩ **Serves 6**

Position an oven rack in the lower third of the oven and preheat the oven to 300°F. Grease the bottom and sides of an 8 by 2-inch round (or a 7 by 10 by 2-inch rectangular) glass or ceramic baking dish with 2 tablespoons of the shallot oil. Place the dish inside a 9 by 13 by 3-inch glass or ceramic baking dish. Put a fine-mesh sieve inside the smaller pan.

Fill a small saucepan, preferably with a spout, with about 4 cups water and bring to a boil over high heat.

Meanwhile, combine the sugar and flour in a bowl and stir until well blended. Crack the whole eggs into the sugar mixture, then add the egg yolks, coconut cream, and salt. Tie the pandan leaves together into a knot and add them to the bowl. Mix everything with your hand, incorporating as little air into the mixture as possible (don't be tempted to use a fork, a whisk, or, even worse, an electric mixer). The best way to do this is to grab a handful of the mixture, including the pandan knot, and make a tight fist,

continued

squeezing it so hard that the liquid oozes out of your grasp. Keep doing this for a few minutes until no egg whites are visible and the mixture is evenly colored. (If you are not used to doing this, the mixture will feel cold and icky in the beginning. But by the end, something inside you will be a little sad that it's over so soon.) Squeeze every bit of the batter out of the pandan knot and discard the knot.

Using a rubber spatula, scrape the batter into the sieve over the prepared baking pan. Don't shake the sieve. Instead, use your hand or the spatula to press and smear the egg mixture against the mesh until all that is left in the sieve are tiny specks of egg white that refuse to break down any further. Place the baking pan on the oven rack. By this time the water in the saucepan should be ready. Pour the water into the large baking pan to come halfway up the sides of the smaller pan. Bake until the custard is just set and the center still ever so slightly jiggly when the pan is shaken, about 1 hour and 15 minutes.

Brush the top of the custard with the remaining 2 tablespoons shallot oil. Turn off the oven, leaving the custard in the oven, and turn on the broiler. Broil with the oven door open wide, rotating the water pan almost constantly, until the top of the custard is thoroughly golden, 2 to 3 minutes. If the surface of the custard bubbles and domes during the broiling, puncture the bubbles with the tip of a knife and press out the air. (Otherwise, the domed parts will burn before the rest is properly browned.) Remove the large baking pan, with the custard still in it, from the oven. Sprinkle the fried shallots on top and leave the custard to cool in the water bath to room temperature before cutting it into six slices and serving.

Sweet roti

โรตีหวาน ROTI WAN

1 recipe roti dough (page 335), aged in the refrigerator for 48 hours, then brought to room temperature

About ½ cup ghee or vegetable oil

¼ to ⅓ cup sweetened condensed milk

4 teaspoons granulated sugar

Crisp, flaky, slightly chewy, sweet, gooey, sandy—you get all of these sensations at once when you bite into freshly made roti prepared the classic way: drizzled with sweetened condensed milk, sprinkled with sugar, and rolled up into a loose scroll.

To create the desired texture and to make stretching possible, you need to age the dough for 48 hours. This allows it to develop both flavor and gluten. I find this aspect of roti making more important than the theatrical swinging, stretching, and slapping of the dough that professional roti makers do. That's fun to watch, of course, and it serves a purpose, but an average person would need months of doing nothing but swinging and stretching dough to master the technique.

You can achieve the same result by stretching roti dough the way the Austrians stretch their strudel dough: on the table. It makes for a painfully boring party trick, but it gets delicious roti into your mouth in minutes instead of months. Different roti vendors in Bangkok have different ways of shaping their roti. The one I've recommended here is the easiest of all. ◆ **Makes 4 roti**

Put a roti dough ball in the middle of a large work surface, making sure it is surrounded by at least 6 inches of empty space on all sides. Using a rolling pin or the heel of your palm, flatten the dough into a 4-inch round of even thickness. Gently stretch the dough as thinly and as evenly as possible. The easiest way to do this is to pull from the center and work your way toward the edges, pressing the edges down against the work surface to secure the initial stretch, then stretching again until you have a large, paper-thin round (the edges will be slightly thicker than the middle, but as long as they are no more than ¼ inch thick, don't sweat it). The round should be 15 to 18 inches in diameter. Leave the dough there for now.

Heat 1 tablespoon of the ghee in a 10- to 12-inch frying pan over medium heat. When the ghee is hot, quickly fold all four edges of the stretched dough toward the middle to form a roughly 5-inch square. Holding the square by the top corners, quickly lay it, seam side down, in the hot frying pan. Fry, pressing down the dough with a spatula as you go, until golden brown on the underside, about 2 minutes. Flip the square and fry, adding another 1 tablespoon of ghee to form a shallow pool of oil (not to keep the roti from sticking to the pan, but to ensure flakiness), until the second side is golden brown, about 2 minutes longer. Transfer to a plate, seam side up. Drizzle about 1 tablespoon or slightly more of the condensed milk evenly over the surface and sprinkle with 1 teaspoon of the sugar, then roll up the roti like a yoga mat. Repeat with the remaining dough, condensed milk, and sugar. Enjoy while still warm and crisp.

Durian ice cream

ไอศกรีมทุเรียน AI-SA-KRIM THURIAN

5 egg yolks

1½ cups whole milk

½ cup granulated sugar

2 tablespoons tapioca syrup or light-colored honey

2 tablespoons Thai tapioca starch or cornstarch

¼ teaspoon salt

2 teaspoons light rum

1 cup heavy cream, kept chilled

¾ cup very soft, fully ripened fresh or thawed, frozen durian pulp, pureed until smooth and kept chilled

1 (3-ounce) package strawberry-flavored gelatin dessert, prepared according to the package instructions, poured into a shallow mold, cut into 1-inch cubes, and kept chilled

Durian isn't called the king of fruits for nothing. Every year when the hot season lets up and the rain falls more frequently, countless cultivars of the thorny monarch flood Bangkok's markets. And Bangkokians fall to their knees.

As durian fanatics will tell you, there's nothing like fresh durians, especially straight from the orchard. And when durians are at their most voluptuous, freshest, and sweetest, eating them out of hand is the only option that makes sense.

Frozen durians, on the other hand, require a strategy. They're the only option I have during the months I'm not in Bangkok. All of the durians I've seen at Asian stores in the United States, even those that look like they have just been picked, always show signs—obvious to all certified durian aficionados—of having been frozen and then thawed.

But a frozen durian has its uses, too. One of the ice cream pioneers of Bangkok, especially durian ice cream, is Lieo Lieng Seng (Ratchawong 555), an old shop specializing in Teochew cuisine. Although it long ago moved out of its original location in a historic corner of Chinatown, I still occasionally visit its new location to enjoy the food and to relive the memories of the meals I had as a kid with my parents—meals that always ended with a scoop of rich, smooth durian ice cream with a piece of strawberry gelatin on the side. That's the Bangkok style of serving ice cream that is as old-school as it gets.

This is my own take on durian ice cream. It has a tiny bit of rum, which not only doesn't compete with or cancel out the aroma of durian—the whole point of it all—but elevates it. The alcohol also helps prevent iciness. ◆ **Makes 1 quart**

Fill a large bowl with ice and water and nest a 2-quart stainless-steel bowl in the ice bath. Whisk the yolks together in a bowl that can hold twice the volume of the yolks. Set both bowls near the stove.

Combine the milk, sugar, tapioca syrup, tapioca starch, and salt in a 2-quart saucepan and set over medium heat. When steam begins rising from the surface but the mixture has not come to a boil, with one hand, pour half of the hot milk mixture into the yolks while whisking constantly with the other hand. Use a heatproof rubber spatula to scrape every bit of the yolk mixture back into the saucepan, then cook over low heat, stirring and scraping the sides and bottom of the pan constantly with the spatula. When the mixture is thick enough to coat the spatula, after about 20 minutes, scrape it into the stainless-steel bowl. Stir until the mixture cools to room temperature. Stir in the rum, cream, and durian puree, then strain the custard through a fine-mesh sieve into an airtight container with a lid. Cover and refrigerate for 8 to 10 hours.

Transfer the chilled custard to an ice cream maker and freeze according to the manufacturer's instructions. Transfer the ice cream to an airtight container and freeze until firm, at least 2 hours. Serve the ice cream with the strawberry gelatin. Any leftover ice cream will stay fresh in the freezer for up to 2 weeks.

The GFB

You can't judge a book by its cover. You can't judge a street vendor by her outward demeanor, either. Thanks to GFB, I learned this early on.

When I was a grade school student in Bangkok, I would spend my weekends at my maternal grandparents' house. As part of an effort to reinforce the English that I was learning in school, Grandpa decided that on each visit, he and I would walk together to a nearby newsstand to buy the weekend issue of a local English-language newspaper that included two crossword puzzles, one for people like Grandpa, who possessed advanced English skills, and one for children like me. On the way back, we would always get a bag of assorted fried snacks to eat (Grandpa claimed that the crackly sounds you hear in your head when you munch on something crunchy make it easier to solve crossword puzzles, and who was I to think otherwise?). We would then spend Saturday afternoons working on our respective puzzles while snacking.

I barely remember now what the newsstand looked like, and the memories of working on those crossword puzzles have also faded with time. But my recollection of the fried-snack stand, Grandma Fried Bananas, as they called the old woman who ran it, and of what I witnessed there remains vivid.

I don't remember when or why I started using the initials GFB to refer to this famous fried-banana street vendor. I'm pretty sure it wasn't because I was too lazy to say or write out the words in full. Maybe it was because on some level I was afraid of saying her name—you know, like Voldemort. After all, I'd never seen a street vendor as fearsome as GFB. Then again, I'd never seen such a tiny stand with so many customers waiting in line to buy, either.

GFB was one fine cook. All of her snacks were perfectly seasoned and fried. Everything went into hot oil; none came out oily. Everything looked plain; none tasted anything but extraordinary. There was always an extra layer of flavor, a spicy, herbaceous element that I was only able to identify much later as the quintessential Thai seasoning paste of garlic, white peppercorns, and coriander roots. GFB's sweet potato fritters were the best I'd ever eaten. Each stick had an impossibly crisp exterior and a warm, starchy, mildly sweet interior that was worth every bit of anxiety I felt as I waited in line.

GFB's stand was proof that a business can be successful in the absence of customer service. She wasn't there to be your buddy, and she made it clear you knew that. Every day, she would stand there, wielding her deadpan aloofness as if it were a sword. And every day, people would line up, eager to be stabbed with it just so they could leave with a bag of her taro fritters, corn and shrimp fritters, sweet potato fritters, banana fritters, fried tofu, or curry puffs.

My grandfather was one of those people who couldn't live without GFB's fried snacks. He had learned the ropes years earlier, so by the time I came on the scene, he was well versed in GFB's unwritten protocol, which was less about what to do and more about what *not* to do.

The first thing to keep in mind was that GFB was not interested in your opinions on, well, *anything*. One man once brought back fried bananas in a bag made out of old newspaper, a common takeout container among street vendors back then. "There's a blurred-out photo of a murder scene on this bag," he said. "I can still see the blood, and it's so gruesome it has ruined my appetite." Everyone in line looked down at the ground in stunned silence. "Can you transfer these fried bananas to a different bag— one with entertainment news perhaps?" the man asked, as he handed the bag of fried bananas to GFB.

That question was quickly followed by GFB telling the man that if he didn't get out of her face right that minute, she would make sure he ended up in tomorrow's papers, bloodstained and blurred out. That—and a few new colorful words for the human reproductive organs—was all I heard before Grandpa quickly covered my ears.

Then, as Murphy's Law would have it, while GFB was bagging some sweet potato fritters for us, I made the mistake of saying to Grandpa—a little too loudly—that it would be nice to have the thinner, skin-on pieces, which were crispier than the voluptuous, fleshy ones. Before I could finish the sentence, Grandpa told me in a gentle (but oddly squeaky) voice that maybe we should just let "Auntie" take care of that for us. It was hard to tell if GFB heard what I said, and although I knew Grandpa would have protected me, I still recoiled inside from fear.

Luckily, I didn't unleash GFB's patented brand of wrath that day. I caught a glimpse of mild exasperation that was quickly replaced by a stone-cold expression. Maybe I was too small and she'd rather take on someone her own size, or maybe she just didn't care. I often wondered if there was any humanity behind that cold, heartless façade. In my juvenile imagination, I once even entertained the possibility of her being from another planet.

But perhaps my view of GFB didn't match what my grandfather had long known. During the months after my protocol gaffe up until the day GFB mysteriously vanished when news broke of how the shophouses in the area would be converted into an office building, every one of our orders for sweet potato fritters consisted of nothing but the extra crispy, skin-on ones— without fail.

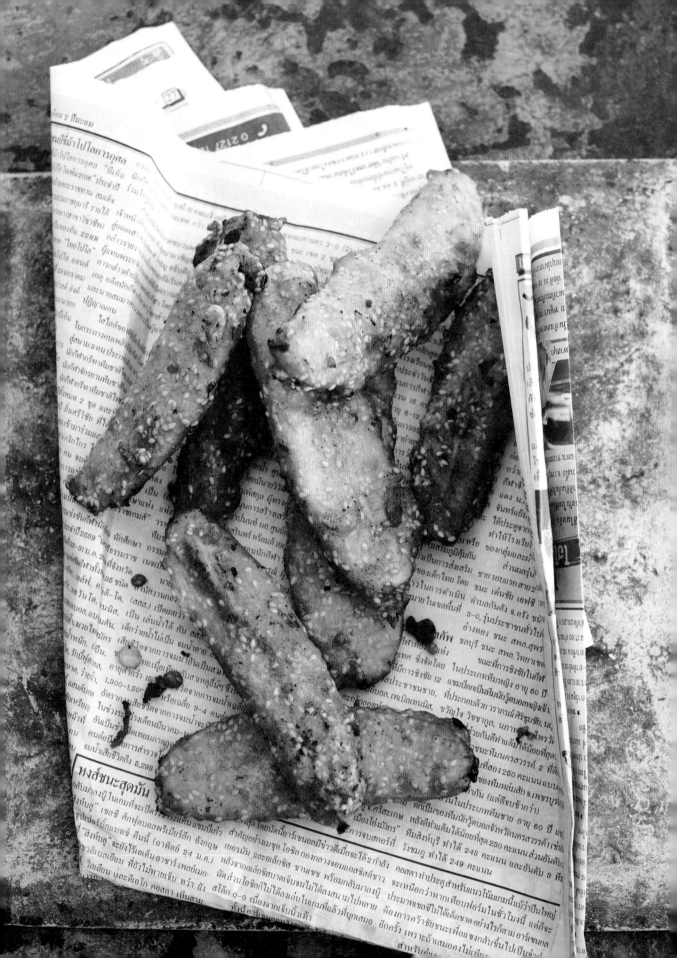

Fried bananas

กล้วยทอด **KLUAI THOT**

Vegetable oil, for deep-frying

1 cup plus 2 tablespoons
Thai rice flour

½ cup granulated sugar

½ cup unsweetened dried
fine coconut flakes

1 tablespoon white
sesame seeds

1½ teaspoons salt

¾ cup limestone solution
(page 336)

8 nam wa bananas or Burro
bananas, peeled and each
cut lengthwise into 3 slices,
or 4 semiripe plantains,
peeled, halved crosswise,
and each half cut lengthwise
into 3 slices

You need the short, stout Thai *nam wa* bananas or Burro bananas, as they are traditionally used to make this ubiquitous street snack. They are firmer, stickier, and tangier than the regular Cavendish bananas or the baby bananas you find at the supermarket, and these different types are too different to be considered interchangeable here. If you can't find *nam wa* or Burro, semiripe plantains are the best substitute. **Serves 4**

Pour the oil to a depth of 2 inches into a wok or Dutch oven and heat to 350°F. Set a cooling rack on a sheet pan and place it near the stove.

While the oil is heating, in a large bowl, whisk together the flour, sugar, coconut, sesame seeds, salt, and limestone solution until a thick but smooth batter forms. Add the bananas to the batter and toss to coat evenly.

When the oil is hot, working in batches to avoid crowding, lift the banana pieces from the batter, allowing the excess batter to drip back into the bowl, and add to the oil. Deep-fry until crisp and golden brown, about 3 minutes. Using a mesh skimmer, transfer to the cooling rack. Repeat until all of the bananas are fried. Enjoy the bananas while they are slightly warmer than room temperature.

The Cosmopolitan Cuisine of Bangkok

Foreign fast-food chains have entered Bangkok since the 1970s, enticing us with television commercials showing pizzas with oozing, stringy cheese and happy people eating doughnuts. By the late 1980s, a large variety of American foods had become as much a part of Bangkokian life as a neighborhood noodle or rice-curry shop.

Not everyone is happy about this development, of course. Some see it as a culinary invasion that has created a generation of people who don't appreciate traditional Thai dishes because they're too busy eating a Grand Burger (there was a time when the Quarter Pounder was called the Grand Burger in Thailand; you can ask Vincent Vega for the explanation).

Yet there has *never* been a period in the history of Bangkok when its food was free of foreign influences. Portuguese traditions permeated the royal kitchens of Ayutthaya, giving birth to several dishes that are still enjoyed to this day. Chinese cuisine changed the way the Siamese ate even before the city was established. Japanese culinary customs arrived long before most people came to know what tempura is. King Phutthaloetla Naphalai (Rama II), who ruled in the early 1800s, wrote celebrated rhymes that not only glorified the dishes made by his beloved but also referenced several foreign-influenced dishes and ingredients in the royal court kitchens. One of Thailand's earliest food publications, *Mae Khrua Hua Pa*, was inspired by the nineteenth-century British best-seller *Mrs. Beeton's Book of Household Management*, and contains recipes that employ imported products, such as canned salmon and canned herring, in traditional Thai dishes. These are only some of many examples.

Today's rabid fervor over the need to remove foreign influences from "Thai cuisine" is misguided, as is the notion that we should go back in time to retrieve "pure" Thai food in order to popularize it again. These are modern sentiments that don't reflect the mind-set of the older generations who did not believe the glory of Thai cuisine lay only in the distant past. They saw cooking and eating as free, open-minded, and explorative. They relished the idea that new foods were always waiting to be discovered and embraced.

Thai cooks are the masters of indigenization, and that's precisely why Thai cuisine is one of the best in the world. Give Thai cooks anything from anywhere and they'll figure out how to create something that pleases local palates. Looking over a list of foreign franchises in Bangkok, it seems that those that have thrived—versus ones that have packed up and left—possess the same trait. Admittedly, many other factors contribute to the success and failure of food franchises. But it is irrefutable that the successful ones nearly always offer brilliantly indigenized dishes, such as the mash-up of ice cream sundae and traditional Thai mango and sticky rice served during mango season at Swensen's, Bangkok's best-known ice cream franchise.

The sundae combines mango ice cream and pandan-scented (and tinted), sweet coconut-infused sticky rice. This is not a new concept, as sweet sticky rice has long been a common ice cream topping in Thailand. But when you add fresh mango cubes, a dollop of mango preserve, a generous piping of whipped cream, and some chopped nuts, you've got the best of both worlds in one dish.

Mango sundae with pandan-coconut sticky rice

ไอศกรีมข้าวเหนียวมะม่วง   AI-SA-KRIM KHAO NIAO MAMUANG

PANDAN-COCONUT STICKY RICE

¾ cup Thai white glutinous rice, soaked in water for 2 hours

¼ cup coconut cream, preferably freshly extracted

½ cup coconut milk, preferably freshly extracted

1 tablespoon extra-virgin coconut oil, if using canned coconut cream and milk

½ cup granulated sugar

½ teaspoon salt

1½ teaspoons pandan juice concentrate (page 337), or less if you prefer a paler color

MANGO SAUCE

1 cup Ataúlfo (or Alphonso) mango puree

½ cup granulated sugar

⅛ teaspoon salt

MANGO ICE CREAM

Follow the recipe for Durian Ice Cream (page 300), replacing the durian pulp with the same amount of Ataúlfo (or Alphonso) mango puree, kept frozen.

EMBELLISHMENTS

2 cups ripe Ataúlfo (or Alphonso) mango cubes (½-inch cubes)

½ cup heavy cream, whipped

¼ cup unsalted roasted peanuts or cashews, chopped (optional)

4 fan wafers (optional)

Use the ripest Ataúlfo or Alphonso (Alphonse) mangoes you can find in this recipe. If you're in Thailand, go with ripe *ok rong*, *nam dok mai*, or *maha chanok*. ◆ **Serves 4**

To make the sticky rice, line a steamer tier with a double layer of cheesecloth. Drain the rice, transfer it to the steamer tier, mounding it slightly, and steam over boiling water until it has barely turned glossy, about 20 minutes. (Alternatively, spread out the rice into a thin layer on a metal splatter guard, place it over a saucepan three-fourths full of boiling water, cover the rice with an overturned stainless-steel bowl, and steam as directed.) When the rice is ready and still very hot, quickly combine the coconut cream, coconut milk, oil, sugar, and salt in a 1-quart saucepan and bring to a boil over medium-high heat, stirring to dissolve the sugar. Remove the pan from the heat, stir in the hot rice and the pandan concentrate, and mix until blended (the mixture will be soupy). Cover and let cool, undisturbed, for 1 hour.

To make the mango sauce, while the sticky rice is steeping, in a 12-inch frying pan, stir together all the ingredients and cook over medium heat, stirring constantly, until it is the consistency of loose jam, 10 to 12 minutes. Let cool to room temperature.

Put scoops of the ice cream into four dessert dishes. Spoon some mango cubes to one side and some sticky rice to the other side. Top the ice cream with the mango sauce, then pipe or dollop the whipped cream on the sauce. Sprinkle the nuts on top, and decorate each bowl with a fan wafer. Serve immediately.

Thai iced tea

ชาเย็น CHA YEN

My paternal grandfather got around Bangkok in a gray 1954 Fiat with suicide doors. On the knob of the window crank by the driver's seat was a plastic bag of Thai iced tea, hanging by a rubber band tied to one of its corners. As he drove, he would bend over and sip the tea through a straw sticking out of the opposite corner.

It was like that every day—my grandpa, his car, the knob of the window crank, and the tea in a plastic bag, hanging by a rubber band and bouncing up and down to the rhythm of the moving car. Bangkok's notorious traffic made him nuts, and the tea was his way of dealing with the daily commute. Once home, Grandpa would pull into the garage and get out of the car. His right thigh would always be soaking wet from the condensation that had dripped onto his pants from the tea bag. Grandma would shake her head, laughing. Every day.

My paternal uncle got around Bangkok in a chartreuse two-door 1969 Opel. On the knob of the window crank by the driver's seat was a plastic bag of Thai iced tea, hanging by a rubber band tied to one of its corners, bouncing up and down to the rhythm of the moving car. Bangkok's traffic drove him nuts, too, and his wife hated it when he cussed. Sipping the tea seemed to help temper his anxiety and his cussing. Once home, Uncle would pull into the garage and get out of the car, his right thigh wet from the condensation that had dripped onto his pants from the tea bag. His wife would smile and say something about a fallen fruit, a tree, and the short distance between the two.

My father drove me around town on our dates in a retro orange 1970 two-door Volkswagen Beetle. On the knob of the window crank by the driver's seat was a plastic bag of Thai iced tea, hanging by a rubber band, bouncing up and down to the rhythm of the moving car. But sooner or later the Bangkok traffic would come to a standstill, and my father would sigh over and over and I would sometimes whine. On the knob of the window crank by the passenger's seat was a plastic bag of Thai iced tea, hanging by a rubber band, completely still in the gridlock. But shortly we'd start singing the French drinking song he'd taught me. *Chevaliers de la table ronde.* We'd bend over and sip our tea. *Goûtons voir si le vin est bon.* We'd sip again. *Goûtons voir, oui, oui, oui.* Another sip. *Goûtons voir, non, non, non.* Another sip. *Goûtons voir si le vin est bon.* And finally, a big gulp. That was how we dealt with Bangkok's traffic. Once home, we'd get out of the car. Dad's right thigh and my left thigh would be wet from the condensation dripping onto our pants from the tea bags. Mom would look at us, laughing.

continued

3 tablespoons Thai tea mix (Hand Brand, Pantai, or Por Kwan brand)

2 cups boiling water

1 tablespoon granulated sugar

¼ cup sweetened condensed milk

½ cup evaporated milk

3 cups crushed ice

My cousin picked me up from the airport the last time I went to visit Bangkok from Chicago. He drove a white 2011 Honda Civic with no window cranks or knobs. Between the front seats was Thai iced tea in a large to-go paper tumbler—the standard vessel for cold beverages these days. We chatted and caught up. He picked up his iced tea, held it in front of his face, wondered out loud how in Hades there could be traffic at one o'clock in the morning, sipped his tea, and put the cup back down. We talked. He sipped his tea. Eventually we arrived at my condo and got out of the car. The crotch of his pants was visibly wet from the condensation from the bottom of the paper cup dripping onto it. I looked at him and—oddly—felt I couldn't have possibly loved my family more. ♦ **Serves 2**

Put the tea in a heatproof 1-quart measuring glass. Pour the boiling water over it and stir with a spoon. Using the back of the spoon, press as much flavor out of the tea mix as possible for about 30 seconds. Stir in the sugar and leave the tea to steep and cool down to lukewarm.

In a small pitcher, whisk together both milks. Divide the ice evenly between two large glass tumblers. Pour the tea through a small mesh sieve directly into the tumblers. Top each tumbler with the milk mixture, dividing it evenly.

Serve immediately with the two components layered. Stir down the milk with the straw as you sip. Consume with care, as dripping condensation can cause embarrassing wet marks on clothing.

Homemade Variation

The recipe above gives you Thai iced tea exactly how it is made in Thailand—food coloring in the tea mix and evaporated milk out of a can and all. However, if you'd like to make your own Thai iced tea from scratch, as I do from time to time, replace the commercial Thai tea mix with black tea leaves (or red rooibos to get a faint orange color) and add 4 star anise pods, cracked, and 4 whole cloves to the water as you steep the tea. Proceed as directed above, replacing the evaporated milk with half and half and adding ⅛ teaspoon vanilla extract, if desired. The sweetened condensed milk, however, must stay.

Basic
Recipes

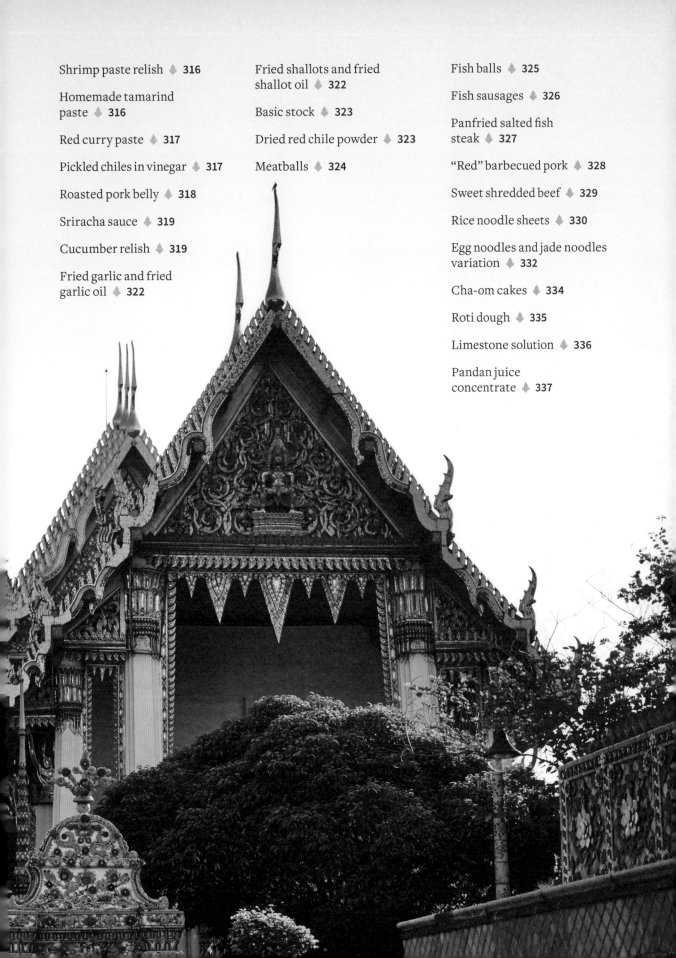

Shrimp paste relish

น้ำพริกกะปิ NAM PHRIK KAPI

4 large cloves garlic

5 or 6 bird's eye chiles

1 tablespoon packed
Thai shrimp paste

1 to 3 teaspoons packed
grated palm sugar or
1 to 2 teaspoons packed
light brown sugar

2 teaspoons fish sauce

¼ cup fresh lime juice

4 or 5 pea eggplants,
smashed with a pestle
just until they split up
(optional)

2 teaspoons grated lime zest
(optional)

This relish is usually kept quite simple. Shrimp paste, garlic, chiles, fish sauce, and lime juice go into the bare-bones version. Sugar is optional. Some cooks don't add it at all and lament the fact that nowadays most versions of the relish are too sweet. I grew up with shrimp paste relish that's primarily sour and salty, so I usually add a smidgen of palm sugar not to sweeten the relish but to round out the flavor and lessen the sharp edges. The most common way this relish is served is in the classic ensemble featuring fried mackerel and assorted side vegetables (page 110). ♦ **Makes ¾ cup**

In a mortar, grind the garlic, chiles, and shrimp paste to a smooth paste. Add the sugar (you decide how much), fish sauce, lime juice, and pea eggplants and mix well. Stir in the lime zest.

Use immediately, or refrigerate in an airtight container for up to 1 week, then bring to room temperature before serving.

Homemade tamarind paste

น้ำมะขามเปียก NAM MA-KHAM PIAK

1 (14-ounce) block Thai
seedless tamarind

1¾ cups warm water

Tamarind is one of the most prominent sources of acidity in traditional Thai cooking, so you will be reaching for it quite often when you make the recipes in this book. You can buy the diluted paste of the tamarind pods, which is sold in small plastic jars and is often labeled "tamarind concentrate" or, misleadingly, "tamarind juice." But commercial tamarind paste is nearly always too watery for my liking, so I often make my own from seedless tamarind that comes in block form. It's more economical this way, and it gives you more control of the amount of liquid you add to a recipe. ♦ **Makes 2 cups**

In a bowl, combine the tamarind block and water and let stand for 15 minutes. Then, using your hand, break up the tamarind until it is reduced a thick puree. Pass the puree through a fine-mesh sieve held over a bowl, using the back of a sturdy spoon to force every bit of pulp through the mesh. Use a rubber spatula to scrape off the pulp that clings to the underside of the sieve. Discard the stringy veins in the sieve.

Transfer the sieved pulp to a glass jar and cap tightly. Store in the refrigerator for up to 1 week or in the freezer for up to 6 months.

Red curry paste

น้ำพริกแกงเผ็ด  NAM PHRIK KAENG PHET

4 teaspoons coriander seeds

1 teaspoon cumin seeds

5 large dried Thai long or guajillo chiles, cut into 1-inch pieces, soaked until softened, and squeezed dry

4 dried bird's eye chiles, soaked until softened and squeezed dry

½ teaspoon white peppercorns

1 tablespoon finely chopped galangal

1 tablespoon thinly sliced lemongrass (with purple rings only)

1 teaspoon finely chopped makrut lime rind

1 teaspoon packed Thai shrimp paste

1 tablespoon finely chopped cilantro roots or stems

5 large cloves garlic

¼ cup sliced shallots

This paste is the base for the classic Thai curry that has come to be known internationally as "red curry" due to its reddish color. This so-called Red Curry is, of course, just one among the countless other types of Thai curries, many of which sport the same color. However, *kaeng phet* happens to be one of the most common and the most popular type of curry in Bangkok; its paste base is also one of the most versatile which can be used to flavor several non-curry dishes.
Makes ½ cup

Toast the coriander and cumin seeds in a small frying pan over medium-low heat, stirring often, until fragrant, about 2 minutes. Transfer the seeds to a mortar, add the chiles and peppercorns, and grind until smooth. One at time, add to the granite mortar the galangal, lemongrass, lime rind, shrimp paste, cilantro roots, garlic, and shallots, grinding to a smooth paste after each addition. Use immediately, or transfer to an airtight container and freeze for up to 3 months.

Pickled chiles in vinegar

น้ำส้มพริกดอง NAM SOM PHRIK DONG

2 cups distilled white vinegar

4 or 5 fresh Thai long, jalapeño, or serrano chiles, cut crosswise into ¼-inch-thick slices

This is a common table seasoning mostly for noodle soups, noodle stir-fries, and rice soups. **Makes 3 cups**

Combine the vinegar and chiles in a tightly capped glass jar. Both the chiles and the vinegar can be used right away, but for the best result, let the mixture stand at room temperature for 24 to 36 hours before using, to allow the chiles to mellow and pick up the flavor of the vinegar.

Store in the refrigerator for up to 2 months; after that time the vinegar will still be good—and will remain good for months—but the pickled chiles will have become mushy and lost their flavor and should be picked out and discarded.

Roasted pork belly

หมูกรอบ MU KROP

1 (8 by 8 by 3-inch) piece of boneless pork belly with the skin on, rinsed and patted dry

2 teaspoons salt

½ ground white pepper

1 teaspoon Chinese five-spice powder

1 tablespoon distilled vinegar

Vegetable oil for deep-frying

A perfect piece of this Chinese barbecue classic must, to me, have these characteristics: flavorful, firm yet tender meat, a juicy fat layer, and bubbly, crackly, and ever-so-slightly blistered skin. This is hard to achieve. But when I feel like making it at home, this is the method that, after having tried many, I find to be the most reliable, and—this is important—the most effective in producing crispy skin that stays crispy for hours. ⬥ **Makes between 1½ to 2 pounds**

Place the pork belly, meat side down, in a saucepan wide enough to fit it comfortably. Pour in just enough water to cover the pork; boil, covered, over medium-high heat for 15 minutes. Remove from the pan and let cool to room temperature.

Turn the pork on its skin so the meat side is up. Combine 1 teaspoon of the salt, the pepper, and five-spice powder. With a sharp knife, make crosshatch slashes on the meat about ½ inch deep and 1 inch apart. Rub the prepared mixture all over the meat (not the skin) on the sides and deep into the grooves. Wrap the meat part with a piece of foil, leaving the skin exposed. Combine the remaining 1 teaspoon salt and the vinegar and brush the mixture all over the skin. Put the pork, with the foil still covering the meat part, on a plate and refrigerate for 12 to 24 hours.

Pour the oil to a depth of ½ inch—just enough to cover the skin once it's puffed up—into a wok or Dutch oven and heat to 350°F. Carefully lower the pork, skin side down, into the hot oil and immediately stand back. (There will be some serious splattering, so you may want to cover the wok.) Move the pork around every minute to ensure even cooking. Once the skin is bubbly and golden brown, about 6 to 7 minutes. Using tongs, turn the pork over and lightly brown the bottom and the sides, no more than 2 minutes total. Remove from the heat and transfer to a cooling rack or a plate. Let cool, skin side up, to slightly warmer than room temperature before using in a recipe.

Sriracha sauce

12 ounces fresh red Thai long chiles, stemmed

2 heads garlic, separated into cloves and peeled

¼ cup distilled white vinegar

¾ cup water

1 cup plus 2 tablespoons granulated sugar

3 tablespoons salt

Sriracha is used as a dipping sauce, seasoning sauce, and often a base for other sauces. This recipe produces Thai-style Sriracha sauce, which is different from and cannot be used interchangeably with the widely known American-made Sriracha sauce ("rooster sauce"). ⬦ **Makes 2 cups**

Process the chiles, garlic, vinegar, and water in a blender until smooth. Strain the mixture through a fine-mesh sieve placed over a 2-quart saucepan. Using a sturdy wooden spoon or rubber spatula, press as much liquid out of the mixture and through the sieve as possible. Add one-third of the pulp from the sieve to the liquid in the pan and discard the remaining pulp.

Whisk the sugar and salt into the mixture in the pan. Bring to a boil over medium heat, stirring occasionally. Lower the heat to a simmer and cook uncovered, stirring often, until the sauce is reduced to about 2 cups and has thickened slightly, 12 to 15 minutes.

Remove the pan from the heat and let the sauce cool completely. Transfer the sauce to a glass jar, cap tightly, and refrigerate for 2 days before using to allow the sauce to mellow. The sauce will keep in the refrigerator for up to 1 month. To ensure against spoilage, be sure to use a clean spoon every time you scoop the sauce out of the jar. The sauce can also be frozen for up to 6 months; thaw in the refrigerator.

Cucumber relish

1 cup granulated sugar

1 cup distilled white vinegar

¼ cup water

½ teaspoon salt

1 cup thinly sliced English, pickling, or Persian cucumber

2 ounces shallots, halved lengthwise, placed cut side down, and cut lengthwise into paper-thin slices

2 fresh Thai long, jalapeño, or serrano chiles, cut crosswise into ¼-inch slices

2 tablespoons packed cilantro leaves

This relish usually accompanies Thai dishes of South Asian or Middle Eastern origins with warm dried spices and rich components like ghee, cream, and yogurt. The sweet and vinegary dressing, the crisp and cool cucumber slices, and the fresh chiles complement these dishes very well. ⬦ **Makes 2 cups**

Combine the sugar, vinegar, water, and salt in a 1-quart saucepan and bring to a gentle boil over medium heat, stirring just until the sugar dissolves. Remove from the heat and let cool completely, then transfer to a bowl.

Just seconds before serving, add the cucumber, shallots, chiles, and cilantro and stir to combine. Do not mix them in beforehand, or the cucumber slices will become limp and release moisture that will dilute the dressing.

Fried garlic and fried garlic oil

กระเทียมเจียว-น้ำมันกระเทียมเจียว **KRA-THIAM JIAO-NAM MAN KRA-THIAM JIAO**

2 heads garlic, separated into
cloves and peeled

¾ cup vegetable oil

Most of the time, fried garlic and fried garlic oil are used together as an accent ingredient for various dishes, most notably noodles. But since they're not always used together, or in equal amounts, I treat the fried garlic and fried garlic oil (the oil in which the garlic is fried) as two entities. Storing them separately also helps the fried garlic stay crisp longer. **Makes ¾ cup fried garlic and ¾ cup garlic oil**

Pound the garlic in a mortar into small uniform bits the size of a match head. Transfer the garlic to a 6- or 8-inch frying pan, add the oil, and set over medium heat. Cook, stirring occasionally, until the oil is sizzling, about 5 minutes. Turn the heat to medium-low and continue to cook, stirring often, until the garlic turns light brown, 2 to 3 minutes longer. Remove the pan from the heat and immediately pour the contents through a fine-mesh sieve held over a small heatproof bowl. Transfer the garlic to a second small bowl. Let the garlic and the oil cool to room temperature.

Transfer the garlic and oil to separate airtight containers and store in a cool, dry place. The fried garlic will keep for up to 3 weeks and the oil for up to 2 months.

Fried shallots and fried shallot oil

หอมเจียว-น้ำมันหอมเจียว **HOM JIAO-NAM MAN HOM JIAO**

4 shallots, about 1 ounce
each, thinly sliced lengthwise

¾ cup vegetable oil

Fried shallots and shallot oil are used in traditional Thai cooking and in dishes with strong ties to the Thai Muslim communities. The key is to start out with everything at room temperature and to cook the shallots slowly over moderate heat. **Makes ½ cup fried shallots and ¾ cup shallot oil**

Combine the shallots and oil in 6- or 8- inch frying pan and set over medium heat. Stir the shallot slices with a wooden spatula to separate them. Cook, stirring occasionally, until the oil is sizzling, about 5 minutes. Turn the heat to medium-low and continue to cook, stirring occasionally, until the shallots turn the color of honey, 5 to 7 minutes. Remove the pan from the heat and immediately pour the contents through a fine-mesh sieve held over a small heatproof bowl. Let the shallots and the oil cool to room temperature.

Transfer the shallots and oil to separate airtight containers and store in a cool, dry place. The fried shallots will keep for up to 3 weeks and the oil for up to 2 months.

Basic stock

น้ำซุป NAM SUP

4 pounds raw chicken
carcasses or pork neck or
spine bones

4 quarts water, or as needed

4 Chinese celery stalks or
2 cups chopped regular
(Pascal) celery

1 yellow onion

¼ cup white peppercorns,
cracked

8 large cloves garlic

8 cilantro roots, smashed,
or 1 cup coarsely chopped
cilantro stems

1 pound daikon, cut into
3-inch cubes (optional)

This recipe is for a basic chicken or pork stock. If you will be using the stock for a noodle soup, blanch the chicken carcasses or pork bones in boiling water for 1 minute, then rinse under cold water and drain well before proceeding to make the stock as directed. **Makes 4 quarts**

Combine all of the ingredients in a stockpot and bring to a boil over high heat, skimming off any foam that forms on the surface. Lower the heat to a simmer, cover, and cook for 3 hours, replenishing the water along the way as needed to maintain the original level.

Remove from the heat and strain the stock through a fine-mesh sieve into one or more clean containers. Skim off the fat, if using immediately. You can also leave the stock to cool and then refrigerate it for up to 1 week or freeze for up to 6 months, removing the hardened fat on the surface before reheating.

Dried red chile powder

พริกป่น PHRIK PON

1 cup loosely packed dried
bird's eye chiles, stemmed

5 large dried Thai long or
guajillo chiles

You can't walk into a noodle shop in Bangkok without seeing dried red chile powder in the table seasoning caddy that's set out for you. But you can also use pulverized toasted dried chiles in salads, dips, sauces, and many other things. You can buy prepared dried red chile powder at most Thai grocery stores, but I like to make my own because it's fresher and I can make sure that the dried chiles that go into it are in good condition and not moldy. Making my own chile powder also allows me to customize the level of spiciness. Some brands use all bird's eye chiles, which are very hot, or more of them than long chiles, which are moderately hot, and the end result is so hot you can't use too much of it. In dishes where you want both the heat and the color of the dried chiles, this can be an issue. **Makes 1 cup**

Toast the chiles in a small frying pan over low heat, stirring constantly, until fragrant and brittle, about 3 minutes. Pour onto a plate and let cool completely, then transfer to a mortar or food processor and grind to the consistency of coarse cornmeal.

Use immediately, or transfer to an airtight container and store in a cool, dry place for up to 6 months.

Meatballs

ลูกชิ้น LUK CHIN

2 pounds lean boneless beef eye of round; boneless, skinless chicken breasts or thighs; or boneless pork loin with all the fat trimmed off, chilled

½ cup crushed ice

2 tablespoons salt

2 teaspoons ground white pepper

2 teaspoons granulated sugar

1 teaspoon baking powder

¼ cup Thai tapioca starch or cornstarch

This is a recipe for Asian-style meatballs. Commercial ones are firm, perfectly smooth, and bouncy. Think uncased frankfurters but firmer, chewier, smaller, and rounder. But without an industrial-strength emulsifying machine, your homemade meatballs will not be supersmooth like commercial ones. And without the use of additives such as borax, they won't be firm and elastic enough to bounce like a ball when thrown to the floor.

Still, high-quality homemade meatballs can be achieved. The first step is to start out with a piece or pieces of meat rather than ground meat. This recipe can be used with beef, pork, or chicken, and the leaner and fresher the meat is, the firmer and bouncier your meatballs will be. Before you begin, assemble the tools you will need: a 12- to 14-cup food processor; an instant-read thermometer; a wide, shallow 4-quart saucepan; a mesh skimmer; and a couple of large bowls and a small bowl. ◆ **Makes 2¼ pounds; about 120 one-inch meatballs**

Put the bowl and the blade of your food processor in the freezer. Cut the meat into ½-inch cubes and spread the cubes in a thin layer in a large lidded storage container or plastic bag, seal closed, and freeze until a very thin layer of frost appears on the surface of the meat but the meat is still soft, about 15 minutes, assuming the temperature of your freezer is at 0°F or lower.

Meanwhile, fill a wide, shallow 4-quart saucepan with water, set over medium heat and heat just until the water reaches 50°F to 60°F, using an instant-read thermometer to check the temperature. Adjust the burner as needed to keep the temperature in this range at all times. Set a large bowl on one side of the stove and a small bowl of cold water and a thin-edged spoon on the other side.

When the meat is ready, put it in the food processor, add the ice, salt, pepper, sugar, baking powder, and tapioca starch and process to a pale, smooth, very sticky paste, stopping to scrape down the sides of the bowl along the way. To prevent overheating, the processing should be done in the shortest time possible, preferably no more than 3 minutes. When the paste is ready, the meat should register less than 15°F for the best results. If it doesn't, pop the meat, still in the food processor bowl, into the freezer for a few minutes to bring down the temperature.

Moisten one hand with the water in the small bowl, grab a handful of meat paste, and make a tight fist to extrude the paste through the opening between your thumb and index finger into a smooth ball about 1 inch in diameter. (You are turning your hand into an extruder.) With the other hand, moisten the spoon and quickly scoop up the ball at the base, rounding the bottom, and then gently drop it into the water. Repeat until you have shaped about half of the paste, moistening your hand and the spoon along the way whenever the paste gets too sticky. Once you have produced enough meatballs to cover the water surface in a single layer, flip them around until the entire surface of each ball is opaque. Using a mesh skimmer, transfer the balls to the large bowl near the stove. You do not want the meatballs fully cooked at this point, as they will be cooked again. Repeat to make more meatballs until you run out of meat paste, adding the balls to the same bowl after they are partially cooked.

If necessary, add water to the same saucepan so it is half full, then turn up the heat and heat the water until it registers 80°F. Fill the second large bowl with ice-cold water and set it near the stove. When the hot water is ready, working in batches to avoid crowding, cook the partially poached meatballs, flipping them often, until they are no longer pink inside when split open, about 10 minutes. (A meatball will have to sacrifice its life for the doneness test in each batch.) Using the skimmer, transfer the meatballs to the ice water and let them soak just until they cool to room temperature—no longer. Using the skimmer, transfer the cooled meatballs to a storage container. Repeat until you have cooked all of the meatballs. (Don't throw away the poaching water; it's a delicious broth.)

The meatballs are now ready to use as directed in individual recipes. Or store, covered tightly, in the refrigerate for up to 48 hours or in freezer for up to 3 months.

Fish balls

ลูกชิ้นปลา LUK CHIN PLA

2 pounds skinless firm white saltwater fish fillets, chilled

4 egg whites, well chilled, if not using fish favored in Bangkok (see headnote)

¼ cup crushed ice

2 tablespoons salt

2 teaspoons ground white pepper

2 teaspoons granulated sugar

⅓ cup Thai tapioca starch or cornstarch

The process of making fish balls is similar to how meatballs are made. The difference is that fish meat needs more help to yield firm, bouncy results, unless you use the types of saltwater fish favored by professional fish-ball makers in Bangkok, such as king mackerel (*pla insi*), dorab wolf-herring (*pla dap lao*), and yellowtail fusilier (*pla hang lueang*) when they're as fresh as possible and have never been frozen. If you can't source one of these types or find them fresh, purchase the firmest, freshest white saltwater fish fillets you can find and use egg whites along with tapioca starch to help achieve a good texture.

⬇ **Makes 2¼ pounds; about 120 one-inch balls**

Make the paste (adding the egg whites with the seasonings) and shape, cook, and store the balls as directed for meatballs, above.

Fish sausages

อื่อก๊วย HUE KUAI

Fish paste for fish balls (page 325)

The same fish paste that you use to make round fish balls can be shaped into a sausage-like log, poached (or poached and then deep-fried), cooled, and cut into slices for serving in noodle dishes. ◈ **Makes four 6-inch sausage rolls; about 144 slices**

Prepare the fish paste as directed, paying close attention to the consistency and final temperature of the paste. Cut four 8-inch squares of parchment paper or aluminum foil (do not use waxed paper). Divide the fish paste into four equal portions. Spoon a portion onto a parchment square, positioning it near the edge closest to you. Shape the paste into a 6-inch-long log of even thickness, leaving 1 inch of paper uncovered at each end. (Don't worry about the log not being round at this point. Focus instead on it being of even thickness.) Starting from the side nearest you, fold the edge over the log and then roll up the log snugly in the parchment paper, being careful not to apply so much pressure that the fish paste oozes out the ends. Tie each end of the parchment tube securely with kitchen string to form a tight sausage roll. Repeat with the remaining fish paste portions and parchment squares.

Fill a 4-quart saucepan halfway with water, set over medium-high heat, and heat the water until it registers 60°F on a thermometer. Gently lower the fish rolls into the water and adjust the heat to resume the temperature, which will have dropped slightly. In about 1 minute, the fish sausages should be firm enough to manipulate into uniformly cylindrical rolls. Using a pair of rubber spatulas, squeeze and mold the rolls into shape as they are poaching. The fish sausages should be cooked through in 20 minutes.

Using a mesh skimmer, transfer the sausage rolls to a flat plate, let cool to room temperature, and unwrap. You can use the sausage as is, or you can deep-fry them in vegetable oil heated to 375°F until medium brown, about 5 minutes, then let them cool to room temperature. Most noodle shops in Bangkok offer both versions in a single bowl. Cut the poached or deep-fried sausages on a 45-degree angle into slices a scant ¼ inch thick to serve.

Variation

Mix ½ cup finely chopped green onion (green parts only) or Chinese garlic chives into the fish paste before forming it into logs.

Panfried salted fish steak

ปลาเค็มทอด PLA KHEM THOT

1 large bone-in king mackerel steak, about 8 ounces and ¾ to 1 inch thick

¼ cup salt

2 tablespoons homemade lard (page 28) or vegetable oil

In Thailand, king mackerel is one of the most common types of fish used to make salted sun-dried fish. But most firm, oily saltwater fish, such as salmon, will work well. I have streamlined the process here so that you can get the same result using fish steaks as opposed to whole fish, which take much longer to salt and to dry and require a more complicated procedure. To use homemade salted fish in a recipe, plan ahead, because the salting process takes 72 hours. Serve the fish hot with rice or plain rice porridge (page 21) or use as directed in individual recipes. ⬧ **Makes one 6-ounce fish steak**

Cover both sides of the fish steak with the salt. Don't worry if not all of the salt sticks to the fish. Place the fish in a glass dish, cover with plastic wrap, and refrigerate for 72 hours, flipping the steak over once after 24 hours.

Rinse the salt off the fish steak with cool running water and pat dry. Place the steak on a plate, cover it with a domed mesh food cover, and let it dry in the sun, flipping the steak often, until dry to the touch on both sides; the timing will depend on the weather. Alternatively, place the fish steak on a rack set on a sheet pan and dehydrate in a 120°F oven until dry to the touch on both sides, 4 to 5 hours. (At this point, the salted fish can be wrapped in plastic wrap and refrigerated for up to 2 weeks or frozen for 6 months.)

To cook the salted sun-dried fish, heat 1 tablespoon of the lard in an 8-inch frying pan over medium-high heat. When the lard is hot, add the fish steak and fry until golden brown on the first side, about 3 minutes. Adding the remaining 1 tablespoon lard to the pan, if necessary, flip the fish and cook until the second side is golden brown, 2 to 3 minutes longer. Serve at or slightly warmer than room temperature. Enjoy in small bites, treating it more like a salty condiment rather than a main protein.

"Red" barbecued pork

หมูแดง MU DAENG

1 to 2 ounces raw beet or
2 drops red food coloring

1½ pounds trimmed boneless
pork butt (Boston butt)

1 tablespoon Chinese rose
wine (mei kuei lu chiew) or
rice wine (shaoxing)

1½ teaspoons hoisin sauce

1½ teaspoons oyster sauce

1½ teaspoons Thai sweet
dark soy sauce

1½ tablespoons packed
grated palm sugar or
1 tablespoon honey

2 cloves garlic, ground to
a smooth paste

Unless otherwise advertised, Chinese-style barbecued pork in Bangkok is made according to the Teochew tradition, unlike in most Chinatowns in the West, where the Cantonese tradition is common. The former, which is what I am making here, is drier—but by no means unpleasantly so—and isn't coated in a sweet, glossy glaze.

I've found boneless pork butt (aka Boston butt) to be the best cut for the job. Although pork loin is acceptable, it is not recommended, and you should definitely steer clear of pork tenderloin, which is too lean and has the wrong texture.

Commercial barbecued pork is nearly always reddish from the addition of red food coloring. Some recipes for home cooks suggest tomato sauce or ketchup to avoid using artificial coloring. Beet juice from raw beets (the juice of canned or cooked beets doesn't have enough staining power) is what I use, however. You need only a small amount to turn the pork a perfect reddish brown, plus it doesn't interfere with the taste of the pork the way tomato sauce or ketchup does. That said, the red color isn't important. Some barbecued pork shops in Bangkok, don't use any red food coloring. ◆ **Makes 1 pound**

If using the raw beet, put it in a blender and add as little water as possible to get the blades moving, then process until pulverized. Transfer the contents of the blender to a fine-mesh sieve set over a small bowl and press against the pulp to extract the juice. Measure out 1 tablespoon juice to use for the pork. Discard the pulp and any remaining juice. If using the food coloring, set it aside for now.

Cut the pork with the grain into strips 3 to 4 inches thick (and about 6 inches long). Transfer them to a bowl and prick thoroughly with a fork. Add the beet juice or food coloring, wine, hoisin sauce, oyster sauce, soy sauce, sugar, and garlic and mix well, coating the strips evenly. Cover tightly and refrigerate for at least 6 hours or up to 12 hours.

To grill the pork, prepare a low fire in a charcoal or gas grill. If using charcoal, allow it to burn until the coals are covered with gray ash. Grill the pork strips, flipping them every 2 to 3 minutes, until they are firm to the touch and slightly charred on the outside, 20 to 30 minutes. Alternatively, broil the pork. Position an oven rack at the very bottom of the oven and preheat the broiler. Line a large sheet pan with aluminum foil. Arrange the pork strips on the prepared pan and place the pan on the oven rack. With the oven door ajar, broil the pork, flipping the strips every 2 to 3 minutes (really!), until they are firm to the touch and slightly charred on the outside, about 30 minutes. Regardless of which method you use, be sure to keep an eye on the pork at all times. You can't walk away from it, as it burns easily.

Transfer the barbecued pork to a baking pan and cover tightly with aluminum foil or plastic wrap. Let stand for 20 to 30 minutes before serving or using in a recipe. To store, place in an airtight container and refrigerate for up to 3 days or freeze for up to 3 months.

Sweet shredded beef

เนื้อฝอยหวาน NUEA FOI WAN

1 teaspoon salt

1 (8-ounce) lean top round steak, about ¾ inch thick

¼ cup packed grated palm sugar plus 1 tablespoon packed dark brown sugar, or ¼ cup packed dark brown sugar

3 tablespoons fried shallot oil (page 322)

¼ cup fried shallots (page 322)

Though made primarily of meat and classified as a savory dish, sweet shredded beef—candied beef floss, if you will—isn't meant to be enjoyed heartily as a main protein. If anything, it should be seen as a condiment—an umami-rich condiment that's so sweet it's usually enjoyed in small amounts as part of a set meal or a meal ensemble in which there are always salty and/or sour components to complement and counterbalance its sweetness . ⬇ **Makes about 1¼ cups**

Rub 1 teaspoon salt evenly over both sides of the steak. Grill or broil the steak until well-done, then let rest for 15 minutes.

Cut the steak with the grain—a bit counterintuitive here—as thinly as you can into wide slices 2 to 3 inches long. Then, using your hands, shred the slices lengthwise into thin strands. Transfer the strands to a 12-inch frying pan, add the sugar and shallot oil, and set over medium-high heat. Stir constantly with the blunt end of a wooden spatula to separate the beef into fine strands. When all of the moisture is gone and the strands look glossy, about 6 minutes, add the fried shallots. Set aside to cool to room temperature before using.

Rice noodle sheets

ก๋วยเตี๋ยวเส้นใหญ่ KUAI TIAO SEN YAI

FORMULA 1

2 cups Thai tapioca starch

1 cup Thai rice flour

½ teaspoon salt

3 cups water, at room
temperature

¼ cup vegetable oil, or
nonstick cooking spray
(not olive or coconut oil)

FORMULA 2

1¼ cups Thai tapioca starch

1¾ cups Thai rice flour

½ teaspoon salt

3 cups water, at room
temperature

¼ cup vegetable oil, or
nonstick cooking spray
(not olive or coconut oil)

You know the old adage about real estate: Location, location, location. With this recipe, it's precision, precision, precision. If I've learned anything from my many tests on this particular recipe, it's this: There's absolutely no room for improvisation or substitution.

In Bangkok, the making of these noodles is nearly always given over to noodle factories. Even the city's older, artisanal, multigenerational, much-lauded noodle shops that make their own meatballs don't make these rice noodles themselves. Ordinarily, I'd tell you to do as Bangkokians do and buy them from the store. If you can't find them fresh, I'd suggest buying the widest dried rice noodles you can find (9 millimeters or ⅓ inch) and cook them like you do dried pasta.

But in some cases, store-bought rice noodle sheets, at least those sold in the Chicago area, won't do. They are too thick and too doughy for the job. The process of making them can be tedious and the emphasis on precision can seem discouraging, but once you have finished, there's something wonderful about seeing a stack of soft, elastic, glistening rice noodle sheets that you've just made yourself.

I have devised two formulas. Both are made the same way, but the ingredients are in different amounts. Formula 1 is specifically designed to be chewy and elastic enough for Rice Noodle Parcels with Chile-Lime Sauce (page 39). Formula 2 is better suited for a stir-fry or soup, such as Wide Rice Noodles in Fermented Soybean Broth with Seafood (page 237). For the former, leave the finished noodles whole; for the latter, cut the noodles—the whole stack all at once—into strips 1 inch wide, then peel them off of each other and loosen up the strands before using.

Before you get started, assemble all of the tools you will need: a whisk; a ¼-cup measuring cup; a round metal cake or pie pan, preferably nonstick, with a perfectly level bottom free of dents and dings that measures exactly 8 inches in diameter (it's okay if the top flares outward) and is no more than 2 inches high (any higher and it will be difficult to get the noodles out); a steamer tier that sits perfectly level in the steamer pot and is large enough to accommodate the 8-inch pan; and a pastry brush.

⬥ **Makes 2 pounds; 16 (8-inch) rounds**

Select the formula you will be making, then whisk together the tapioca starch, flour, salt, and water in a bowl until perfectly smooth. Cover the batter and let rest at room temperature for 30 minutes. You should have 4 cups batter, which means if you use precisely ¼ cup of it to make one noodle sheet, you will end up with sixteen sheets of equal weight and size. This is the reason you need the ¼-cup measuring cup.

Fill a steamer pot with water, keeping the water level about 4 inches below the bottom of the steamer tier, and bring to a boil over high heat. Lower the heat until the water is boiling only gently. Coat the bottom of the cake pan lightly with the oil. Whisk the batter again, as the tapioca starch and flour will have settled on the bottom, then pour ¼ cup of the batter into the pan and swirl the pan so the batter coats the bottom evenly. (This may be a bit hard to do because of the oil, so do your best.) Put the pan in the steamer tier and swirl it again so the batter coats the entire surface as quickly as possible before it firms up. Cover and steam for exactly 1 minute. Uncover the steamer and brush or spray the top of the noodle sheet with a very thin layer of oil. Remove the tier from the steamer and use a rubber spatula to ease the noodle sheet out of the pan onto a flat plate. Cover the finished noodle with a kitchen towel.

Repeat the process another fifteen times, stacking the noodle sheets on top of one another as each is finished. Be sure to whisk the batter each time before you start the next noodle. Regrease the bottom of the pan as needed, and always brush the top of the noodle sheet before you remove the tier from the steamer. The noodle sheets can remain covered with a kitchen towel at room temperature for no more than 3 hours. They are best used fresh and should not be stored.

Egg noodles and jade noodles variation

เส้นบะหมี่ SEN BAMI/BAMI YOK

4½ cups all-purpose flour, plus more for dusting

3 eggs

½ teaspoon salt

1 tablespoon vegetable oil

¼ cup lukewarm water

Sen bami is among the most common noodles found at most Chinese Thai noodle shops. They almost always come fresh, formed into small skeins each perfect for a single serving, and blanched briefly to achieve the tender yet chewy texture.

Not all of the so-called egg noodles are made with eggs, however; sometimes *sen bami* is made from just wheat flour, salt, water, and lye water—sometimes a little bit of yellow food dye—similar to Japanese ramen. This formula produces very tough and crumbly dough that requires a lot of skill and manual labor to knead it until smooth, supple, and ready to be rolled out and cut. At home, I'm happy with homemade egg noodles—with eggs in them—prepared quite simply and in the same way Italian pasta is. To achieve an even chewier, bouncier texture, replace 1 tablespoon of the flour with vital wheat gluten. **Makes 1 pound**

Shape the flour into a mound on a work surface and make a well in the center. In a bowl, beat together the eggs, salt, oil, and water with a fork until blended and pour the mixture into the well. With the help of a bench scraper, mix the ingredients together, working the flour into the liquid until a stiff dough forms that cleans the board. Then, knead the dough until smooth and supple, 5 to 6 minutes. Form the dough into a ball, flatten it into an 8-inch disk with smooth edges, and wrap tightly with plastic wrap. Let rest for 30 minutes.

Set up a manual pasta machine according to the manufacturer's instructions. Divide the dough into ten equal portions. Working with one portion at a time, keeping the other portions covered, set the pasta machine rollers to the widest setting and lightly dust the rollers with flour. Flatten the dough portion into a rectangle about 3 inches wide and pass it through the rollers. Fold the dough into thirds, like a business letter, and pass it through the rollers again. Repeat three or four times, lightly dusting the rollers and the dough with flour as needed to prevent sticking. Adjust the rollers to the next narrowest setting and pass the dough through the rollers. Continue to pass the dough through the rollers, progressively narrowing the setting each time and dusting the rollers and dough as needed, until you have run the dough through the narrowest setting. Lightly dust the finished sheet with flour and set it aside on a lightly dusted work surface. Repeat with the remaining dough portions.

Once all of the dough portions have been rolled, you can use the cutting attachment with the thinnest setting to cut the sheets into noodles. The thinnest cutters are not thin enough for me, however. I fold each sheet loosely into thirds and then use a sharp knife to slice it crosswise into very thin strips. The choice is yours.

Gently separate the noodles, dust them lightly with flour, and set them aside on a floured sheet pan to dry for 5 to 6 minutes before cooking according to individual recipes.

Jade Noodles Variation

To make jade noodles, replace the water with ¼ cup undiluted spinach juice from blending 8 ounces fresh spinach in a blender, preferably high-speed, pressing out the juice through a fine-mesh sieve, and discarding the solids.

Cha-om cakes

ชะอมทอดไข่   CHA-OM THOT KHAI

6 ounces fresh or thawed, frozen cha-om leaves (from 12 ounces chao-om stalks if using fresh leaves)

6 eggs

½ teaspoon salt

2 tablespoons homemade lard (page 28) or vegetable oil

Cha-om stalks can be found in the produce section of well-stocked Thai grocery stores. Buy twice the weight the recipe calls for, as you will be using only the leaves. The stalks are dotted with sharp thorns, so you need to remove the leaves from the stalks with care. With one hand, pinch the tender shoot at the tip firmly between your thumb and index finger. With your other hand, pinch the stalk in the same manner directly below your first hand and then firmly slide the thumb and finger of your second hand down the length of the stalk, removing the leaves as you go. The thorns on the stalk point downward, so it is important to pull the leaves downward to avoid injury. Once the leaves have been removed from a stalk, snap off the tender shoot at the tip and use that, too. The stalks have no use, so discard them.

Alternatively, you can buy vacuum-sealed frozen *cha-om* leaves, which come already prepared. To thaw them, leave them on the counter for 20 to 30 minutes or put them in a colander and run them under warm tap water. The leaves will be wet when thawed by either method, so squeeze them dry before using.

Nothing can mimic the unique scent and taste of *cha-om*. But if you absolutely can't find it, I recommend samphire (also known as sea beans or sea asparagus) or asparagus, cut into very thin matchsticks. A combination of collard greens and arugula, cut into narrow ribbons, performs well, too.

Some people, on the other hand, see this dish as an omelet with *cha-om* leaves as an add-in. They call it *khai jiao cha-om* ("omelet [featuring] *cha-om*"), and they prepare it as an omelet with a small amount of *cha-om*. *Cha-om* cakes are, to me, panfried *cha-om* leaves with beaten eggs acting as the binder and giving body and oomph to the cakes. And this recipe gives you *cha-om* cakes as I think they should be: *cha-om* leaves as the main star and the eggs in the supporting role.

Cha-om cakes are usually served alongside a relish, most commonly Shrimp Paste Relish (page 316); they're also used in a variant of Central Thai sour curry that's wildly popular in Bangkok (page 82).

Makes two 6-inch round cakes

If using fresh *cha-om* leaves, rinse them well; if using either fresh or thawed, frozen leaves, squeeze them dry. Crack the eggs into a bowl and beat them with a fork until blended. Add the leaves and salt and mix well with the fork.

Put 1½ teaspoons of the lard in an 8-inch frying pan and set over medium heat. When the lard is hot, tilt the pan so the lard evenly coats the bottom, then pour in half of the egg mixture. Use a wide spatula to flatten and spread the mixture into a 6-inch cake of even thickness. When the bottom of the cake is firm and light brown, about 2 minutes, use the spatula to lift up the cake just high enough to allow you to slip another 1½ teaspoons lard underneath it. Then, instead of lowering the cake back down, flip it and continue to cook, pressing on it constantly with the spatula, until the second side is firm, light brown, and no liquid oozes out when the cake is pressed, 2 to 3 minutes. Transfer to a plate. Repeat to make a second cake with the remaining egg mixture and 1 tablespoon lard and add to the plate.

Let the cakes cool completely, then use as directed in individual recipes. The cakes are best consumed fresh, but they can be stored in the refrigerator for up to 2 days.

Roti dough

แป้งโรตี PAENG ROTI

1 cup all-purpose flour

1 cup bread flour

2 teaspoons granulated sugar

½ teaspoon salt

3 tablespoons vegetable oil

½ to ¾ cup water

Be sure to plan in advance, because this dough requires 48 hours to age in the refrigerator in order to be able to be stretched very thinly.

◆ **Makes enough for 4 roti**

Combine both flours, the sugar, salt, and 1 tablespoon of the oil in a bowl and stir with your hands to mix. With one hand, gradually add the water to the flour mixture while mixing everything together with the other hand, halting the addition of water when a shaggy ball of dough has formed that cleans the bottom and sides of the bowl. (Be sure not to use more than ¾ cup water.)

Divide the dough into four equal portions (a kitchen scale helps here), then form each portion into—this is crucial—a smooth, *crack-free* ball. Place the balls in a food storage container with a lid. Pour the remaining 2 tablespoons oil over the dough balls and flip them around so they are evenly coated with the oil. Cover the container and refrigerate for 48 hours. The dough needs to come to room temperature before it can be used.

Limestone solution

 น้ำปูนใส NAM PUN SAI

4 ounces food-grade red limestone paste

4 cups water

There's a lot of confusion about limestone solution in Thai recipes. Most of the time, recipes call for the amount of solution needed without explaining how to prepare it. When cooks fail to achieve the recipe results the writers intended, it is usually because the writers and the cooks have different levels of concentration in mind. In developing the recipes in this book, I have adhered strictly to the following ratio, which, because it is highly concentrated, makes it easier to control the amount of liquid in a recipe.

Limestone paste is inexpensive and can be found at most Southeast Asian grocery stores or online. It can be reused multiple times, and the prepared solution keeps at room temperature for months. To keep the concentration constant, take as much solution as you need out of the jar, replace it with the same amount of fresh water, shake the mixture, and let the paste sink to the bottom again. You know the solution has lost its potency when the white, cloudy film that usually forms on its surface upon storage disappears. When that happens, get a fresh batch of limestone paste and repeat the process. ◆ **Makes 4 cups**

Whisk together the limestone paste and water in a large glass jar until the limestone paste fully dissolves. Leave it undisturbed until the limestone paste sinks to the bottom and the solution becomes completely clear, about 1 hour. The solution is now ready to be used in a recipe. To store, cap tightly and keep at room temperature.

Pandan juice concentrate

น้ำใบเตย NAM BAI TOEI

4 ounces pandan leaves (fresh or frozen)

1 cup water, if using a blender

This is the most concentrated form of pandan juice, and it is the best way to deliver the scent and color of pandan leaves to a recipe without also introducing too much moisture, which could ruin whatever you are making. Prepare the concentrate no more than 24 hours before using, and use it up in one go, as it doesn't store well in the refrigerator or freezer. ◈ **Makes about ¼ cup**

Chop the pandan leaves into 1-inch pieces. If you have a juicer, preferably the masticating type, run the leaves through it and collect the juice. The juice is ready to use.

If you don't have a juicer, transfer them to a blender, add the water, and process until pulverized. Pass the puree through a fine-mesh sieve into a clear glass jar or glass measuring cup, using a rubber spatula to press out every drop of the juice. Cover the jar or cup and refrigerate, undisturbed, for 24 hours. Carefully remove the container from the refrigerator. You will see a clear demarcation between the diluted green water and the dark green pandan concentrate that has settled at the bottom. Pour off all of the light green water and keep only the darkest, most concentrated extract to use in a recipe.

Notes on
Ingredients

Banana Blossom

Basil, Thai Sweet

Banana Blossoms (HUA PLI 🔸 หัวปลี): These rugby ball–shaped, reddish purple flowers come with several tough petals concealing tiny immature bananas. These outer petals are too tough to eat and the little bananas too bitter. Both need to be removed layer by layer until you get to the tender, light-colored core that is the palatable part. A banana blossom oxidizes and turns brown once it is cut open, so it needs to be submerged in acidulated water right away until it is used. Banana blossoms are sold fresh in the produce section of many well-stocked Asian stores specializing in Southeast Asian ingredients; they also come trimmed and packed in brine in a glass jar. The type that comes in brine is acceptable in recipes in which the blossoms are cooked. However, in this book, banana blossoms are served as a side vegetable and, therefore, need to be fresh.

Basil, Holy (BAI KA-PHRAO 🔸 ใบกะเพรา): This basil comes in two varieties, reddish and green, both with soft, fuzzy hair on their stems and leaves. Both are perfectly interchangeable. Holy basil is used in stir-fries and in some spicy curries, and, in Thailand, it is the sine qua non ingredient in Thai spicy basil stir-fry (*phat ka-phrao*; page 93). But if it is not available where you live, Mediterranean or Thai sweet basil will perform adequately in its place.

Basil, Lemon (BAI MAENG LAK 🔸 ใบแมงลัก): In this book, lemon basil, which has narrow, ovate, pale green leaves and a pleasing citrusy scent, is used to accompany Rice Vermicelli with Fish Curry (page 171). In Thailand, this is the only basil you will usually see paired with this dish. In its absence, Mediterranean or Thai sweet basil is a better substitute than holy basil.

Basil, Thai Sweet (BAI HORA-PHA 🔸 ใบโหระพา): With purple stems and dark purple flowers, Thai sweet basil is probably the best-known Asian basil around the world. It has a sweet, unassertive flavor and fragrance that allows it to stand in for both holy basil and lemon basil (those two, on the

Cha-om

Chiles, Dried Thai Long

Chinese Broccoli

other hand, don't always perform well in its place), making it the most versatile of the three main basil varieties used in Thai cooking. Fortunately, it's also the most widely available outside of Thailand.

Cha-om (BAI CHA-OM ◆ ใบชะอม): The *cha-om* plant is a small shrub with thorny stalks, tender tips, and fragrant leaves. Only the leaves and tips are used in cooking, most commonly in panfried cakes, stir-fries, and soups. Look for fresh *cha-om* stalks in the produce section and frozen leaves in the freezer section of Southeast Asian grocery stores. For tips on working with both fresh and frozen *cha-om*, see the recipe on page 334 for cakes made with *cha-om*.

Chiles, Dried Bird's Eye (PHRIK KHI NU HAENG ◆ พริกขี้หนูแห้ง): Small and potent, these are red bird's eye chiles (see entry) that have been dried whole. They are used in curry pastes, dipping sauces, and in a wide variety of dishes. Although dried bird's eye chiles and dried Thai long chiles (see entry) are sometimes interchangeable, the amounts called for often differ, as the bird's eyes are much hotter.

Chiles, Dried Thai Long (PHRIK CHI FA HAENG ◆ พริกขี้ฟ้าแห้ง): Used primarily to impart flavor and color to chile pastes and curry pastes, these are red Thai long chiles (see entry) that have been dried whole. If you cannot find them, dried *guajillo* chiles (Hatch or New Mexico) can be used in their place. Dried bird's eye chiles can also be substituted, but because they are more fiery, you will need to reduce the amount.

Chiles, Fresh Bird's Eye (PHRIK KHI NU ◆ พริกขี้หนู): Also colloquially referred to as Thai chiles, these small, superhot chiles are used in countless Thai dishes and seasoning ingredients. Red bird's eye chiles are a bit milder and sweeter, with a more noticeably floral aftertaste, whereas green ones have a faint herbaceous scent. Unless otherwise specified, both can be used interchangeably.

Chiles, Fresh Thai Long (PHRIK CHI FA ◆ พริกขี้ฟ้า): Typically ranging in length from 2 to 4 inches, these slender chiles are milder than bird's eye chiles. They come in red, green, and orange, and are ideal in condiments or curry pastes where you want bright color but less heat than bird's eyes would deliver. If you cannot find red or green long chiles, jalapeño or serrano chiles are acceptable substitutes.

Chinese Broccoli (PHAK KHANA ◆ ผักคะน้า): A Chinese leafy green with stalks slimmer and more tender than Western broccoli, this versatile vegetable is used extensively in Thai cooking. The deep green leaves and stalks are cut up and used in stir-fries or steamed or blanched and added to one-plate rice meals or noodle dishes. In the United States, Chinese broccoli, which is often labeled *kai lan* or *gai lan* (its Cantonese name), can be found at most Asian grocery stores and some mainstream supermarkets.

Chinese Flowering Mustard Greens

Cilantro Roots

Chinese Flowering Mustard Greens (PHAK KWANG TUNG 🍴 ผักกวางตุ้ง): Variously labeled as *yu choi sum*, *yu choi*, or *choi sum*, this large, leafy vegetable is often confused with Chinese broccoli. The fact that the two—not interchangeable in general and in any of the recipes in this book—are nearly always sold side by side in the produce section of most Asian stores only makes it more confusing. Flowering mustard greens have dark yellowish green leaves that are thinner and more tender than those of Chinese broccoli. Its stalks are also generally thinner and juicier than those of Chinese broccoli. And while Chinese broccoli comes most often with small white flowers, with some new varieties sporting yellow flowers, the flowers of Chinese flowering mustard greens are always bright yellow. This vegetable is generally used in stir-fries, soups, and stews; it can also be blanched and used in noodle dishes or as a side vegetable for relishes.

Chinese Garlic Chives (BAI KUI CHAI 🍴 ใบกุยช่าย): Also known as Chinese chives, garlic chives, and green nira grass, Chinese garlic chives have dark green flat blades (unlike round, hollow Western chives) and a mild garlic flavor. They're generally used in stir-fries and to make fillings for savory buns; they're also routinely served raw as a side vegetable for fried noodles, most commonly pad thai.

Cilantro Roots (RAK PHAK CHI 🍴 รากผักชี): The roots of cilantro plants are regularly used as an aromatic in Thai cooking, primarily as part of the base for dishes and marinades. Look for bunches of cilantro with the roots attached in Southeast Asian groceries. Although less fragrant, cilantro stems can be used in place of the roots.

Coconut Cream (HUA KA-THI 🍴 หัวกะทิ): This is the fatty, thick, opaque layer of cream that separates and rises to the top of the first extraction of grated mature coconut, with the thinner coconut milk below it. In the case of canned coconut milk, the cream is the thick, rich layer than floats at the top of the can. To retrieve the cream, open the can without shaking it and scoop the cream off the top. Some Thai brands sell 100 percent coconut cream in a can, but I've found this product to be inconsistent and, therefore, not always reliable. At its worst, it causes the dish to be much more oily than intended. I've found extra-virgin coconut oil, a widely available ingredient used in some recipes in this book, to be a much more practical solution; just a small amount of it helps get canned coconut cream to perform almost like freshly extracted coconut cream.

Coconut Milk (NAM KA-THI 🍴 น้ำกะทิ): This is the thinner liquid extracted from the finely grated meat of a mature coconut that settles below coconut cream (see entry). Prepared coconut milk is widely available in cans, usually containing 13½ or 14 ounces. It is also sold in aseptic boxes in the United States. In every case, make sure you buy unsweetened coconut milk without emulsifiers, thickeners, or other additives. If you will not be scooping the cream from the top, always shake the can or box before opening.

Fingerroot

Galangal

Garlic, Pickled

Curry powder (PHONG KARI ⬙ ผงกะหรี่): Curry powder is a spice blend that finds its way into several dishes with ties to either the Thai Muslim communities or the Thai Chinese communities. Generally, the blend includes turmeric, coriander, cumin, cinnamon, cloves, and cayenne. However, formulae vary from brand to brand; so do the amounts of cayenne and, proportionately, the levels of heat contained therein. Curry powder made by Southeast Asian brands comes in mild, medium, and hot. For the recipes in this book, the mild (also labeled "sweet") type is to be used, and the best brand to use in order to achieve the intended results is any brand from Thailand or at least a brand manufactured in Southeast Asia.

Fingerroot (KRACHAI ⬙ กระชาย): A long finger-shaped rhizome that goes by many other names—lesser ginger, wild ginger, Chinese keys, *krachai*—fingerroot can be found at well-stocked Asian supermarkets fresh, vacuum-packed, frozen, or brined whole or slivered in jars. All of these work well in a curry paste in which the texture of the rhizome is not as important as its scent and flavor. There is no substitute for fingerroot, so if you can't find it in any form, leave it out.

Flour, Glutinous Rice (PAENG KHAO NIAO ⬙ แป้งข้าวเหนียว): This is flour finely milled from medium-grain white glutinous—aka sticky or sweet—rice. It's used in both sweet and savory dishes. Unless otherwise indicated, no other type of flour, including regular rice flour (see entry), can be used in its place. For the best results, use a Thai brand, such as Erawan, for the recipes in this book.

Flour, Rice (PAENG KHAO JAO ⬙ แป้งข้าวเจ้า): This is flour finely milled from long-grain white rice. It is used primarily in noodle and dumpling doughs, savory and sweet batters, steamed desserts, and sometimes as a thickener. Unless otherwise indicated, no other type of flour, including glutinous rice flour (see entry), can be used in its place. For the best results, use a Thai brand, such as Erawan, for the recipes in this book.

Galangal (KHA ⬙ ข่า): Also known as blue ginger, galangal is a rhizome used in Thai cooking most commonly as a curry paste ingredient and to infuse soups. It is available fresh and frozen at most well-stocked Asian stores. Although fresh ginger looks similar to galangal, it cannot be substituted for it. Unlike ginger, galangal does not need to be peeled before using.

Garlic, Pickled (KRA-THIAM DONG ⬙ กระเทียมดอง): Every culture that uses pickled garlic in the kitchen pickles it differently. In the United States, Thai pickled garlic is sold in jars, with whole heads submerged in a solution of vinegar, sugar, and salt. That's the only type of pickled garlic that can be used for recipes in this book. Look for it in Southeast Asian groceries.

Ghee (NAM MAN NOEI ⬙ น้ำมันเนย): Used in Thai Muslim dishes, ghee is a type of clarified butter common to South Asian cooking. It is available in South Asian grocery stores and well-stocked supermarkets.

Limestone Solution (NAM PUN SAI 🔸 น้ำปูนใส): Used as a key ingredient in some recipes (curry puffs, fried dumplings, fritters) to promote crispiness, this simple solution is made by mixing water with limestone paste and then allowing the paste to settle at the bottom of the container, leaving the usable clear liquid at the top. See page 336 for directions on preparing it. Limestone paste usually comes in small plastic tubs (about 4 ounces) and can be found in the dry goods aisle of most groceries specializing in Southeast Asian ingredients. The paste is usually pink, but occasionally it comes in white; both are interchangeable.

Mace Blades, Whole (DOK JAN THET 🔸 ดอกจันทน์เทศ): A mace blade is the outer sheath of the nutmeg seed. Its flavor is similar to nutmeg, though more subtle and gentle. In the Thai kitchen, mace is primarily used to flavor curries. Look for mace blades in the spice section of South Asian and Southeast Asian groceries and well-stocked supermarkets.

Makrut Lime

Makrut Lime (MAKRUT 🔸 มะกรูด): Also known as kaffir limes, *makrut* limes grow on large, thorn-lined shrubs native to tropical Asia. The leaves and the rind of immature *makrut* limes are core ingredients in Thai food. Although once difficult to find outside of Southeast Asia, the lime leaves, both fresh and frozen, are starting to be stocked by more and more Asian grocery stores in the United States. The juice is hardly used in cooking, and when it is, such as in the recipe for Sweet-and-Sour Curry of Water Spinach and Fish (page 103), only very small amounts are needed.

Mango, Sour Green (MAMUANG DIP 🔸 มะม่วงดิบ): In recipes in this book calling for sour green mango, the only type of mango that can be used is the green (unripe) mango found in South and Southeast Asian grocery stores. Do not use the green-red Tommy Atkins mangoes that are sold at most supermarkets, as they won't give you the desired result. When picking a green mango, choose one that is rock hard. If it gives even just a little when you squeeze it hard, it's not good enough.

Mango, Sour Green

Noodles, Angel Hair Rice (SEN MI 🔸 เส้นหมี่): These are the thinnest type of rice noodles used in Thai cooking. This type of noodle is sometimes referred to as rice vermicelli, but I've decided to call it angel hair because it's roughly the same thickness as the Italian angel hair pasta and also to prevent confusion because *khanom jin* is just as often referred to as rice vermicelli. Wai Wai brand *sen mi*, which comes in a 17½-ounce package, is the only Thai brand widely available in the United States at the time of writing. If you can't find Wai Wai brand *sen mi* at a brick-and-mortar Asian grocery store, you'll need to mail order them, as there are no acceptable substitutes—not even other thin white noodles that may resemble them.

Noodles, Egg (SEN BAMI 🔸 เส้นบะหมี่): Though "egg noodles" is a common umbrella term for these wheat-based noodles, just as often they're called "wheat noodles," which may be a more accurate term, as the noodles don't always contain eggs. (The yellow color you see is caused by either the alkaline water that is often added to achieve chewiness or the yellow food dye that some manufacturers add to the dough.) These long, fresh yellow noodles are available in a variety of thicknesses and appearances. Some are round and thin, much like Italian capellini; some are wider and flat, much like Italian linguine albeit flatter; some are squiggly; some are straight. But they're always found in the refrigerated section of most Asian stores, wound into bundles and packed into clear plastic bags. For homemade egg noodles, see page 332.

Noodles, Fresh Wide Rice (KUAI TIAO SEN YAI 🔸 ก๋วยเตี๋ยวเส้นใหญ่): These fresh rice noodles are sold in large sheets, which are oiled and stacked, and in broad noodles ¾ to 1 inch wide. Look for them in the refrigerated section of Asian grocery stores. Alternatively, you can make your own fresh rice noodles using the recipe on page 330, or you can purchase the widest dried rice noodles available (about 9 millimeters or ⅓ inch), cook them as you would dried pasta until soft (rice noodles should not be cooked al dente), and then drain them. If using dried noodles, use half the amount, so if a recipe calls for 1 pound fresh wide rice noodles, use 8 ounces dried noodles.

Noodles, Thin Rice (KUAI TIAO SEN LEK 🔸 ก๋วยเตี๋ยวเส้นเล็ก): Also known as pad thai or *phở* noodles, these long, thin, flat dried rice noodles come in different widths, ranging from 3 to 9 millimeters (roughly ⅛ to ⅓ inch). For the recipes in this book, the thinnest width (3 millimeters) is ideal (unless you use them to replace wide rice noodles, as described in the previous entry).

Noodles, Vermicelli Rice (SEN KHANOM JIN 🔸 เส้นขนมจีน): In this book, rice vermicelli refers to what the Thais call *khanom jin*. In the United States, *khanom jin* is only available dried in the noodle aisle of most Asian stores specializing in Southeast Asian ingredients. If you can't find dried *khanom jin*, the type of dried rice vermicelli used to make the Vietnamese noodle soup, *bún bò huế*, is a good substitute. Cook the noodles in the style of pasta according to the package directions. Be sure to add more water than you think prudent, as the dried noodles release quite a lot of starch as they cook. Once they are cooked, drain them well in a colander, hold them under running hot water to wash off any residual starch, and drain again before using.

Oranges, Bitter (SOM SA 🔸 ส้มซ่า): Also known as Seville oranges, bitter oranges have a sour, tart, bitter flavor. Only the green (immature) fruits are used in Thai cooking. For more information on bitter oranges and a substitute for them, see page 53.

Pandan Leaves

Pandan Leaves (BAI TOEI ⬦ ใบเตย): These leaves, which come from the pandan (or pandanus) plant that grows throughout tropical Southeast Asia, are prized for their highly fragrant aroma. They are used to flavor both savory and sweet dishes, and the juice extracted from them imparts fragrance and color to desserts and drinks. Pandan leaves are available fresh and frozen. If you have purchased frozen leaves, hold them under running hot water to thaw before using.

Preserved Cabbage (TANG CHAI ⬦ ตังฉ่าย): Also known as pickled Chinese cabbage, this full-flavored ingredient is used in Chinese-style clear soups and noodles only sparingly due to its saltiness. Available in most Asian grocery stores, it is sold finely chopped in earthenware or translucent plastic crocks and ready to use without further preparation.

Preserved Radishes (HUA CHAI PO ⬦ หัวไช้โป๊): These are daikon radishes that have been pickled and then dehydrated just until they have shriveled but are still moist. They come whole, slivered, or finely chopped in a clear plastic bag and are available in Asian grocery stores in two types, salted (salty with hardly any sweetness) and sweet (both salty and sweet).

Red Fermented Tofu (TAO HU YI ⬦ เต้าหู้ยี้): These are tofu cubes that have been inoculated with fungal spores and then allowed to ferment slowly until they have taken on a texture and scent similar to that of ripened soft cheese. Red yeast rice is added for color. Used for both its flavor and color in a handful of recipes in this book, this bold-flavored tofu comes in glass or clear plastic jars and can be found at most Asian groceries.

Rice, Jasmine (KHAO HOM MALI ⬦ ข้าวหอมมะลิ): Prized around the world, this fragrant long-grain white rice is the most commonly consumed rice in Thailand. This strain of rice was so named due to its resemblance to the jasmine flower. However, despite what many erroneously believe, the resemblance has to do with the off-white color (the original Thai name of the rice is *khao dok mali*, "white [like] jasmine"), not the fragrance. The aroma of jasmine rice is actually more similar to that of pandan leaves, as both have the aroma compound 2-acetyl-1-pyrroline. For the best results, use a brand from Thailand.

Rice, White Glutinous (KHAO NIAO ⬦ ข้าวเหนียว): Grown and consumed primarily in north and northeastern Thailand, this medium-grain rice that becomes pleasantly sticky when cooked is most commonly prepared by steaming it in a basket over a pot of boiling water (see page 18). No other type of medium- or short-grain rice can be used in its place in any of the recipes in this book. For the best results, use a brand from Thailand.

Salted Duck Eggs

Salted Duck Eggs (KHAI KHEM ⬦ ไข่เค็ม): Appreciated for their saline pungency, salted duck eggs can be found in most Asian grocery stores, usually cooked and vacuum-packed and thus ready to use. If the eggs you purchase are not already cooked, boil them for about 10 minutes before using.

Salted Fish Steaks (PLA KHEM 🌶 ปลาเค็ม): The most commonly used salted fish in Thai cooking is king mackerel, which is salted whole, dried in the sun, and then sliced crosswise into bone-in steaks. The steaks are usually panfried in a shallow pool of oil until cooked through and golden brown on both sides and then enjoyed in tiny bites as a condiment-like accompaniment to rice or rice porridge. The salty meat—think salt packed with umami—is also sometimes used as a seasoning ingredient. Salted king mackerel steaks can be found in most Asian groceries, packed in oil or vacuum-packed and frozen. However, commercial salted fish steaks tend to be low in quality—they're overly salty and smelly—and I've been making my own salted fish at home; see page 327.

Salted Soybean Paste, Dark (TAO JIAO DAM 🌶 เต้าเจี้ยวดำ): These are soybeans that have been salted and slowly fermented until they turn into a brown, very salty, coarse paste with an intense aroma. Used as a seasoning ingredient, the paste comes in glass jars or bottles and can be found in most Asian groceries. Salted soybean paste from Thailand—what I recommend that you use—usually comes in tall glass bottles. The colors can range from dark yellowish brown to dark reddish brown; all of them work fine.

Salted Soybeans, Light (TAO JIAO KHAO 🌶 เต้าเจี้ยวขาว): Like dark salted soybean paste (see entry), these are soybeans that have been salted and fermented but for a shorter time. That means the beans are much lighter in color (pale yellow) and retain their shape; they are also much less salty and have a nuttier, lighter aroma than their darker counterpart. It's important to note that the two products cannot be used interchangeably. Look for these salted soybeans in glass jars, labeled "Yellow Soybean Paste" or "Yellow Soybean Sauce," even though they are neither paste- nor sauce-like in appearance, at groceries specializing in Southeast Asian ingredients.

Shrimp Paste (KAPI 🌶 กะปิ): Made from planktonic shrimp (krill) that have been salted, fermented, ground, and dried into a salty, brown-purple paste, this classic Thai ingredient is used in many curry pastes, dips, and sauces. For the recipes in this book, seek out shrimp paste imported from Thailand sold packed in round plastic tubs.

Soy Sauce, Dark (SI-IO DAM 🌶 ซีอิ๊วดำ): This dark-colored soy sauce is salty with no hint of sweet (unlike sweet dark soy sauce; see entry). It lends salinity and adds color to savory dishes. For the best results, use a Thai brand, such as Healthy Boy (Chinese dark soy sauce, for example, tends to be very dark and will turn the dishes in this book a much darker shade of brown than intended). Also, it's wise to check the label before purchasing, as dark soy sauce can be easily confused with dark sweet soy sauce. Make sure molasses is not on the list of ingredients.

Soy Sauce, Sweet Dark (SI-IO DAM WAN ♦ ซีอิ๊วดำหวาน): Also dubbed "black soy sauce" due to it being nearly black in color, this thick soy sauce with a treacly sweet, salty, smoky flavor lends its flavor to noodle stir-fries, sauces, and other preparations. For the best results, use a Thai brand, such as Healthy Boy or Dragonfly. To make sure you purchase the right kind of dark soy sauce, look for molasses on the list of ingredients, a sure sign that this is indeed sweet dark soy sauce and not dark soy sauce (see entry).

Soy Sauce, Thin (SI-IO KHAO ♦ ซีอิ๊วขาว): Also known as white soy sauce and light soy sauce, thin soy sauce has a thinner consistency, a milder taste, and a lighter color than its thicker, darker counterparts. Never substitute a different type of soy sauce for Thai thin soy, as it will darken the color of the dish or sauce beyond what the recipe intends. The only type of Thai sauce that can be used interchangeably with thin soy sauce is Golden Mountain seasoning sauce (not to be confused with Maggi seasoning sauce) from Thailand, sold in a green-capped bottle.

Sriracha Sauce (SOT SIRACHA ♦ ซอสศรีราชา): This garlicky hot sauce is often served with fried seafood dishes, but it can be used as a dipping sauce or seasoning sauce for just about anything. It's very important to note that in all of the recipes in this book where Sriracha sauce is called for, the only sauce you must use is the kind of Sriracha sauce that's used in Thailand, which is runnier, sweeter, and milder than any of the U.S.-made Sriracha, such as Huy Fong Sriracha. Shark and Sriraja Panich are the most common brands of Thai Sriracha in the United States, and they can be found at many well-stocked Asian stores or online. To make your own Sriracha sauce, see page 319.

Sugar, Chinese Rock (NAM TAN KRUAT ♦ น้ำตาลกรวด): Often called "rock candy," these irregular lumps of crystallized sugar are routinely used in Chinese cooking and some Thai dishes, especially warm desserts, of Chinese origin. The colors of this type of sugar range from opaque white to dark amber; all work in the recipes in this book. You can find rock sugar at most Asian stores. To use, crush the lumps in a mortar, or crack them into tiny pieces with a heavy object, so the sugar can be measured more easily and also melt more quickly.

Sugar, Palm (NAM TAN TANOT ♦ น้ำตาลโตนด): In Thailand, palm sugar most often comes in soft, sticky form—similar in consistency to peanut butter—and has the flavor of light caramel. This type of palm sugar is extremely hard to find in the United States, though you may spot it at some Thai grocery stores in a big city with a large Thai population, such as Los Angeles. Palm sugar in solid form that's shaped like half a burger bun or a flying saucer (*nam tan puek*) is the most common type found at many Asian groceries in the United States, and, even though it's lighter in color and flavor than the sticky type, it works well in most recipes in this book. In some cases, however, the color and pronounced caramel-like flavor of the sticky palm sugar are needed to create the intended results. In these cases, such as Fire-Roasted River Prawns with Tamarind Sauce and Blanched Neem (page 121) and

Soy-Braised Eggs with Pork Belly (page 135), I augment it with brown sugar. This type of palm sugar needs to be finely grated before using in any recipe.

Sweet Chile Sauce (NAM JIM KAI 🌶 น้ำจิ้มไก่): Literally "dipping sauce [for] chicken," the name of this sweet, sour, and mildly spicy sauce hints at its primary use: to accompany grilled chicken. The sauce is, however, much more versatile; it can be used as a dipping sauce for various savory appetizers as well as deep-fried or grilled meats. Sweet chile sauce comes in tall glass bottles. Once opened, it needs to be refrigerated. For best results, buy a Thai brand, such as Pantai or Mae Ploy.

Tamarind Paste (NAM MA-KHAM PIAK 🌶 น้ำมะขามเปียก): Sometimes labeled "tamarind concentrate" or "tamarind juice," this sour concentrated pulp, which is made from tamarind, a dried pod-like brown legume, is used to add acidity to Thai dishes. Use a Thai brand only, which usually comes packed in a plastic jar. Although mature sour tamarind pods are more or less the same everywhere in the world, different countries have different ways of processing them, so that Indian tamarind paste, for example, is too dark, concentrated, and syrupy for Thai cooking. For the best results, make your own tamarind paste from blocks of seedless tamarind paste packaged in plastic (see page 316).

Tapioca Starch (PAENG MAN SAMPALANG 🌶 แป้งมันสำปะหลัง): Also known as tapioca flour, tapioca starch is a fine white starch extracted from the cassava root. In Thai cooking, it is used as a thickener for stir-fries and soups and in noodles, breads, and sweets to enhance their texture. For the best results, use a Thai brand, such as Erawan, for the recipes in this book.

Water Spinach (PHAK BUNG JIN 🌶 ผักบุ้งจีน): Often referred to by its Cantonese name, *ong choy*, and Chinese water morning glory in English, water spinach has long, hollow stems and bright green arrowhead-shaped leaves. It is used mainly in stir-fries and sometimes salads, and it can be found in the produce section of most Asian grocery stores. While only one type of *phak bung* is commercially available in the United States, several types can be found in the markets of Thailand, and—this is also the case with the various types of basil—each of them is associated with specific dishes. Two main types of *phak bung* are used in cooked dishes in Thailand: one grown in soil, which is the same one found in the United States, and one grown in water (Siamese water spinach, or *phak bung thai*), which so far I've only seen in Thailand. The latter is crunchier and juicier, has more voluptuous stalks with fewer leaves, and tends to retain its crunch better when cooked as opposed to the former, which becomes stringy and chewy if you overcook it by just a minute or two. Even though the type of water spinach—what the Thais call "Chinese water spinach"—can be used in all of the recipes in this book that call for water spinach, if you live in Thailand, you will want to use Siamese water spinach in Wide Rice Noodles in Fermented Soybean Broth with Seafood (page 237) and Sweet-and-Sour Curry of Water Spinach and Fish (page 103), as it is the traditional—and ideal—choice.

Water Spinach

Notes on
Romanization

The romanization of Thai words in this book is based largely on the Royal Thai General System of Transcription (RTGS) as published by the Royal Institute of Thailand in 1999. It should be noted that the system has been devised primarily to serve as the standard for bilingual road signs, maps, and government publications. It exists to help a casual reader pronounce Thai words with reasonable accuracy without inundating him or her with diacritics. Without special characters, the RTGS is also more practical than, for example, the ALA-LC by the American Library Association and the Library of Congress.

The only departure from the RTGS in this book is the use of the English *ch* and *j* to represent the Thai ฉ and จ, respectively. (The RTGS instead employs the English *ch* for both ฉ and จ. However, names with well-established or codified spellings remain strictly RTGS-compatible—for example, Chao Phraya instead of Jao Phraya and Kudi Chin instead of Kudi Jin.) The use of a hyphen in places prone to syllable misdivision, such as *makham* as *ma-kham* (to prevent the incorrect *mak-ham*), is also my own modification of the RTGS.

Note that the digraph *ph* is pronounced like *p* in English and not like *f*. Likewise, the digraph *th* is pronounced more like the aspirated *t* and not the *th* in English. In both cases, the *h* functions as a marker of aspiration to create simplified forms of aspirated *p* and *t* of the International Phonetic Alphabet.

The spellings of the words *satay* and *pad thai* follow the convention of the various English lexica to which they have been added. The Romanization of these words, however, is consistent with the RTGS.

People's names and some other proper names are spelled according to the most reliable attestations available. Otherwise, they are romanized according to the RTGS.

Visit the Royal Institute of Thailand's website for more information on the RTGS.

Acknowledgments

 I would like to thank the following people:

Emily Timberlake for being the most brilliant editor an author could ever hope to work with, for her vision, encouragement, and patience, for understanding what's in my heart, and for believing in me.

David Loftus for trekking around Bangkok—camera in hand—during one of the hottest winters the city has ever seen, for taking such gorgeous photos of the food, and for being an example of professionalism, class, and kindness.

Betsy Stromberg for not only making this book more beautiful than I could have imagined, but also for listening, understanding, and being so kind throughout the process.

Sharon Silva for doing such an outstanding job steering my words in the right direction, saving me from myself, and teaching me how to be a better writer.

Julia Azzarello for her artistic talent and for her willingness to go above and beyond to make the food look as stunning as it does.

Lola Milne for her sweet spirit, intelligence, and professionalism and for being such a joy to work with.

The people who have graciously provided information, insight, and technical knowledge to aid the writing of this book: the ever so wise and knowledgeable Harold McGee for being generous with his time in answering my questions; Suntharee Asavai of Thai Khadi Research Institute whose writings and personal conversations regarding the culinary history of Bangkok have been tremendously enlightening to me, Associate Professor Thanes Wongyannava who is one of the most intelligent and insightful people I've had the privilege of interviewing and whose works have greatly expanded my mind; Ong Bunjoon for setting an example of diligence and scholastic integrity; Thai scholars and writers—greater in number than I can mention here—to whom

I am truly and deeply indebted; Boonyong Panpanichgul of Queens Khao Man Kai for feeding me and my father with the best *khao man kai* we'd ever had and for always being kind in unreservedly sharing with me what he had learned during his decades-long career; Kanittha Sakunthong of Ban Sakunthong for sharing with me her knowledge of the Kudi Chin Community and its centuries-old cuisine; Chanchavee Skulkant of Krua Apsorn for allowing me to enter the sanctum sanctorum of your illustrious restaurant so that I can see firsthand how things are done; Auntie Sri, the street vendor of delicious little sponge cakes well-known around Charoen Krung 42, who, when approached by a stranger with a camera and a notepad in hands sheepishly asking to sit beside her on the sidewalk for an afternoon to learn how she made the cakes, stared confusedly for a few seconds then nodded, smiling, scooting to one side to make room for said stranger who later wrote this book.

Thammasat University along with its Pridi Banomyong Library, my writing haven on the Chao Phraya, who not only is like a person to me but also one whom my heart has loved for so long.

The Joseph Regenstein Library, also a person—a friend—to me, who is my writing haven in Chicago.

Mike Sula, one of the best writers I know, for his friendship and encouragement which have made the world of professional food writing feel like a friendlier, saner place to me.

The kind people who have helped me test the recipes: Dietrich Ayala, Véronica E. Betancourt, Sven Becker, Rosemary Bolich, Chris Cardwell, Carrie Carter, Emma Cham, Shuang Chen, Bart De Pauw, Bob Dolan, Krista Ebert, Kira Fry, Mark Harris, Richard Harwood, Håkan Hedrén, Tania Howard, Ryan James, Tippy Jeng, Rajkumari Junginger, Naphat Kijsamrej, Liana Krissoff, Megan Lee, Pascal Marais, Laura McCarthy, Francesca McLin, Sujitra Pookpanratana, Stephan G. Schoen, Mike Sula, Sirirath Wen, including many more who had volunteered.

The readers of SheSimmers.com whose support has been a source of strength and inspiration to me all these years.

My family in Bangkok for their help in researching this book and for allowing me to publish some of our recipes.

All of my loved ones both in Bangkok and Chicago whose support I can always count on.

My late parents whose love has been the rock of my life.

Bangkok, a city who is at once conventional and quirky, comforting and challenging, indomitable yet hospitable, harmonious and variegated, familiar and ever changing—altogether home, altogether lovely, altogether beloved to me.

Index

C

Cabbage
    Hot Pot, Bangkok Style, 261–62
    preserved, 344
    Salted Soybean–Coconut
      Relish, 109
    Shrimp Paste Relish and Fried
      Mackerel, 110
    Stir-Fried Glass Noodles with
      Chicken and Vegetables in
      Fermented Tofu Sauce, 220
Cakes
    Coconut Rice Pudding Cakes,
      283–84
    Kudi Chin Sponge Cakes, 287, 290
Carrots
    Rice Noodle Parcels with Chile-Lime
      Sauce, 39–40
    Spicy Corn Salad, 124
Cashews
    Crispy Water Spinach Salad, 127
    Fried Rice with Salted Olives, 209
    Mango Sundae with Pandan-
      Coconut Sticky Rice, 307, 308
    Pomelo Salad Bites, 46
    Winged Bean Salad, 129
Catfish
    Sweet Pork–Shrimp Paste Relish
      (Boat Relish), 117–18
Cha-om, 339
    Cha-om Cakes, 334–35
    Sour Curry of Cha-om Cakes and
      Shrimp, 82
Cha-om thot khai, 334–35
Cha yen, 311–12
Chicken
    Basic Stock, 323
    Black Pepper Roasted Chicken, 155
    Braised Chicken in Coconut-
      Galangal Cream Sauce, 105–6
    Chicken and Banana Pepper Curry
      with Toasted Peanuts, 84
    Chicken and Rice, Thai Muslim
      Style, 191–92
    Chicken Curry Puffs, 71–73
    Chicken–Green Banana Curry, 78
    Coconut Rice with Green Papaya
      Salad, Sweet Shredded Beef, and
      Chicken Red Curry, 197–98
    Egg Net Parcels with Pork-Peanut
      Filling, 63–64
    Egg Sausage Soup, 130–31
    Fried Chicken in Pandan
      Leaves, 148

Fried Chicken with Crispy Garlic,
    153–54
Grilled Meatballs with Spicy Sweet-
    and-Sour Sauce, 47
Hot Pot, Bangkok Style, 261–62
Meatballs, 324–25
Poached Chicken on Rice with
    Soy-Ginger Sauce, 217–19
Rice Vermicelli with Chopped
    Chicken Curry and Yellow
    Chile–Coconut Sauce, 177–78
Steamed Dumplings with Chicken-
    Peanut Filling, 33–34
Stir-Fried Glass Noodles with
    Chicken and Vegetables in
    Fermented Tofu Sauce, 220
24-Hour Chicken Matsaman Curry,
    95–96
Chiles
    Chile Jam, 22
    Dried Red Chile Powder, 323
    Green Curry Paste, 90
    Pickled Chiles in Vinegar, 317
    Red Curry Paste, 317
    Rice Noodle Parcels with Chile-Lime
      Sauce, 39–40
    Sriracha Sauce, 319
    Stir-Fried Lump Crabmeat with
      Long Beans and Hot Yellow
      Chiles, 87
    types of, 339
    Yellow Chile–Coconut Sauce, 177
Chile sauce, sweet, 347
Chinese broccoli, 339
    Braised Spareribs in Salted
      Soybean Sauce on Rice, 195–96
    Crispy Angel Hair Rice Noodles with
      Beef and Chinese Broccoli Stalks,
      255–56
    Stewed Pork Hocks on Rice, 205–6
Chinese flowering mustard greens, 340
    Hot Pot, Bangkok Style, 261–62
    Jade Noodles with Barbecued
      Pork, 243
Chinese garlic chives, 340
Chinese winter melon
    Poached Chicken on Rice with
      Soy-Ginger Sauce, 217–19
Cilantro roots, 340
Coconut
    Angel Hair Rice Noodles with
      Coconut Sauce, 231–32
    Braised Chicken in Coconut-
      Galangal Cream Sauce, 105–6
    Coconut Rice Pudding Cakes,
      283–84

Coconut Rice with Green Papaya
    Salad, Sweet Shredded Beef, and
    Chicken Red Curry, 197–98
cream, 340
Fried Taro Dumplings with Shrimp-
    Coconut Filling, 66–67
Mango Sundae with Pandan-
    Coconut Sticky Rice, 307, 308
milk, 340
Rice Crackers with Pork-Shrimp-
    Coconut Dip, 48
Rice Vermicelli with Coconut Sauce
    and Fish Dumplings, 175
Salted Soybean–Coconut Relish, 109
Tapioca and Thai Muskmelon in
    Iced Coconut–Palm Sugar Syrup,
    271–72
Cook shops, 138–39
Corn
    Hot Pot, Bangkok Style, 261–62
    Spicy Corn Salad, 124
Crab
    Fresh Spring Rolls, 35–36
    Omelet Roll with Crabmeat Filling,
      143–44
    Stir-Fried Lump Crabmeat with
      Long Beans and Hot Yellow
      Chiles, 87
Crackers
    Fried Rice Crackers, 20
    Rice Crackers with Pork-Shrimp-
      Coconut Dip, 48
Crullers, Twin, 281–82
Cucumbers
    Beef and Cucumber Curry, 81
    Chinese Sausage–Cucumber
      Salad, 185
    Cucumber Relish, 192, 319
    Plain Rice Porridge with Assorted
      Accompaniments, 185
    Rice in Flower-Scented Water with
      Accompaniments, 166–69
    Salted Soybean–Coconut Relish, 109
Curries
    Beef and Cucumber Curry, 81
    Beef Green Curry, 90
    Beef Yellow Curry on Rice,
      Chinatown Style, 203–4
    Chicken and Banana Pepper Curry
      with Toasted Peanuts, 84
    Chicken–Green Banana Curry, 78
    Coconut Rice with Green Papaya
      Salad, Sweet Shredded Beef, and
      Chicken Red Curry, 197–98
    Mussel-Pineapple Curry, 100
    Pork Belly–Green Juice Curry, 99

Copyright © 2017 by shesimmers.com
Photographs copyright © 2017 by David Loftus

Library of Congress Cataloging-in-Publication Data
Names: Punyaratabandhu, Leela.
Title: Bangkok : recipes and stories from the heart of Thailand / Leela
  Punyaratabandhu ; photography by David Loftus.
Description: First edition. | Berkeley, California : Ten Speed Press, [2017]
  | Includes bibliographical references and index.
Identifiers: LCCN 2016051340 (print) | LCCN 2016056911 (ebook)
Subjects: LCSH: Cooking, Thai. | Bangkok (Thailand)—Description and travel.
  | LCGFT: Cookbooks.
Classification: LCC TX724.5.T5 P859 2017 (print) | LCC TX724.5.T5 (ebook) |
  DDC 641.59593—dc23
LC record available at https://lccn.loc.gov/2016051340

Hardcover ISBN: 978-0-399-57831-1
eBook ISBN: 978-0-399-57832-8

Printed in China

Design by Betsy Stromberg

10 9 8 7 6 5 4 3 2 1

First Edition

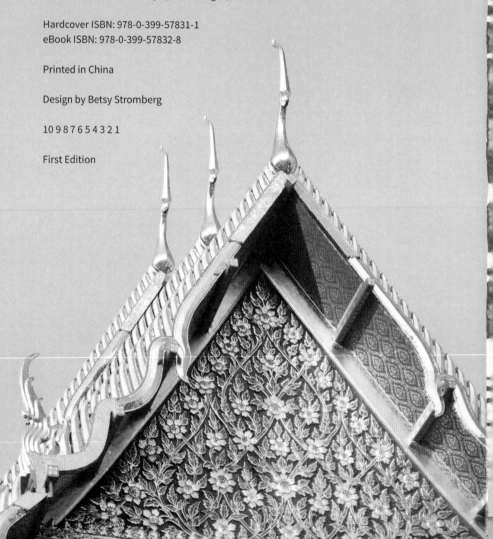